MW01230242

*The International Library of Sociology*

# LUNACY, LAW, AND CONSCIENCE
# 1744 - 1845

*Founded by KARL MANNHEIM*

# The International Library of Sociology

## THE SOCIOLOGY OF MENTAL HEALTH

### In 7 Volumes

# LUNACY, LAW, AND CONSCIENCE
# 1744 - 1845

## The Social History of the Care of the Insane

by

KATHLEEN JONES

First published in 1955 by
Routledge

Reprinted in 1998 by
Routledge
2 Park Square, Milton Park, Abingdon, Oxon, OX14 4RN

Transferred to Digital Printing 2007

The publishers have made every effort to contact authors/copyright holders
of the works reprinted in *The International Library of Sociology*.
This has not been possible in every case, however, and we would
welcome correspondence from those individuals/companies
we have been unable to trace.

*British Library Cataloguing in Publication Data*
A CIP catalogue record for this book
is available from the British Library

Lunacy, Law, and Conscience 1744 - 1845
ISBN 0-415-17802-9
The Sociology of Mental Health: 7 Volumes
ISBN 0-415-17835-5
The International Library of Sociology: 274 Volumes
ISBN 0-415-17838-X

**Publisher's Note**
The publisher has gone to great lengths to ensure the quality of this reprint
but points out that some imperfections in the original may be apparent

# CONTENTS

# PREFACE

THE author is greatly indebted to Professor W. J. M. Mackenzie and Mr. A. B. L. Rodgers, both of the University of Manchester, and to Mr. H. L. Beales, of the London School of Economics; all three helped this manuscript through its varying vicissitudes with unfailing patience, and gave much helpful advice and criticism. Dr. Alexander Walk, Librarian of the Royal Medico-Psychological Association, contributed much from his own store of knowledge on this subject, and made available sources of information which would have otherwise been inaccessible. Professor Anderson of the University of Manchester and Dr. J. E. Nicole of Winwick Hospital, Warrington, were kind enough to offer suggestions and corrections on the psychiatric aspects.

Thanks are also due to the late Mr. E. Robson and Dr. W. H. Challoner of the University of Manchester; Dr. E. Brockbank of the Manchester Royal Infirmary; and Mr. Anthony Tuke, Chairman of Barclays Bank, and heir to a great tradition.

*The University of Manchester,*                          K. J.
*March,* 1954.

# INTRODUCTION

IN the eighteenth century, madmen were locked up in madhouses: in the nineteenth century, lunatics were sent to asylums; and in the twentieth century, the mentally ill receive treatment in hospitals. That is the essence of the change which has taken place in the care and treatment of the insane in the past two hundred years—a change which is more than a matter of terminology; for a 'madhouse attendant' is not the same as a mental nurse, nor is a 'mad-doctor' the professional equivalent of a psychiatrist.

This survey deals with the development of 'madhouses' into 'asylums' during the period 1744–1845. It is primarily an administrative study. In 1744, a section of the insane first received mention as a separate class in the community for whom it was desirable that provision should be made. By 1845, a national system of inspection and supervision of all institutions for the insane had been achieved. After 1845 came the development from 'asylums'—to 'mental hospitals'—a development belatedly recognized by the Mental Treatment Act of 1930; but the events and ideas of 1744–1845 have a unity of their own, culminating in the first great Lunatics Act.

Lunacy reform was not an isolated movement. It was connected with the other reforms of the early nineteenth century—reforms of the penal law, of factory law, new developments in education and public health. Like these other movements, it sprang from a conception of the community's responsibility for the well-being of its members, and revealed a new spirit of humanity in public life. The insane were in fact the first of the handicapped classes to receive legislative protection.

The course of reform followed what was to become a familiar pattern in nineteenth-century England—a pattern which bore a clear relation to the parliamentary system. First came an indefinable sense of public uneasiness at existing conditions. This manifested itself in isolated incidents and local experiments. Improvements were carried out by individual philanthropists and small groups of influential people in two or three of the larger cities. In time, these experiments attracted the attention of certain members of parliament—usually back-benchers in the early days, for the care of the insane did not become in any sense a major parliamentary issue until Ashley intervened. On three occasions within twenty years, the small group of reformers in parliament secured the appointment of a Select Committee which assessed the value of the new methods of treatment, investigated the extent of the need for general reform, and helped to mould enlightened public opinion. Only then was it possible to frame a new law.

A new system was being devised, and there were no precedents. That was why the process of reform involved not one Select Committee, but three, not one Act of Parliament, but a series of Acts over a period of a hundred years.

The subject is not well documented. While the number of medical works on insanity published during this period was considerable, the very fact that no central control existed makes difficult the collation of material on the administrative aspects of the movement. Private madhouses kept no records, lest their defects should be discovered. Workhouses and prisons made no separate account of their insane inmates. Bethlem, the oldest and most famous of the lunatic hospitals, has now no records relating to any period before 1914. A conspiracy of silence covered the whole subject for many years. It is comparatively easy to obtain information about the pioneer institutions, such as the Retreat, which had nothing to hide; but for the others, we are dependent on scattered sources, on accounts of occasional scandals which broke through the barrier of secrecy, and on reading between the lines in partisan accounts.

The words 'insane' and 'insanity' are now generally restricted to those suffering from mental disorder, while the mentally defective are designated separately. In this survey, the words are used in their nineteenth-century sense, which covered both classes. Section 114 of the Lunatics Act of 1845 stated: ' "Lunatic" shall mean every insane person, and every person being an idiot or lunatic or of unsound mind.' This practice has been adopted for verbal convenience—to avoid cumbrous references to 'the mentally disordered and the mentally deficient'—and also for historical accuracy.

The following generally-accepted abbreviations are used throughout in footnotes:

D.N.B.—*Dictionary of National Biography.*
H.L.J.—Journal of the House of Lords.
H.C.J.—Journal of the House of Commons.

# Chapter One

## EIGHTEENTH-CENTURY THEORY

ENGLAND in the early eighteenth century was a country of some five and a half million people who lived for the most part in small towns and villages. There were only two towns of appreciable size—London, with a population of little over half a million, and Bristol, with about fifty thousand inhabitants. Elsewhere, people lived in semi-isolated communities, remote from each other and from any central stream of influence. Travel was slow and hazardous. There were few books, and no national newspapers. Many of the rich were cultured and sceptical; most of the poor were illiterate and superstitious; and some of the poor starved.

From an economic point of view, it was a society undergoing a slow process of disintegration, in the final stages of the decay of feudalism; from a social point of view, it was scarcely a society at all, for it lacked the homogeneity necessary to social action. The medieval conception of charity as a duty which each man owed to his neighbour was dying, and there was as yet nothing to take its place. The community recognized little corporate responsibility for the well-being of its citizens, and inevitably its weakest members—the very poor, the very old, the sick, and the insane—suffered.

There was no clear definition of what constituted insanity, and certainly no recognition of the insane as a separate social class requiring a distinct form of treatment. The problem was a submerged one. Only a small proportion of the total number were recognized as being insane, and the majority were treated as though they were fully responsible for their actions. If their mental condition reduced them to penury, they came within the purview of the Poor Law. If it led them to break the criminal code, they were judged by the penal law. If they wandered abroad from their legal place of settlement without means of support, they were involved in the rigours of the vagrancy laws.

The person who was recognized as insane—that is, the person whose actions were obviously a danger to himself or to others—had no protection in law. If he lived in or near London, he might be sent to Bethlem or 'Bedlam', the only institution of any public standing which dealt with the mentally abnormal. If he were wealthy, he might be sent by his relatives to one of the small private madhouses which combined high fees with a pledge of absolute secrecy, or confined alone with an attendant. If he were poor, he might be kept by his family in whatever conditions they chose, or sent to the workhouse or prison for greater security; but whether he lived in London, or in a small and remote village, whether he was rich or poor, he was almost certain to be confined, neglected, and intimidated, if not treated with open cruelty.

Since the lunatic or idiot was so dependent on those around him, our first task is to inquire what the eighteenth century thought about insanity, and what fundamental beliefs lay behind this treatment. The attitude of the labouring classes will be considered first, and then that of the medical practitioners, who were responsible for what little treatment of insanity there was; the clergy, who considered mind as a function of spirit, and all human misfortunes as falling within their province; and philosophers, who were at this time obsessed with that study of the rational faculties of man which later laid the foundations of the science of psychology.

*(i) The Labouring Classes.*

Society in its more primitive forms sees the manifestations of mental disorder as proof of divine powers, or evidence of divine disfavour. The Bible abounds in cases of reputed demoniac possession, and medieval Christendom, in its orgy of witch-hunting, persecuted thousands whose only crime was that they suffered from mental aberration. The so-called 'Devil's Claw'—a patch of insensitive skin on the body of the supposed witch into which pins and knives might be inserted without causing pain—is to-day widely recognized as a form of localized anæsthesia found in some cases of hysteria;[1] yet it was believed to be an infallible proof of witchcraft, for which the penalty was trial by ordeal, or death at the stake. The harmless lunatic was generally treated with respect in the Middle Ages, as being different from other people, and thus standing in a special relation to the Deity. Piers Plowman refers to the 'lunatik lollers'[2]:

[1] B. Hart, *Psychology of Insanity, p. 5;* see also M. Murray, *The Witch Cult in Western Europe,* p. 86.
[2] 'Lollers' = vagabonds.

# EIGHTEENTH-CENTURY THEORY

Moneyles thei walke
With a good wil, witlees, meny wyde contreys
Ryghte as Peter dude, and Paul, save that thei preche nat.

and the author continues:

Mattheu ous techeth
We sholde have hem to hous, and help hem when thei come.

The penal laws against witchcraft were removed in 1736, and belief in witchcraft had certainly been superseded by rationalism in the minds of the educated classes; but among the uneducated, this belief lingered on, and local trials for witchcraft were not uncommon in the mid-eighteenth century. A case is noted in the *Percy Anecdotes*—'so recently as the year 1759'—in which an elderly woman named Susannah Hannokes was accused at Wingrove in Hertfordshire of bewitching her neighbour's spindle, and was tried by the time-honoured method of weighing against the Church Bible. The Bible appears to have been a comparatively small one, for 'to the no small astonishment and mortification of her accuser, she actually outweighed it, and was honourably acquitted of the charge'. Sir Frederick Eden, writing in 1797, found it 'mortifying to a philosophic mind' that a British jury could be persuaded that the crime of witchcraft existed, and that a woman could converse with the devil in the shape of a cat.[1] It is interesting to note in this connection that Mr. Montague Summers, that modern believer in witchcraft, relating the case of a female witch convicted and hanged in 1670, referred to her as 'this miserable lunatic',[2] apparently regarding mental abnormality as proof that the sufferer was allied to the powers of darkness.

When burning witches became prohibited by law, and witchcraft became a doubtful hypothesis which only the totally uneducated took seriously, the poorer classes turned to other methods of driving the devil out of the lunatic. D. H. Tuke, in his *Chapters in the History of the Insane in the British Isles*, mentions the existence of several wells in the remoter parts of the British Isles where superstitious rites connected with insanity were practised even in the nineteenth century. The usual procedure was a combination of repeated duckings and religious rites—a system which differed little in practice from the 'ordeal by water' formerly used in witchcraft trials, and which had more than a little in common with the 'cold bath' and the 'bath of surprise' which were favourite remedies for

---

[1] F. Eden, *State of the Poor*, pp. 146-7.
[2] M. Summers, *History of Witchcraft and Demonology*, 1926, p. 35.

insanity among the medical profession. At St. Nun's Pool in Cornwall, the sufferer was made to stand with his back to the pool, and was then thrown suddenly into it. After being repeatedly ducked until half-drowned and thoroughly exhausted, he was taken to the church, and certain masses were sung over him. If there was no marked improvement in his condition, the process was repeated as long as life remained. At a well in Scotland, the lunatic was stripped of his clothes, bound hand and foot, immersed in the sacred pool, and then left all night in the chapel. If he managed to free himself of his bonds during the night, there was a good hope of recovery. 'It sometimes happens,' added Tuke's informant, 'that death relieves him during his confinement of the troubles of life.'[1]

If the insane were no longer judicially executed, they were certainly regarded with superstitious fear by the lower classes, who clung to the belief that harsh treatment would drive out the devil. Thus there was no hope of pressure for the amelioration of conditions from this quarter.

*(ii) The Medical Profession.*

Medical qualifications were at this time unstandardized, and the title of 'doctor' bore no settled meaning. A Master of Arts of the Universities of Oxford or Cambridge could still acquire an M.D. degree by expounding a book of Galen in three written or six spoken lectures,[2] the Royal College of Physicians and the Company of Barber-Surgeons held their own examinations, but the examining boards were completely irresponsible, and the standard required was low.[3] The Society of Apothecaries licensed its own men, but anyone who had served a nominal apprenticeship as a druggist might set up in his own right and call himself an apothecary. No legal action against the unqualified practitioner was possible, and none of the licensing bodies had any real authority outside the metropolitan area. One witness before a Select Committee which examined this problem in 1834 spoke of a man who had set up as a 'chemist, druggist, surgeon, apothecary and man-midwife' without qualifications of any description.[4]

Since professional standards were so low, the average medical practitioner contented himself with a rough-and-ready knowledge of the ailments of the body, and had little or no apprehension of the complexities of the mind-body relationship. There were no facilities for research, and

---

[1] D. H. Tuke, op. cit., Chapter 1, *passim*.

[2] A. Chaplin, *Medicine in the Reign of George III*, pp. 18–19.

[3] *A Statement by the Society of Apothecaries*, 1844, p. 20. (Evidence of Sir David Barry and Mr. R. D. Grainger before Select Committee, 1834.)

[4] *A Statement by the Society of Apothecaries*, p. 35.

few ways of disseminating information. Medical knowledge was still dominated by the belief in the four 'humours' of blood, choler, phlegm and bile, and the theory that all human ailments were due to an excess of one or more of these substances. The means employed in driving out the excess humours were in some ways akin to those used in driving out the devil, since they consisted in systematically weakening the patient, and sometimes in a calculated terrorism.

*The Anatomy of Melancholy*, published in 1676, gives a detailed analysis of the beliefs which were commonly held by medical men up to the end of the eighteenth century and beyond. Burton's treatise derived partly from Hippocrates, with a superstructure of religious and superstitious ideology. The original cause of madness was the Fall of Man. "We are . . . bad by nature, bad by kind, but far worse by art, every man the greatest enemy unto himself." Mental and moral defect were synonymous.

Although he attributed the basic causes of insanity to sin and the activities of the devil, Burton also believed that the 'six non-natural things' were contributory causes. These were bad air, the retention of bodily excretions, bad diet, lack of sleep—'which causeth dizziness of the brain, frenzie, dotage, and makes the body lean, dry, hard and ugly to behold', too much or too little exercise, and emotional disturbances.

Burton's outline of physiology was almost entirely derived from Hippocrates. The body consisted of parts contained and containing, the most important of the former being the four humours. The treatment of mental disturbance was a matter of removing the excess of these substances by means of evacuation.

The most readily accessible means of evacuation were 'simples', or purges and vomits. Burton recommended laurel, white hellebore, antimony and tobacco—'divine, rare, super-excellent tobacco . . . a sovereign remedy to all diseases. A good vomit, I confess, if it be well qualified, opportunely taken, and medicinally used; but as it is commonly abused by most men . . . hellish, divelish and damned tobacco.' Senna, aloes, herb mercury and half-boiled cabbage were also useful. Many of these substances had been used in the treatment of insanity in antiquity, and were probably still being used by country doctors in 1845.

Bodily evacuation could also be achieved by blood-letting, and other 'chirurgical' methods, such as the use of horse-leeches, and the practice of raising blisters through the application of plasters and hot irons. 'Cauteries and hot irons are to be used in the suture of the crown, and the seared or ulcerated place suffered to run a good while.' Burton also cited a number of authorities for the efficacy of the ancient practice of trephining, which

LUNACY, LAW, AND CONSCIENCE

involved boring holes in the skull of the sufferer in order to allow the humours affecting the brain to escape.[1]

The Anatomy of Melancholy was widely current in the eighteenth century, and received the public commendation of an archbishop in 1777.[2] The foreword to the 1821 edition shows that, even at that date, Burton's diagnoses and treatment were acceptable.

*(iii) The Church.*

The Church of England was the only considerable religious force in England in the first half of the eighteenth century; nonconformity suffered an eclipse from the Restoration to the advent of the Wesleys, and Roman Catholics were still unpopular, possessing no assessable national influence; but the Church of England was a decaying institution in which the parson was often a gentleman, sometimes a scholar, seldom a pastor, and never a priest. In the country parishes, no doubt, existed men of the calibre of George Herbert, but they did not usually obtain preferment, and their influence was restricted to their own charges. The fox-hunting parson perhaps did little or no harm to the human race, but he was not the man to lead a crusade; the socially eligible parson—like Mr. Tilney in *Northanger Abbey*—found ample leisure from his pastoral duties to take part in the social round; and the obsequious parson, of whom Jane Austen's Mr. Collins is the epitome,[3] had no time or thought to spare for the unfortunate.

It is doubtful whether the majority of the clergy at this time possessed a coherent social philosophy other than that implied in the defence of privilege; but if they turned for assistance to contemporary theology, it merely reinforced their own inclinations. At different periods in history, the Church tends to stress varying aspects of the Christian Gospel, and until the eighteenth century, the laity had lived under the perpetual shadow of Death, Judgment and Hell. Now the emphasis changed. The new philosophical fashion of 'natural law' produced a new theology—a rationalized theology which proclaimed that the world was as God made it, and that doubtless His reasons for doing so were good. The old ideas and the new came together in a synthesized theory of judgment—that human misery was a result of personal sin. What Man, with his limited vision, called evil, was divinely ordained. It followed from this premise that the

[1] Trephining was the forerunner of the modern surgical operation of pre-frontal leucotomy. See W. R. Brain and E. B. Strauss, *Recent Advances in Neuro-Psychiatry*, 5th edition, p. 126.

[2] Archbishop Herring. See Introduction to 1821 edition.

[3] *Northanger Abbey* was published in 1818, and *Pride and Prejudice* in 1813. Both were written some years before publication.

6

poor, the sick, and the insane deserved their fate, and that it was not for Man to interfere with the plans of an inscrutable Deity. 'God moves in a mysterious way' wrote Cowper, and it was not the task of the clergy to plumb the mystery.

This thesis, outlined by Bishop Butler,[1] was taken a step forward by the poet and theological expositor Soame Jenyns, in his *Free Enquiry into the Nature of Good and Evil* (1757). 'The beauty and happiness of the whole,' he wrote, 'depend on the just inferiority of the parts,' and 'the sufferings of individuals are absolutely necessary to human happiness.' Jenyns seems to have envisaged a kind of cosmic hierachy dependent on moral worth, where in a scale ranging from archangels to the lower animals, men appeared high or lowly placed according to their deserts. Each had his use, and each his appointed place.

Such a view of theology made possible a complete acceptance of poverty and disease. The wealthy and powerful owed no duty to the less fortunate members of society. The emphasis had shifted from an immanent God who redeemed Mankind and healed the sick in mind and body to a transcendent God who created and judged in supreme and uncaring isolation.

'Observe him,' said Burton of the lunatic—

> . . . for as in a glass
> Thine angry portraiture it was.
> His picture keep still in thy presence,
> 'Twixt him and thee, there's no difference.[2]

In this respect, Archbishop Herring probably differed from Burton. The clergy saw every possible difference between themselves and the insane. Moral condemnation of the mentally abnormal was as strong a component of eighteenth-century rationalist theology as it was of medical thought, or the inarticulate beliefs of the labouring classes.

### (iv) Philosophy.

Philosophers did not condemn the insane on moral grounds, but this was largely because they ignored them and their problems completely. Many philosophers of the period occupied themselves with the workings of the human mind, but the question of the existence of the whole field of abnormal psychology was never raised. David Hume, in his *Inquiry Concerning the Principles of Morals*, postulated that there were no absolute

---

[1] S. Butler, *The Analogy of Religion*, 1736.
[2] Argument of the Frontispiece, *Anatomy of Melancholy*.

standards, personal merit being merely the possession of qualities 'useful or agreeable to the person himself or to others'.[1] Professor Willey, commenting on Lord Chesterfield's letters to his son, remarks that Chesterfield betrayed a similar belief.[2] The highest good was to be well thought of, and the virtuous man was he who won universal approbation. There was no place in this philosophy of life for those who wished to fight social injustice.

Hartley, in his *Observations on Man*, recognized the existence of certain types of mental aberration. He described hallucinations—'a vivid train of images which forces itself on the patient's eye'—and obsessions—'the frequent recurrency of the same ideas'. He noted in passing the existence of 'violent passions' and 'vapours, hypochondriacal and hysterical disorders'; but his own preoccupation with the 'natural' phenomena— the working of the sane and normal mind—precluded more than a passing interest in these things. His section on 'Imperfections in the Rational Faculty' occupies only nine pages in a work of over six hundred. As a doctor, we are told by his translator,[3] David Hartley 'visited with affectionate sympathy the humblest recesses of poverty and sickness as well as the stately beds of pampered distemper'.[4] Yet neither his medical training, his knowledge of the mind, nor his human instincts induced him to consider in detail the problems of insanity.

That cultured philosopher and man of letters, the third Earl of Shaftesbury, showed an unusual compassion when he wrote in his curiously elliptical style: 'Poor mad people and naturals, how treated? The diversion of seeing Bedlam—what a better laugh? See the malignity of this . . . vulgar, sordid and profane laughter.'[5] Yet he also subscribed to the prevalent philosophy of *laisser-faire*. 'What wouldst thou? That which is good for the world.—Who knows what is good for the world? Who should know but the Providence that looks after it?'[6]

Superstition, moral condemnation, ignorance, and apathy: these were the mental attitudes which dominated the treatment of the insane in the eighteenth century; and they were inevitably reflected in the pattern of administration.

[1] *Hume's Essays and Treatises on Several Subjects*, Edinburgh, 1804, vol. 2, p. 319.
[2] B. Willey, *The Eighteenth-Century Background*, p. 123.
[3] Hermann Andrew Pistorius.
[4] Pistorius, *Notes and Additions to Dr. Hartley's Observations on Man*, 3rd edition, p. 8.
[5] *Life and Letters of the 3rd Earl of Shaftesbury*, 1900 edition, p. 226.
[6] *Life and Letters of the 3rd Earl of Shaftesbury*, p. 96.

# Chapter Two

## EIGHTEENTH-CENTURY PRACTICE

THE main ways in which the insane were confined in the first half of the eighteenth century may be distinguished as follows:

(a) *Those confined under the Poor Laws.* The 'pauper lunatic' was the responsibility of the parish overseer, and was subject to the rigours and inconsistencies which characterized the old Poor Law.

(b) *Those confined under the criminal law.* Insanity was until 1800 ineffective as a defence against a criminal charge. In certain cases, an individual jury might refuse to convict where the prisoner was obviously insane, but as a general rule, the criminally insane went to gaols and Bridewells in exactly the same way as other prisoners.

(c) *Those confined under the vagrancy laws.* The common vagrant was at this time heavily penalized. Poor Law legislation drew a sharp distinction between the respectable pauper who applied for relief in his own parish, and the pauper who wandered abroad begging. Since each parish had to provide for the relief of its own paupers by means of a rate, it followed that each was concerned to prevent casual vagrants from becoming a charge on its funds, and any beggar who was found in a place other than his legal place of settlement was treated with the utmost severity. Administering the vagrancy laws was one of the functions of the local justice of the peace. Vagrants were usually sent to the county Bridewell.

(d) *Those confined in private madhouses.* These institutions were run for private profit, and among their inmates were not only the insane, but also a proportion of people wrongfully detained at the instance of their relatives. Private madhouses varied in size from those taking only two or three patients to those which accommodated three or four hundred. A few of the larger ones took military or naval cases, or received pauper lunatics sent in by the parish overseer because their presence in the workhouse was disturbing to the other inmates. In these cases, the establishments were subject to the inspection of the authorities concerned, but the average private madhouse was such an unpleasant place that the inspection was likely to be a nominal one. Other patients—and these were the vast majority—were without any form of legal protection. The only possible defence which could be raised against the illegal detention of a sane person was by means of a writ of Habeas Corpus,[1] but this means was not often employed, and such was the secrecy with which the proprietors of private madhouses surrounded their activities, that it was seldom successful.

(e) *Patients in Bethlem.* Bethlem Hospital in London had been in use since the year 1377 as an institution for the reception of those suffering from acute forms of mental disorder. It was financed by public subscriptions and legacies.

(f) *Single Lunatics.* This term is used, as it was used in the nineteenth century, to indicate all who were confined alone. The state of single lunatics varied enormously, since it depended entirely on the arrangements made by relatives and friends for their confinement. They can be divided into three main classes—patients of some social standing who remained in their own homes and received medical attention; patients who were 'put away' by their families, usually in some deserted place where their existence might be forgotten, and the family scandal allowed to die down; and those in poorer families who were simply tied or chained in a corner of the house to prevent them from becoming a nuisance to other people. A writer in the *Westminster Review* as late as March, 1845, considered that this class was in the worse case of all.

'The portion of the domestic accommodation usually assigned to these unfortunates is that commonly devoted to the reception of coals . . . namely, that triangular space formed between the stairs and the ground-floor. In this confined, dark and damp corner may be found at this very time no small number of our fellow-beings, huddled, crouching and gibbering, with less apparent intelligence and under worse treatment than the lower domestic animals.'

Nothing further can be said at this juncture concerning single lunatics

[1] *Halsbury's Laws of England* states (2nd edition, vol. 9. p. 718): 'The writ may issue at the instance of any person who is wrongfully kept in confinement under the pretence of insanity or unsoundness of mind, to compel the person having the custody of the person alleged to be insane to produce him in court so that the legality of the detention may be inquired into.' This was also the law in the eighteenth century.

and those in private madhouses,[1] as no public records were kept at this period, and the whole object of such confinement was secrecy; but it is possible to form a picture of the conditions under which the insane lived in Bethlem, and in workhouses and prisons throughout the country.

## I. BETHLEM

*Early History.*

This hospital, which gave the English language a new and descriptive word, was in 1744 the only public hospital in England devoted to the care of the insane.[2] It originally derived its name from a priory of the Order of St. Mary of Bethlehem founded in London in 1247. It was seized by the Crown in 1375 on the grounds that it was in the possession of an alien Order, and was used from 1377 as an institution for the reception of those suffering from acute forms of mental disorder. It was apparently controlled by the Crown until 1546, when the Lord Mayor of London, Sir John Gresham, petitioned Henry VIII to grant the hospital to the City. The Charter was granted on January 13th, 1547—only a few days before the King's death. Eight years later, control passed for a short time into the hands of the Governors of Christ's Hospital, but this experiment in government was apparently a failure. In 1557, the management was transferred to the Governors of the original Bridewell at Blackfriars; this arrangement was later confirmed by Act of Parliament,[3] and endured throughout the joint life of the two institutions until Bethlem was brought under public control in 1853. Governors were elected by the freemen of the City, the Court of Aldermen and the Common Council of the City serving *ex-officio*.

The institution was financed by public subscriptions and legacies; money received in donations and bequests was invested in house property in London, and by the early eighteenth century, when the value of such property was rising, Bethlem was a comparatively wealthy institution, being spared the financial anxieties which beset other ventures in philanthropy.

Patients were liable for their own maintenance unless they were paupers, in which case the responsibility for maintenance fell upon the parish of settlement. Up to the middle of the seventeenth century, 'Toms o' Bed-

---

[1] Conditions in private madhouses are discussed in Chapter 3 in relation to the events of 1763.
[2] See D. H. Tuke, *Hist. of Insane*, p. 45 *et seq.*; Zilboorg and Henrey, *Hist. of Medical Psychology*, p. 564, and O'Donoghue, *Story of Bethlehem Hospital, passim.*
[3] 22 Geo. III, c. 77.

lam'—discharged patients with a recognisable badge[1] which gave them licence to beg in order to pay their arrears—were a familiar sight in towns and villages throughout England. John Aubrey's description is a well-known one:

'Till the breaking out of the Civill Warres, Tom' o Bedlams did travell about the country. They had been poore distracted men that had been putt into Bedlam, where, recovering to some sobernesse, they were licentiated to goe a-begging . . . they wore about their necks a great horn of an oxe in a string or bawdric, which, when they came to an house for almes, they did wind.'[2]

The profession, if it can be called such, suffered greatly from the intrusion of other beggars who counterfeited the distinguishing marks of the Bedlam beggar in order to escape the penalties of the vagrancy laws. A poem composed by a pretended Bedlamite in the seventeenth century sings of:

The lordly lofts of Bedlam
With stubble soft and dainty,
Brave bracelets strong,
Sweet whips, ding-dong,
And wholesome hunger plenty.[3]

'Old Bedlam' was rebuilt after a fire in 1678. The new building was a reproduction of the Tuileries, a fact which is said to have given considerable offence to Louis XIV. It stood on the same site—a flat, low-lying piece of ground at Moorfields, and was partly built over the ancient City ditch, where Liverpool Street station now stands. Prints[4] show an imposing frontage surrounded by pleasant greenery. On either side of the main gate stood the two famous figures of Raving and Melancholy Madness, designed by Caius Gabriel Cibber, and commemorated by Alexander Pope in *The Dunciad*:

Close to those walls where Folly holds her throne,
And laughs to think Monroe would take her down,
Where, o'er the gates, by his famed father's hand,
Great Cibber's brazen brainless brothers stand.[5]

[1] Pictures of the Bedlamite badge and horn may be seen in the Print Room at the British Museum.

[2] J. Aubrey, *Natural History of Wiltshire* (written 1656–91), p. 93.

[3] 'Loving Mad Tom'. *Giles Earle's Song Book*, 1615, and broadsheets.

[4] In the Print Room at the British Museum, and also at the Victoria and Albert Museum.

[5] 'Great Cibber' was Colley Cibber, the actor. D. H. Tuke (*Hist. of Insane*, p. 71) states that a vitriolic reply made to *The Dunciad* by Cibber hastened Pope's death; but as the poem was published in 1728, and Pope died in 1744, this seems far-fetched.

'Monroe' refers to James Monro, son of a Principal of Edinburgh University, who became resident physician of Bethlem in 1728, the year in which *The Dunciad* was written. He held office until 1752, when he was succeeded by his son John; the management of Bethlem remained largely in the hands of an unbroken line of Monros, the office of physician passing from father to son, until 1891.[1]

*Conditions in the Eighteenth Century.*

Bethlem has always had its defenders and attackers. Since most of the early records of the hospital have now been destroyed, we are largely dependent on partisan accounts of the treatment at this time. The official *Story of Bethlehem Hospital*, published as recently as 1913, and written by the chaplain of the hospital, continues this partisanship to some extent, and displays a distressing geniality. '. . . I have a whole budget of literary associations to gossip over as we saunter through the wards,' writes the author. 'Will you allow me to open the pack and spread out some of my attractive wares?' Until 1770, idle and curious visitors were allowed to enter Bethlem at a fee of a penny or twopence a time, in order to watch the antics of the inmates.[2] The official historian's attitude seems to have more in common with them than with the sober and responsible philanthropists who made it their business to investigate conditions in the nineteenth century.

As an instance of the two attitudes, two poems quoted by historians of Bethlem are here reproduced. The first, which appears in the official history, was written by one J. Clark in 1744, and was sold to visitors:

> . . . to our Governors, due praise be giv'n
> Who, by just care, have changed our Hell to Heav'n.
> A Hell on earth no truer can we find
> Than a disturbed and distracted mind.
> . . . our learned Doctor gives his aid,
> And for his Care with Blessings ever paid,
> This all those happy Objects will not spare
> Who are discharged by his Skill and Care.
> Our Meat is good, the Bread and Cheese the same,
> Our Butter, Beer and Spoon Meat none can blame.
> The Physic's mild, the Vomits are not such,
> But, thanks be prais'd, of these we have not much.

[1] See *D.N.B.*
[2] D. H. Tuke, *Hist. of Insane*, p. 73.

Bleeding is wholesome, and as for the Cold Bath,
All are agreed it many Virtues hath.
The Beds and Bedding are both warm and clean,
Which to each comer may be plainly seen,
Except those rooms where the most Wild do lie. . . .[1]

This skilful if naïve propaganda was dedicated to the Governor,[2] Admiral Vernon, and may have served to quiet the consciences of the fashionable visitors.

An anonymous poem written in 1776 is quoted by Daniel Hack Tuke, sometime President of the Royal Medico-Psychological Association, and member of a family famous in the history of lunacy reform:

Far other views than these within appear
And Woe and Horror dwell forever here;
Forever from the echoing roofs rebound
A dreadful Din of heterogeneous sounds.
From this, from that, from every quarter rise
Loud shouts and sullen groans and doleful cries. . . .
Within the Chambers which this Dome contains
In all her 'frantic' forms, Distraction reigns . . .
Rattling his chains, the wretch all raving lies
And roars and foams, and Earth and Heaven defies.[3]

Perhaps the most famous representation of these conditions occurs in the eighth scene of *The Rake's Progress*, which Hogarth painted in the incurable ward in 1733. It shows two fashionable ladies watching the inmates without a visible sign of compassion. The Rake lies on the floor, practically naked, and with his head shaven, while a keeper manacles his feet and another, or an apothecary, examines his head. His expression shows an extreme of cynicism, bitterness, and despair. Another print, dated about 1745 and in the Gardner Collection, shows a similar scene. The patient is again shorn; his hands are chained, and he struggles violently while three keepers hold him down in order to affix a leg-lock to his ankles. A bowl for bleeding or vomit lies in front of the group, and one of the onlookers is a woman—presumably, from her clothes, a female attendant.

An interesting and probably authentic account of the conditions of those whom Tuke's anonymous rhymer called the 'most Wild' occurs in

[1] O'Donoghue, *Story of Bethlehem Hospital*, p. 237.
[2] The House Governor, a paid official.
[3] D. H. Tuke, *Hist. of Insane*, p. 75.

Harrison Ainsworth's *Jack Sheppard*. It refers to the year 1720. Jack Sheppard, who is wanted for murder, risks arrest in order to visit Bethlem to see his mother, who has been driven insane by his crimes:

'Jack absolutely recoiled before the appalling object that met his gaze. Cowering in a corner upon a heap of straw sat his unfortunate mother, the complete wreck of what she had been. Her eyes glistened in the darkness—for light was only admitted through a small grated window—like flames, and as she fixed them on him, their glances seemed to penetrate to his very soul. A piece of old blanket was fastened across her shoulders, and she wore no other clothing except a petticoat. Her arms and feet were uncovered, and of almost skeleton thinness. Her features were meagre and ghastly white, and had the fixed and horrible stamp of insanity. Her head had been shaved, and around it was swathed a piece of rag, in which a few straws were stuck. Her thin fingers were armed with nails as long as the talons of a bird. A chain, riveted to an iron belt encircling her waist, bound her to the wall. The cell in which she was confined was about six feet long and four feet wide.'

This description might be dismissed as over-painted were it not for the fact that reliable investigators in 1815 discovered patients in almost identical conditions.[1]

*Management.*

The management of Bethlem was marred during this period by a series of financial scandals concerning the misappropriation of money and goods by the staff. In 1752, a pamphlet entitled *Low Life: or, One Half of the World does not know how the Other Half Lives*, accused the keepers of stealing food and personal possessions from the patients.[2] In 1772, the House Governor himself was dismissed for obtaining large quantities of provisions from the buttery for his personal use.[3]

*Medical Treatment.*

'Patients are ordered to be bled about the latter end of May, or the beginning of June, according to the weather,' stated Dr. Thomas Monro in evidence before the Select Committee of 1815, 'and after they have been bled, they take vomits once a week for a certain number of weeks; after that, we purge the patients. That has been the practice invariably for

---

[1] See Chapter 6.
[2] O'Donoghue, *Story of Bethlehem Hospital*, pp. 261-4.
[3] O'Donoghue, op. cit., p. 264.

15

years, long before my time; it was handed down to me by my father, and I do not know any better practice.'[1] The control of the Monro family over the medical treatment of the patients was complete and unchallenged, and consisted in an unvarying and indiscriminate use of weakening agents to reduce violence, coupled with the frequent use of mechanical forms of restraint.

### Clothing and Bedding.

Most patients, male and female, appear to have been kept in a state of near or complete nakedness,[2] either because the authorities would not provide clothes, or because the patients might destroy them. Bedding usually consisted of straw for the paupers and unclean patients, since this was cheap and easily cleared away when fouled.[3]

### Diet.

J. Clark's statement concerning the plentiful provision of bread, beer, and 'Spoon Meat'—which presumably means meat broth—were probably coloured to suit the authorities. Patients who were chronically undernourished were more amenable, and one does not feed well a patient who is about to undergo a course of vomits and purges. The financial depredations and raids on the buttery make it unlikely that there was sufficient food to nourish the patients adequately after the Governors' banquets, the requisitions of the House Governor, and the thefts of the keepers had been accounted for out of public funds.

### Visitation.

While casual visitors who paid for admission and came only for entertainment were welcome, serious and responsible visitors who wished to observe and ameliorate conditions were not. Medical practitioners were forbidden to see the patients, and an entry in John Wesley's diary shows that the same prohibition extended to ministers of religion. 'I went to see a young woman in Bedlam; but I had not talked to her long before one gave me to know that none of the preachers were to come here. So we are forbidden to go to Newgate for fear of making them wicked, and to Bedlam for fear of making them mad!'

It is easy to overstate the case against the authorities of Bethlem. They

---

[1] 1815 Report on Madhouses, p. 110.

[2] See p. 95.

[3] O'Donoghue, Story of Bethlehem Hospital, p. 273 and illustration, among many other references.

16

provided care and treatment of a kind when this was otherwise unknown, and had no precedents against which to test their methods. An institution for the reception of the violently insane can never be wholly a pleasant place, and, however enlightened the policy of the authorities, there will always be patients who suffer extremely through delusions of persecution, depression, or squalid habits that defy the most patient and sustained attempts at cleanliness; but the available evidence shows that the policy of the authorities, even by eighteenth-century standards, was very far from enlightened.

## 2. WORKHOUSES AND POORHOUSES

By 1774, pauperism—genuine poverty, as opposed to habitual vagrancy —had assumed alarming proportions. There is probably no other period in English history in which the social classes were so clearly divided. A small book entitled *An Account of the Workhouses in Great Britain in the Year* 1732, compiled apparently from official returns, gives a vivid picture of the treatment of the poor at this time. The rich, who had to pay the rates, were obsessed with the idea that institutions for the poor must be run as cheaply as possible. The Guardians of the workhouse in the parish of St. George's, Hanover Square recorded with some pride that as a result of the 'frugality of management under Honourable Persons' they had succeeded in reducing the cost of maintenance per head to the sum of one and ninepence halfpenny per week. At Maidstone, the Poor Law authorities were satisfied that 'very great numbers of lazy People, rather than submit to the Confinement and Labour of the Workhouse, are content to throw off the Mask and maintain themselves by their own Industry.' 'A Workhouse,' they added, 'is a Name that carries with it an idea of Correction and Punishment.' A prayer 'proper to be used in Workhouses', and couched in the language of the 1662 Prayer Book, includes the plea that the poor may not 'cherish Sin with the Bread of Idleness.'

It is impossible to assess the number of mentally disordered people who were housed in institutions of this stringent and corrective nature. The parliamentary committee of 1807 came to the conclusion that the previous year's estimate of 1765 was a gross under-estimate[1] and in 1828, the figure was put at 9000.[2] Even allowing for the increase of population in the late eighteenth and early nineteenth centuries, it would be safe to say that there must have been four or five thousand people suffering from

[1] *Report of Select Committee on Criminal and Pauper Lunatics,* 1807, Appendix 1.
[2] D. H. Tuke, *Hist. of Insane,* p.173.

17

psychotic disorders or mental deficiency in workhouses before 1789. The significant fact is that their existence was hardly recognized. The *Account of Workhouses in* 1732, which included returns from all the principal Poor Law institutions in the country, mentions them in only two instances, and then in passing. There was no special administrative practice for dealing with pauper lunatics as a class, so that their treatment depended on the policy—or lack of policy—of the local authorities.

*The Position under the Poor Law.*

The basis of Poor Law legislation was the Act of 1601 (43 Eliz. c. 2), which stated that unpaid overseers of the poor were to raise money 'weekly or otherwise by taxation' in each parish for the relief of its own paupers. Outdoor relief was common in most parishes before 1723, the year of the Workhouse Test. It was widely used again towards the end of the century,[1] when the volume of distress became so great that it was impossible for the workhouses to deal with the problem; but in the period under review, outdoor relief was not in general use, and many parishes used the workhouse as a weapon to deter the poor from seeking relief.

The great failure of the Poor Law lay in the apparent inability of its administrators to distinguish between the 'impotent poor' who could not work, and the able-bodied poor who would not. Conditions varied greatly from parish to parish, but the number of authorities was so great, and the administrative area of each so small, that it was impossible for most of them to devise a system of classification which would allow for differentiation in treatment.

A scheme for making more sympathetic provision for the 'impotent poor' was put forward by the Earl of Hillsborough in 1753; he proposed that county hospitals should be set up, and that 'none be admitted into the hospital except the children of parents not able to maintain themselves; all exposed and deserted children, diseased persons who cannot work, and are too poor to purchase medicines; idiots, climatics, lame, old, blind, and others having no means to maintain themselves.'[2] Such a scheme would have been impossible to put into practice without great financial outlay and extensive reorganization of the whole framework of poor relief.

It has been estimated[3] that under the old Poor Law there were between

---

[1] After the passing of Gilbert's Act, 1782, and the introduction of the Speenhamland system.

[2] Eden, *State of the Poor*, pp. 318-9.

[3] S. and B. Webb, *English Poor Law History*, vol. 1.—The Old Poor Law, p. 155.

twelve and fifteen thousand separate parishes and townships, each controlling its own institution for the relief of pauperism. The principles on which relief was organized differed widely. In some of the smaller parishes, the poorhouse was primarily an almshouse for the infirm and aged of respectable character; but in the larger cities, the organized workhouse had superseded the poorhouse, and the succour of the impotent was at best only a secondary aim.

*Diet.*

The *Account of Workhouses* shows that the outstanding characteristic of the workhouse diet at this time was its monotony. Whether generous or meagre in quantity, it was composed almost entirely of starch foods such as bread, pease-pudding, 'hasty-pudding',[1] or 'frumenty',[2] since these were cheap and filling. Milk occurred in most diets only once or twice a week, and the common drink was small beer. Vegetables, other than root vegetables, and fish hardly ever appeared, though the institution run by the Society of Friends at Clerkenwell, and restricted to 'decayed Friends and Orphans' served 'Mackarel, Herrings and Salt-fish in season'. At Hanslope, Bucks, the paupers received for their main meal 'flesh meat' on two days of the week, and on the other five 'a piece of wheaten bread and small beer'. At Bishopsgate Street in London, the main meal consisted of 'rice-milk' on Tuesdays, and 'plumb dumplins' on Wednesdays, with meat twice a week. Since the main object of the workhouse policy was to keep down expenditure, the amount of food allowed was usually small. There were a few exceptions, such as the house at Barking, where the inmates were allowed bread and beer in unlimited quantities at every meal, roast beef on the three great festivals, and plum pudding at Christmas in addition.

*Cost of Maintenance.*

The rules of the institution run by the Society of Friends at Clerkenwell required each inmate to have a householder stand surety for him for the sum of three shillings a week. This may explain the luxury of the occasional provision of fish, since workhouses supported entirely out of the poor rate kept their paupers for very much less. Kingston-upon-Hull and St. Martin's-in-the-Fields, both philanthropic institutions of the old type, spent roughly two and eightpence a week per head. St. George's, Hanover Square, as already mentioned, spent only one and ninepence

---

[1] Porridge.
[2] Barley and water.

halfpenny. At Olney, Bucks, the cost of fuel, food and clothing for thirty paupers was estimated at thirty shillings a week. One of the most insistent complaints concerning the new county asylums for the insane in the early nineteenth century was that the expense was unjustified, since pauper lunatics could be accommodated more cheaply in workhouses.[1] Even the least enlightened of the authorities which controlled county asylums never attempted to feed, clothe, and warm its inmates at so low a cost.

*Work.*

The common justification for the existence of the man on parish relief was his ability to work, and provide at least in part for his own maintenance. Institutions like that at Stroud, Kent, where the infirm and aged were said to be 'wholly removed from the Cares of this Life' and had 'nothing to do but to prepare themselves for the next', were rare and merciful in comparison with the majority. At. St. Andrew's, Holborn, seven old men and women 'of which two are upwards of fourscore and one an Ideot' picked oakum, and were said to be 'continually refreshed by the Balsamick Odour of it'. Oakum-picking and the spinning of mop yarn, both lowly-paid and tedious occupations, were the methods of employment almost universally used.

*Discipline.*

The punishments for not working or for 'mischievous conduct' were frequently severe. They included solitary confinement in a dark room, deprivation of food, and being made to stand on a stool 'with the Crime pinned to their Breast'. A pauper whose mental condition precluded the possibility of normal employment, or led him into erratic conduct would thus be penalized in a way which was likely to aggravate the condition.

Violence and excitability were sternly discouraged in institutions which placed great emphasis on orderliness and quietude. At St. Giles-in-the-Fields, paupers who were 'very clamorous' or who made 'great Disturbances' were debarred from meals until they became amenable. At St. Andrew's, Holborn, those who were guilty of 'prophane Cursing or Swearing' were sent to the stocks. The workhouse at Norwich was accustomed to use leg-locks and manacles on troublesome inmates.[2]

*Medical Attention.*

At. St. Albans, the Guardians recorded with some pride that the sick

[1] See pp. 164–6.
[2] Rigby, *Further Facts Relating to the Care of the Poor* . . . *in the City of Norwich,* 1812, p. 43 and illustration.

were nursed by the women paupers, thus saving fifteen to twenty pounds a year in apothecaries' bills. 'There are many workhouses,' wrote an official at Winchester, 'where medicines are dispensed; but they are generally given without the advice of a doctor.'[1] Where medical attention was provided, the general practice was for the contract to be farmed out to the local doctors, and the lowest tender automatically accepted. The doctor or apothecary gave nominal attention to all paupers, providing his own drugs and medicines, for a sum of perhaps twenty pounds a year.[2] Since a degree of physical debility would render the more troublesome lunatics weaker and thus more amenable, it is unlikely that any sustained attempt would be made to restore them to robust and violent health.

*Classification.*

In general, there was no attempt to separate even the small proportion of the mentally disordered who were recognized as such from the other paupers, for the benefit of either class. Some few of the larger workhouses possessed infirmaries, but these appear to have been mainly used for those suffering from infectious and contagious diseases, such as smallpox and syphilis. Norwich had a 'bedlam' for male and female pauper lunatics in 1812,[3] but it is not known at what date this was instituted. Of St. Margaret's, Westminster, it was recorded: 'The Humanity shewn in this House deserves to be noted . . . a Lunatic that has been discharged out of Bedlam as an incurable has a Brick Cell built on purpose for him, and such as may hereafter in the like circumstances want it.'[4]

*St. Peter's, Bristol.*

The outstanding exception to the rigours of the Workhouse Test as it affected the insane was, ironically, the workhouse where that test was initiated. The records of St. Peter's Workhouse, Bristol,[5] show that it was one of the very few where pauper lunatics were treated as a separate class, and almost certainly the only one where they received treatment as distinct from confinement. Almost from its inception in 1696, the first building, known as the Mint, was used for the 'impotent poor' of the city, and other premises were acquired as a 'manufactory' for the able-bodied.

[1] Kirkman Gray, *History of English Philanthropy*, p. 25.
[2] S. and B. Webb, *English Poor Law History*, vol. 1. The Old Poor Law, pp. 304–8.
[3] Rigby, *Further Facts Relating to the Care of the Poor . . . in the City of Norwich*, p. 67.
[4] *Account of Workhouses*, p. 65.
[5] *Bristol Corporation of the Poor. Selected Records, 1696–1834*, ed. E. E. Butcher, 1932.

By degrees, the aged and those suffering from ailments of a mainly physical nature were housed elsewhere, until the Mint became the general asylum for what was then one of the largest cities in England.

The insane patients seem to have been placed in separate wards almost from the first, an early regulation recommending that 'the lunatic wards be floored with planks'—presumably because stone floors were injurious to the patients' health. Medical attention was provided by surgeons and physicians of local standing, who gave their services voluntarily. A regulation of April, 1768, laid down that they were to visit the 'Frenzy Objects' once a week, and also 'such Objects as shall from time to time be brought in by Warrants of Lunacy.'[1]

The treatment consisted of cold baths, commonly held to be efficacious in maniacal cases, and restraint by straps or the strait waistcoat. No chains were used. Homicidal or other dangerous lunatics were occasionally sent to Bethlem for the better protection of the other inmates.

The policy of the authorities at Bristol stands out in complete contrast to that of almost every other Poor Law authority. They established three principles which laid the foundation for the later development of county asylums: the care of the insane should be the responsibility of the parish or township in which they lived; they should be treated as a separate class, their living conditions being adapted to their special needs; and they should receive treatment, not punishment.

### 3. PRISONS

Bridewells, or houses of correction, were built on the pattern of the original Bridewell raised at Blackfriars in London in 1555. They generally received vagrants and beggars who could not be convicted of any crime save that of wandering abroad or refusing to work. They also housed a number of petty offenders of the kind who under the modern penal system would probably be placed on probation. The chief distinction between a gaol and a Bridewell was that in the former, the inmates were responsible for their own maintenance and for the payment of gaolers' fees, since the gaolers were generally not in receipt of a salary. Many prisoners were forced to remain in gaol as debtors long after the original sentence was served. In a Bridewell, the officials received a salary, and the Poor Law authority was responsible for the maintenance of pauper inmates, who were released at the end of their term of imprisonment. At

---

[1] The patients are commonly referred to as 'objects of charity'—cp. 'those happy objects' at Bethlem, p. 13. For warrants of lunacy, see p. 29.

the same time, conditions were such as to deter the sturdiest of beggars. The Master of the Bridewell at Tothill Fields received the sum of £200 a year, out of which he paid the expenses of the entire house, and made his own salary. He was directed to pay a matron, a chaplain, a porter, and sufficient servants, and to provide the inmates with 'fresh straw every month, and warm pottage thrice a week.'[1]

It would appear from John Howard's *Report on the State of the Prisons* (1777), that the inmates of this Bridewell were comparatively fortunate. 'In many Gaols and most Bridewells,' he wrote, 'there is no allowance of straw for the prisoners to sleep on; and if by any means they get a little, it is not changed for months together, so that it is almost worn to dust.' In writing of the Blackfriars Bridewell, he added, 'The night-rooms are supplied with straw. No other Prison in London has any straw or other bedding.'

'There are several Bridewells . . . in which the prisoners have no allowance of food at all. In some, the keeper farms out what little is allowed them: and where he engages to supply each prisoner with one or two pennyworth of bread a day, I have known this shrunk to half, sometimes less than half, the quantity, cut or broken from his own loaf.' In many cases, there were no tools or materials with which the prisoners might work and earn their keep. 'Some keepers of these houses, who have represented to the magistrates the wants of their prisoners, and desired for them necessary food, have been silenced with these inconsiderate words, "Let them work or starve." When these gentlemen know the former is impossible, do they not by that sentence inevitably doom poor creatures to the latter?'

When Howard undertook his lengthy and self-imposed travels on behalf of the prisoners, he found hardened criminals, shiftless vagrants and petty offenders confined together with the insane. 'Idiots and lunatics . . . serve for sport to idle visitants . . . where they are not kept separate (they) disturb and terrify other prisoners. No care is taken of them, though it is probable that by medicines and proper regimen, some of them might be restored to their senses, and to usefulness in life.'

At Kingston-upon-Hull Bridewell, Howard found 'two rooms below and two upstairs, about twelve feet square, very offensive; no fireplace. Courtyard only twenty-two feet by ten; not secure, and prisoners not permitted to go to the pump: no sewer: no allowance: no straw . . . .' He visited this Bridewell on three occasions between 1774 and 1779, and found the same 'poor, raving lunatic' there each time. At Swaffham

[1] S. and B. Webb, *English Poor Law History*, vol. I. The Old Poor Law, p. 86.

County Bridewell, the lunatic whose existence was noted in 1774 was still there in 1779. At the county gaol, Lancaster, he 'saw only one poor lunatic; who had been there many years, and is since dead.' These instances may be multiplied from his report.

Howard notes in the Appendix to his report, added in 1779, that an Act of 1763 provided for the separation of insane prisoners from others, stating that 'persons of insane mind and outrageous behaviour' were not to 'go in common with the other prisoners'.[1] This is another example of segregation of the insane for the benefit of the sane, since vagrants and petty thieves were to receive what amounted to preferential treatment. This Act appears to have been generally ignored, since most County Bridewells were too small and too badly run to admit of diversity in accommodation; but the reformer's recommendation, that all Bridewells should have 'two wards for the sick, with medical relief' was very far from realization. In many cases, the sick and insane lacked not only medical relief and separate quarters, but even fresh air. 'One reason why the rooms in some prisons are so close is perhaps the window-tax, which gaolers have to pay; this tempts them to stop up the windows and stifle the prisoners.'[2]

*Criminal Lunatics.*

Criminally insane persons were confined to gaol, apparently for life. The only prominent judicial opinion of the period drew such a stringent definition of what constituted criminal insanity that only those beyond the hope of cure could possibly be included in it. At the trial of a man named Arnold in 1723 for the attempted murder of Lord Onslow, Mr. Justice Tracey made the following pronouncement:

'It is not every kind of frantic humour, or something unaccountable in a man's behaviour, that points him out to be such a man as is exempted from punishment; it must be a man that is totally deprived of his understanding and memory, and doth not know what he is doing, no more than an infant, than a brute or wild beast; such a one is never the object of punishment.'[3]

This definition necessarily excluded all cases which were not characterized by chronic and continued incoherence, or the lower grades of mental deficiency, so that the vast majority of those who would now be considered criminally insane and sent to institutions of the Broadmoor

---

[1] 3 Geo. III, c. 27.
[2] *Howard on Prisons*, p. 71.
[3] R. v. Arnold, 1723. *English and Empire Digest*, vol. 14, p. 56, para. 223.

type were punished as ordinary criminals. Those who came within the definition of what became known as 'the Wild Beast Test' were in scarcely better case. They were confined to gaols where the conditions were, if possible, even worse than the Bridewells. At Ely, Howard noted, the gaol was until 1763, in ruins; to prevent them from escaping, the gaoler secured the felons by 'chaining them down on their backs on a floor, across which were several iron bars; with an iron collar with spikes about their necks, and a heavy iron bar over their legs'. An 'excellent Magistrate' named James Colyer brought the plight of the prisoners to the notice of the King, 'upon which His Majesty was much affected, and gave immediate orders for a proper inquiry and redress;' but in 1774, the new gaol had an offensive sewer, no water, no infirmary, and no straw for the inmates to sleep on, so that the extent of the redress was apparently not very great. At Bury St. Edmunds, the felons lived by night and day in 'a large dungeon down three steps' and were chained by staples fixed to their bedsteads. In places such as these, the criminally insane—who were completely lacking in any power to look after themselves—were confined without attention and without food except what they might obtain through charity. Such was the nature of their 'exemption from punishment'.

# Chapter Three

## THE GROWTH OF PUBLIC CONCERN

THE reform movement began imperceptibly, through a series of apparently disconnected events, each of which aroused the public interest in some aspect of the treatment of the insane. In 1744, dangerous lunatics were specially considered by a select committee set up to revise the vagrancy laws; in 1763, the general public was alarmed by revelations concerning the conditions in private madhouses, and a movement to obtain statutory control was initiated; in 1789, the nature of the King's illness became generally known, and the topic of insanity was widely discussed in a context which excluded the attitude of moral condemnation. It was scarcely possible—at least in Tory circles—to assume that the head of State was being punished for his sins. Finally, there was an apparent rise in the incidence of insanity among men of letters which increased the public interest in the subject.

It is doubtful whether many people in the eighteenth century sensed the connection between these events; for, as we have seen, the idea of insanity as a single social factor had not yet been evolved. It is only in the light of later developments that these happenings assumed a relevance to each other.

### I. LUNATICS UNDER THE VAGRANCY LAWS, 1744

*Select Committee of 1742–4.*

A parliamentary committee was set up on December 7th, 1742, to consider the treatment of 'rogues and vagabonds' and the revision of the vagrancy laws. It was appointed during Carteret's period of power, but it may safely be assumed that Carteret was not personally interested. 'What is it to me who is a judge and who a Bishop?' he is reputed to have said, 'It is my business to make Kings and Emperors, and to maintain the balance of Europe.[1] Even had he been interested in vagabonds and lunatics—an unlikely surmise—it is doubtful whether he could have commanded sufficient support in parliament to make that interest effective. Carteret was the King's man, and parliament was at this time united against him.

The committee seems to have included men of contrasting personalities. One of its members was George Grenville, who had entered parliament after the general election of the previous year. Grenville, was called by Robert Walpole 'a fatiguing orator and an indefatigable drudge.'[2] Contemporaries agree that he was a stern and formal man, lacking an understanding of human nature. 'I would rather see the devil in my closet than Mr. Grenville,' declared the King some years later, when Grenville was Prime Minister.[3] One would expect Grenville to condemn vagrants, but not to sympathize with insanity. Another member was Horace Walpole, son of Sir Robert, and later to become fourth Earl of Orford. Walpole's literary interests were already strongly developed, following a long stay in Italy; though over twenty years were to elapse before the publication of *The Castle of Otranto* (1764), we might assume that his bent lay in this direction, rather than in that of public affairs. He too had entered parliament in the previous year, and it seems likely that his appointment on this committee served only as an introduction to parliamentary business. Nicholas Fazakerly, the Jacobite member for Preston, was also nominated. Fazakerly was a barrister of some reputation, with strong local loyalties. He had become Recorder of Preston in 1742, and in both local and national politics was a staunch, albeit cautious, adherent of the Tory party.

Lord Sydney Beauclerk was a more colourful character. On the maternal side, he was descended from the last Earl of Oxford; his paternal grandparents were Charles II and Nell Gwyn. The *Dictionary of National Biography* has nothing to say of Lord Sydney save that he was 'a notorious fortune-hunter' and the father of Topham Beauclerk, a friend of Dr. Johnson. It seems unlikely that the problems of poverty and insanity would interest him. As the fifth son of an illegitimate child—even though of royal descent—he doubtless found his own problems of social status and financial resources sufficiently engrossing.

At least four members of the committee were barristers—Fazakerly,

[1] Mahon, *History of England*, vol. III, p. 135.
[2] J. H. Jesse, *Celebrated Etonians*, vol. I, p. 233.
[3] Albemarle, *Memoirs of the Marquis of Rockingham*, vol. II, p. 50.

Edward Clive, William Hay, and Nathaniel Gundry. They represented the necessary legal element in the discussion. Only one member appears to have had an interest in social reform—Hay, who was an active county magistrate, and who twice brought in a Bill for the better relief of the poor. A county magistrate saw much of the practical side of social administration, since he dealt with vagrants, paupers, criminals and insane persons at first hand.

The size and diversity of this committee suggests two things: first, that no small group of members pledged to a clear-cut plan for improvement was in existence; and second, that the issues involved were not a matter of party controversy. In 1742, the Pretender and his son were still active on the continent, and the Hanoverian succession not yet fully established; yet the committee included both the King's friends and those who were potential enemies. Thus there is nothing to suggest that this was more than a routine investigation to find ways of mitigating a common nuisance.

*The Act of 1744 (17 Geo. II, c. 5).*

The act which resulted from the recommendations of this committee was passed under the ægis of those cultured mediocrities, the Pelhams. The mental attitude of the framers of the Act can be judged from the preamble:

'Whereas the number of Rogues, Vagabonds, and other Idle and Disorderly Persons daily increases, to the great Scandal, Loss and Annoyance of the Kingdom. . . .'

Among the anti-social persons to whom the Act applied were:

'Persons who threaten to run away and leave their Wives and Children to the Parish. . . . Persons found in Forests with Guns. . . . All Minstrels, Jugglers. . . . All Persons pretending to be Gipsies, or wandering about in the Habit or Form of Egyptians. . . .'

Section 20 dealt with the violently insane—'those who by Lunacy or otherwise are so far disordered in their Senses that they may be dangerous to be permitted to go Abroad'—as simply one more group of people whose activities had to be restrained for the common good.

Under this Act, any person could apprehend a vagrant, and the local justice of the peace was directed to order the payment of a reward of five shillings to the informer. The vagrant was to be sent on a magistrate's warrant to a Bridewell 'there to be kept to Hard Labour for any Time not exceeding One Month'.

# THE GROWTH OF PUBLIC CONCERN

There were certain differences between the treatment of the common vagrant and that of the person of unsound mind, though these differences were more apparent in theory than in practice.

*Section* 20.

The section of the Act which applied to the insane was as follows:

'It shall and may be lawful for any two or more Justices of the Peace where such Lunatick or mad Person shall be found, by Warrant under their Hands and Seals, directed to the Constables, Churchwardens and Overseers of the Poor of such Parish, Town or Place, to cause such Persons to be apprehended and kept safely locked up in some secure Place . . . as such Justices shall appoint; and (if such Justices find it necessary) to be there chained. . . . The Charges of removing, and of keeping, maintaining and curing such Persons during such Restraint (which shall be for and during such time only as such Lunacy or Madness shall continue) shall be satisfied and paid . . . by Order of two or more Justices of the Peace, directing the Churchwardens or Overseers where any Goods, Chattels, Lands or Tenements of such Persons shall be, to seize and sell so much of the Goods and Chattels, or to receive so much of the annual Rents of the Lands and Tenements, as is necessary to pay the same; and to account for what is so sold, seized or received at the next Quarter Sessions; or, if such Person hath not an Estate to pay and satisfy the same, over and above what shall be sufficient to maintain his or her Family, then such Charges shall be satisfied and paid by the Parish, Town or Place to which such Person belongs, by Order of two Justices directed to the Churchwardens or Overseers for that Purpose.'

This section has several significant points, and its omissions convey a certain amount of information about the treatment which the insane received.

'. . . *to cause such Person to be apprehended* . . .'

The local magistrates, who possessed neither legal nor medical training, were held to be sufficient judges of the existence of a state of insanity. No medical certification was necessary. It should perhaps be pointed out here that responsible medical certification was hardly possible until after 1858— the date of the Medical Registration Act.

'. . . *two or more Justices of the Peace* . . .'

The warrant for the detention of a vagrant under the other sections of the Act required the assent of only one magistrate. The provision of a joint authority in the case of the insane may have been designed to prevent individual magistrates from indulging in a purely personal grudge against an inconvenient neighbour by using their powers under this section.

'. . . *safely locked up in some secure Place* . . .'

The 'secure place' was almost invariably a gaol or house of correction, since these were the only places which possessed the means of preventing the inmates from escaping.

'. . . *removing* . . .'

If he was not a resident of the parish in which he was apprehended, the insane person would be removed to his legal place of settlement, if this could be established, so that the responsibility for his maintenance might devolve on the latter parish.

'. . . *keeping, maintaining and curing* . . .'

No machinery was set up for curative treatment or medical attention of any kind. The only form of treatment apparently envisaged was that of mechanical restraint in the form of chains.

'. . . *during such Time* . . . *as such Lunacy or Madness shall continue* . . .'

Since no medical evidence was necessary to establish that the state of insanity had ceased to exist, the onus of judgment rested presumably on the justices or the gaolers. Two social dangers were implicit in this unsatisfactory clause: a person who regained his sanity might be confined indefinitely if he offered resistance when chained, or fell foul of his gaoler; alternatively, a person suffering from cyclical insanity, the course of which is separable into distinct and recurrent phases, might be released during a lucid spell, to become again a public danger soon after his release.

Behind the framing of this section, and of much subsequent legislation, lay the belief that insanity was one distinct mental state differing so widely from 'normal' mental health that it was easily discernible to the lay eye. It was also believed to be a continuous state. In fact, no state of insanity consists of continued and unabated violence. Many such states are intermittent in their manifestations, while in others exhaustion terminates the intolerable strain placed on the physical system.

'. . . *The Charges* . . . *shall be satisfied and paid* . . .'

The first charge on the estate of the insane person was to pay 'what shall be necessary to maintain his . . . family'. Only when this charge had been adequately met could the local authority distrain his goods and property to pay for his maintenance.

'. . . *to account for what is so seized* . . *at the next Quarter Sessions* . . .'

A legal check was to be kept on the administration of property appropriated by the overseers or churchwardens to satisfy maintenance charges, but no provision was made for safeguarding any other property of the insane person during his confinement under the provision of this Act.[1] Such property might be seized by an unscrupulous relative without fear of legal action.

The 1744 Act could hardly be called a positive advance on previous law or practice. It excited no public interest, and gave rise to no controversies. The sole achievement lay in the fact that some of those suffering from insanity were for the first time recognized as requiring separate legislative provision.

## 2. PRIVATE MADHOUSES, 1763-74

It was nineteen years before the question of the insane was again raised in parliament, and then in connection with the private madhouses. On this occasion, we have the first hint of outside pressure being brought to bear on the House of Commons. The public interest was aroused by two cases in which a writ of Habeas Corpus had been issued as a means of liberating the inmate of a private madhouse suspected of being wrongfully detained. This procedure was seldom successful, since many devices —such as changing the patient's name, using secret cells which could not be detected by an investigator, or declaring that the patient had escaped— could be used to defeat it.

Judging from reported cases, the usual practice was to require that the relatives and a physician appointed by the Court should be given access to the patient in the madhouse, in order to ascertain whether a state of insanity really existed. If they reported that the patient was sane, the proprietor of the madhouse was then required to produce the patient in court.

In the case of Rex v. Turlington (1761)[2] a motion was made on behalf of the relatives of Mrs. Deborah D'Vebre for a Habeas Corpus to be directed to Turlington, the keeper of a private madhouse in Chelsea. Mrs. D'Vebre had been sent there at the instance of her husband. A rule was made that a physician, together with the patient's nearest blood relation (a gentleman named Peter Bodkin) and her attorney should 'at all proper times and reasonable hours respectively be admitted, and have free access to Mrs. Deborah D'Vebre . . . at the madhouse kept by Robert Turlington in Chelsea'.

[1] Protection for the property of the small category of Chancery Lunatics was more effective. See Appendix II.
[2] *English Reports*, vol. 97, p. 741.

# LUNACY, LAW, AND CONSCIENCE

Two days later, an affidavit from the physician was read in Court. It stated that he 'saw no reason to suspect that she was or had been disordered in her mind: on the contrary, he found her to be very sensible, and very cool and dispassionate'. Mrs. D'Vebre was thereupon produced in Court, and allowed to leave with her attorney.

In another case (Rex *v.* Clarke, 1762)[1] the attempt to serve a writ of Habeas Corpus was defeated by an affidavit from the appointed physician that the patient, Mrs. Anne Hunt, was in an acute state of mental disorder, and had in fact been sent to the madhouse on his own advice.

The interest aroused by the Turlington case and the Clarke case caused a growing degree of public concern which was fanned by the publication of a now famous article in the *Gentleman's Magazine* of January, 1763.

'When a person is forcibly taken or artfully decoyed into a private madhouse,' stated the anonymous writer, 'he is, without any authority or any further charge than that of an impatient heir, a mercenary relation, or a pretended friend, instantly seized upon by a set of inhuman ruffians trained up to this barbarous profession, stripped naked, and conveyed to a dark-room. If the patient complains, the attendant brutishly orders him not to rave, calls for assistants, and ties him down to a bed, from which he is not released until he submits to their pleasure. Next morning, a doctor is gravely introduced who, taking the report of the keeper, pronounces the unfortunate person a lunatic, and declares that he must be reduced by physic. If the revolted victim offers to argue against it by alleging any proofs of sanity, a motion is made by the waiter for the doctor to withdraw, and if the patient, or rather the prisoner, persists in vindicating his reason, or refuses to take the dose, he is then deemed raving mad; the banditti of the whole house are called in, the forcing instruments brought, upon which the sensible patient must submit to take whatever is administered. When the poor patient thus finds himself deprived of all communication with the world, and denied the use of pen and paper, all he can do is to compose himself under the unhappy situation in the hope of a more favourable report. But any composure under such affliction is immediately deemed a melancholy or sulky fit, by the waiter, who reports it as such to the doctor in the hearing of the despairing prisoner, whose misery is thus redoubled in finding that the doctor prescribes a repetition of the dose, and that from day to day, until the patient is so debilitated in body that in time it impairs his mind . . . What must a rational mind suffer that is treated in this irrational manner? Weakened by physic,

[1] *English Reports*, vol. 97, pp. 875-6.

emaciated by torture, diseased by confinement, and terrified by the sight of every instrument of cruelty and the dreadful menaces of an attending ruffian, hardened against all the tendernesses of human nature . . .'

The writer concluded with an appeal to parliament to frame regulations designed to prevent the imprisonment of sane people; and parliament responded on the 27th of January by the appointment of a Select Committee of the House of Commons.

### The Select Committee of 1763.

The Bute administration was in its last few months of office;[1] it included Lord Halifax—a man of 'popular manners, loose morals and small ability',[2] Henry Fox, who as leader of the House of Commons was accustomed to bribe members for their support, and is reputed to have spent £2,500 for this purpose in one day;[3] and Sir Francis Dashwood, leader of the Medmenham Monks, that strange society which mixed blasphemy with eroticism and Black Masses with artistic appreciation.[4] It was an extremely unpopular administration, and may have given way to public demand on this matter as a way of attempting to preserve its own existence; but there are two other factors worthy of consideration. One is the personality of Dashwood, who, in spite of his private excesses, had a long and honest political career. A close friend of Dashwood's was Charles Churchill, poet and ex-clergyman, who forsook his Orders for the society of the Medmenhamites, and died in the following year (1764) in circumstances strongly suggesting mental derangement.[5] It is possible that Dashwood, who was then Chancellor of the Exchequer, may have favoured some form of action which would protect the insane. The other factor was the interest of George Grenville, who had been a member of the Committee of 1742. Grenville had been Secretary of State for the Home Department for a few months before that position was appropriated by Henry Fox, and at the time when the Committee was appointed he was at the Admiralty. Both positions would have given him some insight into the conditions of private madhouses, since 'naval maniacs' were sent to these institutions, and the Home Department would have taken an interest in the Turlington and Clarke cases.

Grenville was a member of the Select Committee, as was his brother-in-

---

[1] Bute resigned on April 7th, 1763.
[2] Hunt, Pol. Hist. of England, vol. x, p. 35.
[3] Hunt, op. cit., vol. x, p. 40.
[4] See Chapter 5 in Clubs of the Georgian Rakes, by L. C. Jones.
[5] L. C. Jones, Clubs of the Georgian Rakes, chapter 5, and Albert, Hist. of Eng. Lit., p. 257.

law, the elder Pitt;[1] other members were Lord North, Henry Fox, Soame Jenyns—whose belief in 'the divine right of things as they are' has already been mentioned—John Wilkes and Sir Richard Glyn. Glyn was Lord Mayor of London, and it may have been at this time that he accepted the office of President of Bethlem, a post which he held for many years.[2] Another member with a strong interest in the medical aspects of the problem was T. Harley, later President of St. Bartholomew's Hospital.[3] The Committee represented all shades of political opinion from the extreme Toryism of Jenyns to the extreme Radicalism of Wilkes. The selection of members appears to have been made on a non-party basis in order to make the Committee as representative as possible; but the chairman was a Whig—Thomas Townshend,[4] son of that Viscount Townshend who had been a rival to Carteret, and uncle of Charles Townshend, Chancellor of the Exchequer in the Grenville Government a few months later. Thomas Townshend's mother was a Pelham. He was a man, according to his biographer, of 'scholarly accomplishments and great social charm.'[5] He might be described as a popular back-bencher with front-bench contacts; unlike his friends and relatives on the front bench, he had time and thought to spare for an out-of-the-way subject. What led Townshend to interest himself in the abuses of private madhouses is not known; it may have been personal contact with a distressing case, or his support may have been enlisted by others less influential. That it was a strong interest may be deduced from the fact that his son, Thomas Townshend junior, continued the struggle for legislative reform after him.

The report of this Committee makes curious reading. Townshend and his colleagues apparently found it necessary to proceed with extreme discretion, since London madhouses confined the relatives of many prominent people, and also because a number of well-known members of the medical profession had financial interests in private madhouses. Accordingly, they confined their investigations to two houses—Miles', at Hoxton, and Turlington's, in Chelsea—and to the detailed study of only one case in each house. They stressed in their short report that these were not selected cases, and that hundreds of similar examples existed, but stated that they refrained from publishing further cases out of consideration for the families of sufferers. One of the witnesses before the Committee was

---

[1] Pitt married George Grenville's sister, who was thus the mother of the younger William Pitt.

[2] See successive issues of the *Royal Kalendar*.

[3] *Royal Kalendar*, 1779.

[4] Thomas Townshend senior, 1701-80. M.P. for Winchelsea and Cambridge University.

[5] *D.N.B.*

Dr. Battie of St. Luke's, who was asked if he had ever met with cases in which persons of undoubted sanity were confined as lunatics.

'He said, It frequently happened.'

Dr. Monro of Bethlem, who bore a strong antipathy to Battie,[1] then gave evidence. He flatly contradicted Battie's statement, and stated that no such cases existed.

The allegations concerning the two madhouses investigated were that persons had been confined there on the representation of relatives without adequate medical examination, and that they were prevented from communicating with the outside world, being denied visits from friends and the use of writing materials.

Mrs. Durant had been a patient in Miles' Madhouse at Hoxton. She complained that she had been carried there eight years previously—in 1755—and that, during her confinement, which lasted three weeks, she received no medical treatment and no medicines. She was refused all opportunity of communicating with her friends, and was finally released at the instance of her mother, Mrs. Gold, who visited the house with a justice of the peace named Mr. Lediard; the latter then struck off her chains, and ordered her release.

The next witness was Mrs. Gold, who corroborated her daughter's story. She stated that she had received an anonymous letter which informed her that her daughter had gone away three weeks earlier with her (Mrs. Durant's) husband, and had not been heard of since. On receipt of this communication, Mrs. Gold visited her son-in-law, and demanded to know where her daughter was. Since she could not obtain a satisfactory answer, she applied to Mr. Lediard, who succeeded in obtaining a confession from Durant.

The evidence was not conclusive; it rested on the statement of a principal witness who had admittedly been suffering from mental disorder at the time, and dealt with a period of only three weeks, some eight years previously. At the same time, it illustrated the ease with which confinement could be procured, the complete lack of treatment, and the secrecy which surrounded the whole proceedings.

The case of Mrs. Hawley provides more valid evidence, since the Committee declared her to be unquestionably of sound mind, and the allegations were admitted by both the madhouse proprietor and his agent.

Mr. Turlington informed the Committee that he kept a house at Chelsea for the reception of lunatics, but that he usually left the management

[1] See p. 50.

of the house and the manner of the admission of patients to his agent, Mr. King. He admitted that all persons who were brought to the house for confinement were taken in, whether they appeared sane or otherwise. No register of patients was kept, and no physician visited the house.

Mr. King in evidence said that he remembered Mrs. Hawley. She had been confined at the representation of a woman purporting to be her mother, and the reason given was that she was an habitual drunkard. He did not remember that she had been refused writing materials, but when pressed, agreed that it was the established rule of the house that none of the inmates should be allowed to send letters to their friends or relatives. Finally, to clarify the issue, Mr. King was asked a general question: whether, if two strangers should come to his house, the one calling herself the mother of the other, and charging her daughter with drunkenness, he would confine the daughter upon the representation of the woman calling herself the mother, though she was a stranger to him, and the daughter herself was apparently sober at the time?

'He said, he certainly should.'

The report of this Committee leaves a great many questions unanswered. Why, in the case of Mrs. Durant, was the magistrate not called to give evidence? Who wrote the anonymous letter to Mrs. Gold, and for what purpose? What was the verdict of a competent medical authority on Mrs. Durant's mental condition, and was she a reliable witness? In the case of Mrs. Hawley, who was the woman who alleged herself to be her mother, and what was her purpose in securing Mrs. Hawley's confinement? The evidence was not given in a legal manner, since in the first case it depended on the testimony of a woman whose balance of mind was disturbed, and the proprietor was apparently not given the opportunity of refuting the charges; in the second case, if the report is an accurate transcription, the method of arriving at a decision consisted in confronting the proprietor and the agent with allegations based on hearsay. Above all, out of the thousands of cases which might have been considered, why were only these two relatively mild cases brought to light? The impression left on the reader is that, although the Committee was bound to investigate, it did not want to investigate too deeply.

*Bills for the Regulation of Private Madhouses.*

The secrecy confronting any would-be investigator, and the pressure brought to bear by interested parties, may be guessed at in the light of the fact that it was eleven years from the time when the Committee made its report to the time when provisions limiting the powers of madhouse proprietors became law.  A Bill was introduced in the Commons in 1773 by Thomas Townshend junior[1] with these words:

'I wish gentlemen would enquire particularly into the abuses which actually are committed, and make themselves masters of this subject which I conceive, Sir, to be equally serious and important. Some facts have reached my knowledge which would awaken the compassion of the most callous heart; and I am assured such cruelty and injustice is shown to individuals who are often confined from interested motives, that cannot be equalled in any other European state.'[2]

Townshend alleged that the delay in bringing the matter before parliament was due to 'the part the gentlemen of the long robe[3] took against it.'

The Bill was seconded by Mr. Herbert Mackworth, Member of Parliament for Cardiff:

'Private madhouses are indeed become a very great nuisance, and I have evidence in writing sufficient to shock the most hardened heart. I am glad to find an hon. gentleman so able has undertaken this matter; and I wish with him that we may have the assistance of the long robe. . . . The scenes of distress lie hid in obscure corners; but if gentlemen were once to see them, I am convinced that they would not rest a day until a Bill for their relief was passed; and for my part, I solemnly protest that I will neither mind time nor trouble, but will employ every hour until some relief may be obtained. The gentlemen of the long robe have been against us: they are the powerful quarter that opposed a Bill of this sort: but I trust, when they are acquainted with the abuses which I have actually seen, they will render every assistance possible towards the completion of so charitable an undertaking.'

The 'gentlemen of the long robe' were seemingly not moved by these references to their opposition. The Bill passed the Commons on May 10th, but was summarily rejected by the House of Lords. A Bill, from which the clauses giving the Commissioners the power to revoke licences had been deleted, was passed in the following year.  ·

*The Act for Regulating Private Madhouses, 1774 (14 Geo III, c. 9).*

The provisions for enforcing the regulations contained in this Act were

---

[1] Thomas Townshend junior, 1733–1800. Later Baron Sydney of Chislehurst.
[2] *Parl. Hist. of Eng.*, February 1st, 1773.
[3] i.e., the legal profession.

so ineffectual that it remained almost a dead letter. It did not apply to pauper lunatics in madhouses, to single lunatics, or to public subscription hospitals. The preamble ran:

'Wheres many great and dangerous Abuses frequently arise from the present State of Houses kept for the Reception of Lunaticks, for Want of Regulations with Respect to the Persons keeping such Houses, the admission of Patients into them, and the Visitation by proper Persons of the said Houses and Patients: and whereas the Law, as it now stands, is insufficient for preventing or discovering such Abuses. . . .'

No person was to take charge of more than one lunatic for profit without a licence. In the metropolitan area ('within the cities of London and Westminster and within seven miles of the same, and within the County of Middlesex') licensing was to be carried out by five Commissioners elected from their number by the President and Fellows of the Royal College of Physicians; the Commissioners were to meet annually in the Hall of the College for this purpose. No Commissioner was to be directly or indirectly concerned in the keeping of a licensed house, on pain of a penalty of fifty pounds. They were to visit all such houses 'between the Hours of Eight and Five in the Day-time', and were to make notes in writing of the condition of the patients.

'In case the Commissioners upon their Visitation shall discover any Thing that, in their Opinion, shall deserve Censure or Animadversion, they shall, in that case, report the same; and such Part of their Report and no more shall be hung up in the Censor's Room of the College, to be perused and inspected by any Person who shall apply for that Purpose.'

A keeper who refused to admit the Commissioners forfeited his licence. Notice was to be sent to the Secretary of the Commissioners by the keeper within three days of the reception of a patient.

Outside the metropolitan area, licensing was to be carried out by the justices at the Quarter Sessions. Two justices and a physician were to be nominated at the Quarter Sessions to visit and make reports on the same terms as the Commissioners in the metropolitan area.

The Act applied only to a limited section of the insane, but even so, had many weaknesses. The most glaring of these was the omission of any power by which the Commissioners might refuse to grant licences on the grounds of ill-treatment or neglect of patients. A keeper would forfeit his licence if he refused to admit the official visitors; but as long as he admitted them, whatever the conditions, they could take no action except that of displaying their report in a place where few could see it and none would have their attention drawn to it.

Visits were to be made 'between the Hours of Eight and Five in the Day-time', and no provision was made to ensure that the proprietors— who might also be members of the Royal College of Physicians—were not warned beforehand. The visit might be a purely cursory one, since the Commissioners were untrained, unpaid (save for nominal expenses) and not instructed what to look for. Since they could not visit at night, they would have no adequate opportunity of inspecting the sleeping conditions.

The proprietors were obliged to send notice of reception within three days, but no medical certificate was needed, and there was no penalty for failure to comply.

*Significance of the 1774 Act.*

Even if the visitation envisaged by the Act had been carried out systematically and conscientiously, the proprietors of private madhouses would have remained almost as free from the fear of legal penalties as before. The Act said nothing on the subject of the medical supervision of patients, diet, overcrowding, mechanical restraint, or deliberate brutality of treatment. Its primary purpose was to provide safeguards against illegal detention, but it failed even in this simple object, since there was no means of forcing the proprietor to comply with the orders of the Commissioners.

Although its provisions were administratively weak, the Act of 1774 served a purpose. It established five important principles in lunacy legislation:

1. Licensing by a public authority of private institutions run for profit.
2. Notification of the reception into such institutions of a person alleged to be insane.
3. Visitation by Commissioners, whose method of appointment was prescribed by parliament.
4. Inspection to ensure that those wrongfully detained were released, and that those rightfully detained were treated with humanity.
5. Supervision by the medical profession.

It was many years before these points were covered by effective legislation. As in most branches of social reform, the reformers themselves were not entirely aware in these early days of what they wished to achieve. Only as one set of laws was found inadequate, and a new law designed to cover the deficiencies of the old, did a coherent policy emerge.

After 1774, the Townshends took no active part in lunacy reform. The elder was in his seventies when the Act was passed, but although he remained a member of parliament until 1780, the year of his death, he naturally played a less active part in parliamentary affairs in his later years. The younger Townshend moved from the back bench to the front; he was a Lord of the Treasury in the Rockingham ministry of 1766, and subsequently held a number of important offices, including those of Secretary for War and Secretary of State, in Whig administrations. In the latter capacity, he was responsible for the decision to send convicts to Australia, and became Baron Sydney of Chislehurst in 1783. These preoccupations inevitably crowded out his earlier interest; perhaps too, he felt that he had done all that could be done in face of the strong opposition of the Upper House. The younger Townshend's colleagues in framing the Bill of 1774 were fairly undistinguished men: George Venables Vernon, later Lord Vernon of Kinderton, whose chief claim to fame is that he was the half-brother of a future Archbishop;[1] Constantine Phipps, a politician and explorer who was one of the 'King's friends';[2] Beaumont Hotham, the member for Wigan, of whom there is no record that he ever made a speech in the House of Commons. Hotham was a barrister, but his knowledge of law is said to have been so meagre that whenever a difficult legal point arose, he referred the case rather than making a decision of his own.[3] None of these was likely to lead a movement for reform. So the matter lapsed until interest in the treatment of the insane came from a new and unexpected quarter.

### 3. THE KING'S ILLNESS AND THE REGENCY QUESTION

The nature of the King's illness did not become public knowledge until 1788, when the attack was so severe that he became incapable of carrying out affairs of state for several months. The Prince of Wales later described the onset of the attack to his friends:

'He told us that he was present when the King was first seized with his mental disorder: that His Majesty caught him with both his hands by the collar, pushing him against the wall with some violence, and asked him who would dare to say to a King of England that he should not speak out, or who should prevent his whispering. His Majesty then whispered.'[4]

[1] Vernon's half-brother, as Archbishop of York, was a governor of the unreformed York Asylum. See pp. 83–92.

[2] D.N.B.

[3] D.N.B.

[4] Quoted by Jesse, *Memoirs of the Life and Reign of George III*, vol. III, p. 45.

The King's doctors, who included Dr. Warren and Sir Lucas Pepys, were not optimistic about a swift recovery; but the fate of the administration hung precisely on this point. If the King's illness lasted more than a few months, a Regent would have to be appointed. The obvious candidate for the Regency was the Prince of Wales, and he left little doubt in the mind of his adherents that, once he was established, his first action would be to dismiss the younger Pitt and his colleagues, and to install the 'Carlton House set', headed by Charles James Fox, in their place.

*The Appointment of Dr. Willis.*

The Opposition backed Dr. Warren and Sir Lucas Pepys; Pitt and his associates needed another and more optimistic opinion of the King's state of mind to preserve themselves in office. Accordingly Dr. Francis Willis was called in. Willis was a former vicar of Wapping who had left his calling in order to practise as a physician, and who was at that time the proprietor of a private madhouse in Lincolnshire.

The King appears to have taken an instant dislike to him. 'Aware of Dr. Willis being a clergyman, he taxed him at his first interview with having abandoned his sacred calling for profit—a rebuke to which the latter rejoined that the Saviour had cured demoniacs. "Yes," said the King, "but He did not get £700 a year for it." ' [1] Fulke Greville recounts that the King offered Willis any preferment he wished if he would return to his former calling. [2]

Opinions on the competence of the new doctor varied. Lord Sheffield dismissed him with 'Dr. Willis . . . is considered by some as not much better than a mountebank, and not far different from some of those that are confined in his house' [3]—while Hannah More described him on the other hand as 'The very image of simplicity, quite a good, plain, old-fashioned country clergyman'. [4]

Mountebank or not, Willis had one great virtue in the eyes of Pitt and his colleagues; he was certain that he could restore the King to sanity within a few months. His first step was to acquire ascendancy over the mind of his patient by intimidatory means. Fulke Greville tells how the King was immediately separated from his wife and family, and kept in constant fear of the strait jacket. Countess Harcourt goes further:

'The unhappy patient . . . was no longer treated as a human being.

[1] Jesse, *George III*, vol. III, p. 91.
[2] *Diaries of Robert Fulke Greville, Equerry to the King*, pp. 118–19.
[3] Jesse, *George III*, vol. III, p. 265.
[4] D.N.B.

His body was immediately encased in a machine which left it no liberty of motion. He was sometimes chained to a staple. He was frequently beaten and starved, and at best he was kept in subjection by menacing and violent language. The history of the King's illness showed that the most exalted station did not wholly exempt the sufferer from this stupid and inhuman usage. . . .'[1]

The treatment of the King speaks volumes for the contemporary view of insanity; one party wanted him cured as soon as possible, and the other would have been glad to see that cure delayed; but neither protested that the person of the monarch should not be subjected to indignities of this description.

By the end of 1788, the King's insanity was being openly discussed in clubs and coffee-houses. There was despondency at White's, the Tory stronghold, and exultation at Brooke's, where the Prince of Wales and the Duke of York freely discussed their father's illness, and made it a subject for merriment. The only person for whom one can have sympathy is the King himself, the unwitting pawn in party manœuvres; but the matter had one good and lasting effect: for the first time, insanity and the treatment of insanity formed a burning topic of public discussion. The subject had been brought out of concealment in a way which defeated the conspiracy of silence.

Willis was still optimistic, though the King's malady continued unabated. At length Pitt's hand was forced, and he rose in the Commons at the beginning of the new session on December 4th, 1788, to inform members that they were 'again assembled in the same unhappy circumstances which he had been under the melancholy necessity of communicating at their last meeting, the continuance of His Majesty's illness still preventing any measures either for opening the sessions or proroguing the parliament, and rendering it for the present impossible for His Majesty personally to attend to any public business; . . . and in this situation, the Privy Council had thought it their duty to call before them His Majesty's physicians, and to examine them on oath concerning the state of His Majesty's health.'[2]

*The Select Committee of 1789.*

A Select Committee was appointed four days later. It consisted of twenty-one members, of whom five had strongly conflicting interests in the matter. Lord North represented the interest of the King; William Wilberforce was a close personal friend of Pitt. He had not yet embarked

---

[1] Jesse, op. cit., vol. III, p. 257.
[2] H.C.J., December 4th, 1788.

on his career as 'the authorized interpreter of the national conscience',[1] though it was three years since his conversion to the religious life put an end to his practice of gambling with the Carlton House set; Lord Grenville, son of George Grenville, who had sat on the two former Committees on lunacy questions, was a cousin of the younger Pitt, and although only thirty, had held office continuously for the past six years. He was a man respected by both parties, and was appointed Speaker of the House of Commons in the following year. Fox and Sheridan were the leaders of the Prince of Wales' party—his personal friends and gambling associates. Sheridan had followed his literary and dramatic triumphs by becoming member of parliament for Stafford in 1780, and had held office in the Rockingham government of 1782 and the coalition of 1783.

It it interesting to note that both Sheridan and Grenville had legal training. Sheridan had been entered at the Middle Temple, and Grenville at Lincoln's Inn, though neither was actually called to the Bar.

The issue before the Committee was a vital one. Sir John Scott (then Solicitor-General, and later better-known as Lord Eldon, the rigid and unyielding Lord Chancellor of Wellington's Government) told Fulke Greville that the Government would back Willis because he stated that recovery was possible within a short time, and that it was essential to stave off the Regency question.[2]

Dr. Warren fanned the flames of medical rivalry and party strife by stating that he had no reason to believe that the King's condition was improving. He alleged that Dr. Willis had written reports, 'expressing His Majesty to be much better than I apprehended His Majesty to be at that time, declaring progress in cure that I could not discover,' and that he had tried to coerce him (Warren) into doing likewise by making 'a very unwarrantable use of the name of a Great Person'.[3] The Committee inquired, 'Whether Dr. Warren knows or has any reason to believe that Dr. Willis has signed more favourable accounts of the King's health than Dr. Willis believed to be true?'—and Warren answered briefly, 'I cannot possibly tell what Dr. Willis believes.' He added that the application of blisters by Dr. Willis had 'made His Majesty much more unquiet, and increased the necessity for coercion'.

Willis was called, and the Whig members of the Committee posed a most searching series of questions. Fulke Greville reports: 'By my con-

---

[1] D.N.B.   [2] *Fulke Greville's Diaries*, pp. 159-60.
[3] H.C.J., January 13th, 1789. The context makes it clear that the 'Great Person' was the Queen, who naturally wished to protect the King against attempts to secure a Regency.

versation with Dr. Willis, I found that he had been very closely pressed and questioned by Mr. Burke and Mr. Sheridan—that he was angry with them, and with Mr. Sheridan particularly'.[1]

The Whigs won their point; a Regency Bill was framed, and passed the Commons on February 12th, 1789. Whig ladies wore 'Regency caps' and Regency favours;[2] and it was said in Brooke's that the Whigs had completed their ministerial arrangements in readiness for the moment when the Prince of Wales should have power to eject the Tories. The Duke of York was to be Commander-in-Chief, Sheridan the Treasurer of the Navy, and Fox Secretary of State, while Mrs. FitzHerbert was to be created a Duchess.

The Regency Bill was about to be read for the third time in the Lords when the King frustrated these plans, whether because of or in spite of the treatment of Dr. Willis, by making a recovery. In March, 1789, he was much better; in April, the doctors were dismissed; and on April 23rd he attended a public service of thanksgiving in St. Paul's Cathedral. Dr. Willis returned to Lincolnshire, the Whigs shelved their plans of political triumph, and the Prince of Wales made his peace with his father. A play at Drury Lane in which Mrs. Siddons and John Kemble were appearing was withdrawn after only one performance solely on account of the title —*The Regent*.

The King's recovery seems to have been greeted with relief and satisfaction by the general public. As the first Hanoverian monarch to identify himself with England rather than Hanover, he was fairly popular, and the Prince of Wales, by reason of his extravagances and his connection with the Roman Catholic Mrs. FitzHerbert, was exceedingly unpopular. The King's journey to Weymouth, where he went to convalesce, became a triumphal procession; and although much of the rejoicing may have been officially inspired, and some of it due to the general public's love of a show, there was undoubtedly a spontaneous element also.

The effects on lunacy reform of this first attack suffered by the King are intangible, but nevertheless real. The sympathies of the nation were with the sufferer, and the note of moral condemnation which had previously characterized all approaches to the insane was entirely lacking. Nobody suggested that the King was being punished by heaven for his sins; nobody regarded him as being possessed by the Devil. Insanity had become a respectable malady—one which might happen to anybody;

---

[1] *Fulke Greville's Diaries*, p. 156.
[2] The remainder of this account of the illness of George III is taken from vol. III of Jesse's *Memoirs of the Life and Reign of George III*, unless otherwise stated.

and, which is even more important, one which was susceptible to treatment and capable of cure.

*The Course of the King's Illness.*

The King became ill again twelve years later—in February 1801. The attack was said at the time to have been caused by Pitt's determination to carry Catholic Emancipation against the King's wishes. Dr. Willis and his sons were sent for; again the strait jacket, the cauterizing irons and the herbal remedies were produced. There was despondency among the Tories, and jubilation at Carlton House. Lord Eldon found the King 'In a house at Kew, separated from his family, and with the Willises living with him.'

Pitt, wisely in the circumstances, gave a guarantee that he would not attempt Catholic Emancipation while the King was alive, and the King, freed from the fear that he would be forced into a course of action which he regarded as a betrayal of his Coronation oath, promptly recovered.

In May, his balance of mind was again disturbed for a short period, during which he was alleged to be desirous of retiring to Hanover and abdicating in favour of the Prince of Wales. In January, 1804, there was another attack; and in May of that year, the King appeared at the installation of the Knights of the Order of the Garter wearing a judge's wig with his Garter robes, to the general consternation. In 1805—he was then sixty-seven years of age—his sight began to fail; as a result he became increasingly incapable of living a normal life. The final descent into insanity, from which he did not recover, came in 1810, brought about by the death of his favourite child, the Princess Amelia. Francis Willis had died in 1807, but his sons, Dr. Robert and Dr. John Willis, returned to take charge of the King. He was confined to a suite of rooms at Windsor, where he found solace in Handel's music and the comforts of religion. Madame D'Arblay reported that he imagined himself to be conversing with angels, and the slow drift into religious delusion may have been a merciful end to a troubled reign.

The Regency Bill became law in 1811, and the King lived on until January, 1820, through more than thirty years of intermittent insanity. His death was little more than a reminder of his long-drawn-out life. The *Gentleman's Magazine* provided a fitting commentary:

'That this brave and honest man should have passed the last years of his long reign in darkness, mental and bodily, and should have died uncon-

LUNACY, LAW, AND CONSCIENCE

scious of his country's glory, is enough to tame all human pride. How little sensation his death occasions! It is indeed but the passing of a shadow.'

Two things are notable about the phrasing of this obituary notice; first, the avoidance of the words 'mad' and 'madness', and the substitution of 'mental darkness' in a context which linked it with the King's physical blindness; and second, the description of an insane person as 'this brave and honest man'. This marked a considerable shift of opinion since the days of the witchcraft trials.

All this is in anticipation of the main thread of events, and it is now necessary to go back to the last years of the eighteenth century, when other events also affected the public attitude to the insane.

### 4. INSANITY IN LITERARY CIRCLES

The high incidence of insanity among men of letters during this period is a phenomenon which seems incapable of adequate explanation. Many of the well-known poets and writers were, if not psychotic, at least highly neurotic, and a survey of their lives shows an unprecedented record of fantasy, dissipation and suicide. The career of Charles Churchill has already been mentioned.[1] William Cowper received treatment in Dr. Willis' madhouse at one time, though without apparent effect. Cowper possessed a highly nervous temperament. He long desired a post as a clerk in the House of Commons; but when at last the post was offered to him in 1763, the offer threw him into a torment of doubt and uncertainty. He began to distrust his own emotions and to doubt his ability to assume the necessary degree of responsibility. Within a short time he developed a severe depression with suicidal tendencies. He made many attempts to kill himself, and might have succeeded, had it not been for the devoted nursing of Mrs. Unwin—'My Mary' of the poems. From 1763 to his death in 1779, he suffered recurrent attacks. He was confined for a time in Francis Willis' house in Lincolnshire, and also with a Dr. Cotton at St. Albans; but he escaped the worst rigours of the madhouse system, and was able to continue his literary work in his periods of lucidity. Lord Shaftesbury commented in his diary many years later, when he was a Lunacy Commissioner, 'Have been reading in snatched moments of leisure, *Life of Cowper* . . . he was, when he attempted his life, thoroughly mad: he was never so at any other time. Yet his symptoms were such as

[1] See p. 33.

46

would have been sufficient for any "mad-doctor" to shut him up, and far too serious to permit any Commissioner to let him out. . . . There are, I suspect, not a few persons confined whom it would be just as perplexing, and yet just as safe, to release as the poet Cowper.'[1]

Christopher Smart (1722–71) was another poet of this period who suffered from recurrent fits of insanity, though in a vastly different form. Smart spent two short periods at Bethlem, where he is said to have written the 'Song to David' on the walls with charcoal. Possibly the brilliance of his literary gifts saved him from longer incarceration, since his affliction apparently did not impair his intellectual processes. He suffered from a psychosis characterized by notable religious preoccupation, and lived wildly among the most degraded classes of society—a combination which seems to have been particularly common among the poets of the late eighteenth century. Dr. Johnson defended him:

'His infirmities were not noxious to society. He insisted on people praying with him, and I'd as lief pray with Kit Smart as with anyone else. Another charge was that he did not love clean linen; and I have no particular passion for it.'[2]

Dr. Johnson's own mannerisms, his morbidity, his obsessions and his fear of death have been faithfully portrayed by Boswell. Oliver Goldsmith (1728–74) has been described as 'unstable and pitifully puerile in mind'.[3] Robert Burns (1759–96) suffered from acute fits of depression. William Collins (1721–59) became insane while at Oxford, and was forced to leave the university; he suffered all his life from melancholia. William Blake's genius was accompanied by visions of a hallucinatory nature. Charles Lamb came of a family in which a predisposition to insanity was hereditary, and was for a time confined in a madhouse in Hoxton. His sister Mary, who killed her mother and wounded her father in a fit of homicidal mania, was well-known to Lamb's literary friends, and appears in the essays as 'Bridget'. She was acquitted on a murder charge, and released into her brother's care, spending in a madhouse only the short periods when the mania returned.[4]

Examples of mental instability in literary circles might be multiplied many times. Well might Wordsworth write:

---

[1] August 20th, 1845. Shaftesbury was then Lord Ashley.
[2] D.N.B.
[3] Albert, Hist. of Eng. Lit., p. 249.
[4] A. Ainger, Life of Lamb.

We poets in our youth begin in gladness;
But thereof come in the end despondency and madness.[1]

Among the poets and the novelists of this time, convention counted for little, abnormality was associated with genius, and people lived by the exercise of their emotions. Consequently the mentally disordered received a growing toleration as human beings capable of making a contribution to society.

[1] 'Resolution and Independence,' written May–July, 1802.

# Chapter Four

## EXPERIMENTS IN TREATMENT

THE improvement in the public attitude to insanity was paralleled in three cities—London, Manchester and York—by the setting up of institutions where treatment of a relatively humane nature could be provided. This action arose in each case primarily from the consciousness felt by a small group of citizens of an overwhelming social evil in their midst. St. Luke's Hospital, London, was founded in 1751, the Manchester Lunatic Hospital in 1763, and the York Retreat in 1792. Each formed not only a local but also a national precedent for improvements in treatment and accommodation which were later to find legislative expression.

This was the pioneer stage—the stage of voluntary social action. In these three cities was laid the foundation of nineteenth-century lunacy legislation.

### I. ST. LUKE'S HOSPITAL

This hospital, which was to become in many respects a rival to Bethlem, was founded by public subscription in 1751. A pamphlet entitled 'Reasons for Establishing St. Luke's', published in 1817, makes the following points: Bethlem was overcrowded, and had a lengthy waiting list; the resultant delay in the admission of patients meant that many whose reason might have been saved by early diagnosis and treatment were not admitted until the disease had become incurable. People of means were frequently reduced to poverty by insanity, and the workhouse was an unsuitable place for their reception, since they were not 'pauper lunatics' in the usual sense of the term; finally, if medical students were to acquire a competent knowledge of the forms and treatment of insanity, a hospital must be established where they would be able to observe and study cases under suitable guidance. Bethlem at this time, and indeed until 1844, forbade the visitation of patients by medical students, or by practitioners other than those on the staff.

St. Luke's may thus claim to have been the first teaching hospital in this field of medicine, and quickly developed into an institution rivalling Bethlem in everything but age. In 1758, the physician, Dr. Battie,[1] published an apparently innocuous pamphlet[2] in which he gave an account of his methods of treatment. This was construed by John Monro of Bethlem as an attack on his father, and he published a printed reply in the same year.[3] The paragraph which chiefly gave offence was that in which Battie wrote of insanity, 'This distemper is as little understood as any that ever afflicted mankind, because the care of lunatics is entrusted to empiricks, or at best to a few select Physicians, most of whom think it advisable to keep the cases as well as the patients to themselves.'

'By a few select Physicians,' replied John Monro, 'I presume are intended the Physicians of Bethlem Hospital, whom I consider it as a duty incumbent upon me to defend against any injurious reflections.' He described his father as 'A man of admirable discernment (who) treated this disease with an address that will not soon be equalled.'

Dr. Battie spoke also of the 'impertinent curiosity of those who think it pastime to converse with Madmen and to play on their passions'. Such visitors were strictly forbidden at St. Luke's, while medical practitioners and students were regularly admitted. Battie advocated generally a quiet and natural form of treatment, without violent vomits and purges, and with a sufficiency of simple food, 'not highly-seasoned and full of poignancy.' The practice of inducing repeated vomiting he described as 'a shocking operation, the consequence of a morbid convulsion', and he urged that purges should be given in small doses, at considerable intervals, and with due care for the patient's physical health. He believed that the mental condition of many patients could be alleviated by diversion, and that an asylum should provide 'amusements . . . rendered more agreeable by a well-timed variety'. Although conditions at St. Luke's were far from perfect by later standards, the hospital was at least a centre for the serious study of mental disorder, where attempts were made to

---

[1] See J. H. Jesse, *Celebrated Etonians*, vol. I, pp. 18–25. 'Battius, faber fortunae suae . . . medicus perspicax.'

[2] Published as *Dr. Battie on Madness*.

[3] Published as *Dr. Monro's Reply to Dr. Battie*.

restore the irrational to mental health by other means than those of coercion and neglect. Evidence on the conditions at this hospital was given before the Select Committees of 1807 and 1815, and will be referred to at a later point in the narrative.

## 2. THE MANCHESTER LUNATIC HOSPITAL

The Lunatic Hospital at Manchester formed part of that city's comprehensive scheme for the treatment of mental and bodily illness in patients of means. The parent body was the Infirmary, founded in 1752, and attached to it when completed were the Lunatic Hospital, the Lying-In Hospital, the Eye Hospital and the Lock Hospital, occupying contiguous sites.[1] This chain of hospitals was raised by public subscription, and largely administered by the trustees of the Infirmary.[2]

### Foundation of the Lunatic Hospital.

Persons 'disordered in their senses' were specifically excluded by section 45 of the Infirmary Rules from becoming in-patients, though they were free to attend the clinic for out-patients. This expedient proved unsuitable, since mental patients were unable to attend the clinic without supervision, and their condition needed more than the sporadic treatment available.

The desire to make provision for patients of this type may have received an impetus from the article on the abuses in private madhouses published in the *Gentleman's Magazine* in January, 1763.[3] In August of the same year, the Infirmary trustees appointed a committee to consider what provision might be made for the insane, and the committee's report recommended the raising of a separate building, for which a subscription list should be opened. Patients should have 'advice gratis, paying for all other necessaries', and paupers should only be accepted if maintained by their parish of settlement. The finances of the new hospital should be kept separately from those of the Infirmary; no contribution made to the work of the Infirmary should be applied to the development of the Lunatic Hospital, 'or any other steps taken that will in any manner prejudice the same.'

Before the Committee's report was presented to the Board of Trustees,

[1] *Raffald's Manchester Directory*, and contemporary maps.
[2] Account Book of the Manchester Royal Infirmary.
[3] See pp. 32–3.

an unsigned article appeared in the *Manchester Mercury*, of September 13th, 1763; this advocated public provision for the insane of the city. The writer pointed out that, though the cost of maintaining a pauper lunatic in a workhouse was low, the lack of treatment in these institutions meant that the majority of such cases became incurable, and had to be maintained out of public funds for the rest of their lives. It would thus be to the advantage of the Poor Law authorities to pay a larger weekly sum for treatment in a lunatic hospital, since the chances of the patient's recovery and the restoration of his earning power were much greater. He was also concerned with 'many people in middling Circumstances who labour under the very great Misfortune of having a Parent or a Child thus visited by the Hand of Providence, and who would most thankfully pay any moderate Sum . . . for a Place of Security where their Relations might be properly guarded, receive the best Advice, and meet with the most humane Treatment.'

The phrasing of this article is similar to that of the Committee's report, and it is difficult to believe that the writer had no knowledge of the steps which were being taken to meet this need. A likely explanation is that the article was inspired by one or more members of the Committee as a means of popularizing the scheme, by means of making it appear to spring from public demand.

This hypothesis is strengthened by the fact that, four years later, on January 13th, 1767, the same journal published in its leading column a statement by the trustees, laying before the public their reasons for undertaking the project. They stated that they had 'long been solicited to take the Case of poor Lunatics under Consideration, upon Account chiefly of their being denied Admission into all other Infirmaries, and their being in Common at too great a distance from London to receive any benefit from the two noble Hospitals established there . . .' Their aim was to provide for the cure of patients, not merely for their confinement, and they wished to preserve the moderately well-to-do from the 'Impositions of Private Madhouses'.

*Conditions of Admission.*[1]

Patients were to be admitted on application by two friends or relatives, or by the parish overseer. The charge for pauper lunatics was seven shillings a week, and that for 'Persons of middling Fortune' not less than ten shillings. In 1777, the charge for paupers was reduced to four shil-

[1] Brockbank, *Short History of Cheadle Royal, passim.*

lings, and it was hoped that the Hospital would eventually be able to take poor patients free, though this was never achieved.[1]

*Administration.*

It was reported at the Quarterly Board meeting on September 26th, 1765, that the building was completed, though it had still to be staffed and furnished. The administration was to be organized in common with that of the Infirmary, the same secretary, steward, surgeon and physician serving both. The Infirmary was to provide all medicines—'for which its account shall have credit'. Jonas Wood and his wife were appointed to the positions of master and matron—at first designated 'governor' and 'governess'—at a joint salary of thirty guineas a year. It was also moved at this meeting that 'the printed rules concerning the Hospital for Lunatics for the County of Northumberland'[2] be adopted.

*Medical Treatment.*

It was stated in the original rules[3] that the reception order for every patient was to be signed by the physician and four of the trustees. It appears that the physician was not required to examine the patient before signing the order, since another rule required the patient to be carefully examined, and the physician to be *informed* of any wounds, sores, or bruises. The examination was presumably carried out by the master or one of the keepers, and was concerned only with the physical condition of the patient.

Physical violence was not to be used on the patients, except where it was 'necessary to restrain the Furious from hurting themselves or others'. Mechanical restraint was used, as it was also provided that 'the feet of those in straw or chains be carefully examined, gently rubbed night and morning, and covered with flannel during the winter.' This was designed to prevent mortification due to restriction of the circulation.

Treatment was otherwise mainly medical, and consisted, according to an account written by the Infirmary Physician in 1795,[4] of the usual

[1] Since its removal to Cheadle in 1850, the hospital has been restricted entirely to private patients.

[2] This was a small subscription asylum erected at Newcastle-on-Tyne. See S. Middlebrook, *Newcastle-on-Tyne: Its Growth and Achievements*, p. 161. The treatment was apparently not of a high standard, and the administration left much to be desired. Considerable reforms took place at this asylum in 1824.

[3] *Manchester Royal Infirmary: Rules for the Government of the Infirmary, Lunatic Hospital and Public Baths in Manchester*, pub. 1791.

[4] J. Ferriar, *Medical Histories and Reflections*, vol. III, pp. 83–112.

methods of blood-letting, blistering, purging and drugs. Dr. Ferriar noted that tartar emetic acted 'briskly', and 'had an instantaneous effect in restoring a degree of rationality' in maniacal cases. Blood-letting was practised on the 'young and plethoric maniac whose eyes are turgid and inflamed, who passes the night without sleep, and whose pulse is quick and full', but Ferriar also gave warning that frequent repetition might prove dangerous. Opium was used in 'large doses in maniacal cases'.

### 'Moral' Treatment.

Although the medical treatment represented no advance on the usual methods of the day, the physicians of the Lunatic Hospital appear to have realized that other factors in the treatment of the insane also affected their mental condition. The situation of the various wards, the provision of gardens, the small amenities given as a reward for an increased degree of self-control—all these formed an adjunct to treatment which had not previously been recognized as important, but which was to play an increasing part in the humane treatment of mental disorder in later years.

Complete separation of the sexes was enforced from the opening of the hospital.[1] Special apartments were put aside for the use of convalescent patients, so that they might not be disturbed by those who were noisy or violent. The trustees reported in 1783 that 'those whose condition will admit it are allowed to walk with their friends in a large adjoining garden'. Dr. Ferriar wrote, 'I find it useful to remonstrate, for lunatics frequently have a high sense of honour, and are sooner brought to reflection by the appearance of indignity than by violence, against which they usually harden themselves. . . . Small favours, the shew of confidence and apparent distinction, accelerate recovery.[2]

### Visitation.

Public sight-seeing was specifically forbidden by the rules, as at St. Luke's. The physician was to visit his patients twice a week, or more often if necessary; he was to keep a regular record of all his cases. The House Visitors of the Infirmary were to visit the Lunatic Hospital daily to investigate the behaviour of the keepers and the domestic staff to the patients, and were also to examine the sleeping accommodation. Four trustees were required to sign the certificates of admission and discharge.

---

[1] *Account of the Rise and Present Establishment of the Lunatic Hospital in Manchester*, 1771, p. 17.
[2] Ferriar, *Medical Histories and Reflections*, vol. III, p. 111.

*Diet.*

The diet of the patients in the Lunatic Hospital was the same as that in the Infirmary, and was laid down by the Infirmary Rules in 1769. The 'low diet' was as follows:

Breakfast: One pint of water gruel or milk pottage.
Dinner: One pint of broth and two ounces of roots
    *or* one pint of rice milk
    *or* eight ounces of bread pudding.
Supper: One pint of water gruel or milk pottage, with one ounce of butter or two ounces of cheese allowed on two days of the week.
Bread, and one pint of beer, during the day.

The 'common diet' was similar, except for a substantial main meal consisting of eight ounces of meat and eight ounces of root vegetables, or twelve ounces of baked pudding, with meat broth as an alternative for supper.

*Conclusion.*

Some idea of the standard of treatment given at the Lunatic Hospital may be gained from an examination of its accounts. In 1769, it received 361 patients at a cost of £444 in addition to the payments made. This sum was met from public subscriptions, and indicates that on an average each patient cost about twenty-five shillings more to maintain than his sureties paid in fees. Since the fees were already fairly high, and the accounts were publicly audited each year, it seems reasonably certain that this relatively large sum was actually expended on the provision of a high standard of treatment and accommodation for the patients.

Although the Manchester Lunatic Hospital dealt with its patients more humanely than was commonly the case, its work can only be described as pioneer work in the most limited sense. It is significant of the trustees' faith in accepted practice that they described Bethlem as a 'Noble Hospital' and adopted the rules of the asylum at Newcastle-on-Tyne.

Treatment proceeded by the usual methods, including restraint by chains and manacles, and violent medicines.

The behaviour of the keepers towards the patients was publicly called in question in 1774. A report of the parliamentary debate on the Private

B

LUNACY, LAW, AND CONSCIENCE

Madhouses Bill published in the *General Evening Post* of February 26th, 1774, contained the following paragraph:

'Sir William M—th[1] begged leave to relate a story which happened in the town he resided in (M—r); he said, there was a madhouse in one of the principal streets of the town, where physicians, surgeons, etc., attended every day: that one of the unfortunate people killed the keeper; a fresh keeper was sent for from London, who prescribed a severe beating to any of them that should appear disorderly; the consequence of which was that they soon beat one person to death; another unhappy man happened to take the part of the deceased, and he was scourged to the bone; his arm was broken, and no surgeon whatever sent for, lest he should disclose and discover their villainous proceedings. Shortly after, this person also died of the mortification of his wounds.'[2]

The trustees evidently had little difficulty in filling in the gaps; and they incorporated into the minutes of their next Quarterly Board Meeting (March 7th, 1774), a statement denying the allegations in general, but admitting that 'a Keeper was unfortunately stabbed by one of the Patients, one of the Patients had one of the Bones of his Arm broken by a Blow from a Servant' and another 'found Means to destroy himself within a few hours of Admission'. The physicians and surgeons of the Infirmary added a statement to the minutes of the trustees' meeting, to the effect that 'the Keepers in that Hospital have never to our Knowledge treated the Patients with any undue Severity without being justly reprehended and punished by the Board of Trustees'. This guarded statement implied two things: first, that such ill-treatment might have happened without their knowledge; and second, that some cases of ill-treatment had definitely occurred, and had been brought to the notice of the trustees on previous occasions.

The Lunatic Hospital's claim to a place in the history of lunacy reform depends less on its treatment than on its tentative approach to what later became known as 'the moral management of the insane'. Its insistence on the importance of keeping records and case-histories sprang from the close connection with the Infirmary, and the fact of that connection brought a new factor into the treatment of insanity. For the first time, that treatment was recognized as being allied to the treatment of bodily illness, to be sought without shame or secrecy. The terms 'hospital' and 'patient' were used, and statements were published in the local newspapers.

[1] Sir William Meredith, M.P. for Liverpool Borough.
[2] This speech was not reported in the parliamentary histories.

56

# EXPERIMENTS IN TREATMENT

It was the first attempt to treat insanity in the way that physical disorders were treated—with matter-of-fact compassion untinged by sensation, moral condemnation or concealment.[1]

## 3. THE YORK RETREAT

The Retreat was founded in 1792 by the Society of Friends.[2] It was unique in two ways: first, because it was neither a subscription hospital nor a private asylum, being financed and organized on a non-profit basis by a body of restricted membership; and second, because it evolved a form of treatment based, not on the scanty medical knowledge of the time, but on Christianity and common-sense.

The city of York already possessed a subscription asylum—the York Asylum, founded in 1777. Consideration of the management of this establishment will be deferred, since it was not until 1815 that the conditions under which it operated came fully to light. For the present it is sufficient to say that the conduct of the Asylum was wrapped in secrecy, the Governors and physician resisting any attempt at visitation and inspection. At least one unsuccessful effort was made to secure a public investigation of conditions,[3] but until 1790, would-be reformers could point to nothing more concrete than the general reluctance of the authorities to open the building to responsible inquirers, and the complaints, easily discredited, of ex-patients.

In the latter year,[4] a patient called Hannah Mills was sent to the Asylum, and her relatives, who lived at some distance from the city, recommended her to the care of the Society of Friends. Members of the Society who attempted to visit her were refused admission on the grounds that she was 'not in a suitable state to be seen by strangers', and she subsequently died under circumstances which aroused strong suspicions of ill-treatment or neglect.

The project for the Retreat was a direct result of this occurrence. It

---

[1] B. Kirkman Gray (*Hist. of Eng. Philosophy*, pub. 1905), states (p. 140) that the influence of the Manchester Lunatic Hospital was 'probably . . . negligible'. This appears to have been the general view until the publication of Brockbank's *Short History of Cheadle Royal* in 1934.

[2] See H. C. Hunt *A Retired Habitation*, and S. Tuke, *Description of the Retreat*, passim; D. H. Tuke, *Hist. of Insane*, pp. 115-116.

[3] G. Higgins, *Letter to Earl FitzWilliam*, 1814, p. 4. 'A general belief was prevalent in the county that great abuses did exist in the York Asylum . . . attempts had previously been made to reform it . . . they always failed.' See also *Edinburgh Review* for March, 1817.

[4] D. H. Tuke (*Hist. of Insane*, p. 112), gives the date as 1791. See Hunt, *A Retired Habitation*, p. 5 and note.

LUNACY, LAW, AND CONSCIENCE

was primarily the brain-child of William Tuke (1732–1822), a tea and
çoffee merchant, and head of a Quaker family which had been resident in
York for several generations. He saw that the time was not yet ripe for a
full-scale public inquiry at the Asylum. The Governors of that institution
—who took no part in its management and made no official visits—were
a powerful and influential body in the city.[1] Public opinion was not yet
sufficiently roused to overcome their opposition to reform. Moreover,
reform was impossible until some system of treatment other than that in
operation at the Asylum had been tried and found successful. Experiment
must precede reform.

Tuke's project met at first with opposition from within the Society of
Friends. Some members thought that the incidence of mental disorder
was too low to warrant the construction of a special institution for
Quakers. Some were 'averse to the concentration of the instances of this
disease amongst us', and others thought that York was not a suitable site
for such an institution, being 'not central to the Nation'.

A man of outstanding personality and considerable administrative
gifts, Tuke overrode all objections. His project was approved at the
Quarterly Meeting[2] of the Society in March, 1792, and by the end of
August, nearly £1200 had been subscribed. The Friends proceeded to
buy eleven acres of land at a cost of £1357, and to approve a building
estimate of nearly £2000. These sums were raised by private donation
and covenant from members of the Society by the end of 1797.

It was significant that the new institution was named neither 'hospital'
nor 'asylum'. York already possessed an asylum, operating under conditions which made the use of the term a mockery, and the Retreat was
not a hospital. William Tuke had a strong distrust of the medical profession and its methods.[3] Daniel Hack Tuke states that 'The Retreat' was
suggested by his grandmother, William's daughter-in-law, 'to convey
the idea of what such an institution should be, namely . . . a quiet
haven in which the shattered bark might find the means of reparation or
of safety.'

The pleasantness of the site was described in the first 'Visiter's Book' of
the Retreat by a Swiss doctor named Delarive, who visited the establishment in 1798:

'Cette maison est située à un mille de York, au milieu d'une campagne
fertile et riante; ce n'est point l'idée d'une prison qu'elle fait naître, mai

[1] See Appendix to Higgins' *Letter to Earl FitzWilliam* for list of Governors.
[2] The 'Quarterly Meeting' is a local executive body of the Society of Friends.
[3] *D.N.B.*

58

plutôt celle d'une grande ferme rustique; elle est entourée d'un jardin fermé.'

*Conditions of Admission.*

The Retreat was built to accommodate thirty patients, who were to be either members of the Society of Friends, or recommended by members. There were several grades of accommodation, the cost ranging from eight shillings to fifteen shillings weekly. Patients recommended by private donors of £25, or by Meetings subscribing £100, were admitted at the reduced rate of four shillings. The fact that the institution was not primarily intended to provide for the insane poor was stressed by the rule that patients' servants could be accommodated for a further six shillings a week.

*Administration.*

The first superintendent appointed was Timothy Maude, 'a Friend of great worth as well as medical knowledge, who had retired from practice.' Maude died within three months of taking up his appointment, and for some time William Tuke himself acted as superintendent, while Dr. Fowler was appointed visiting physician. Thomas Fowler seems to have been an unusually open-minded physician for his generation. After a period of trial and error, he came to believe that 'moral' methods of treatment were preferable to those involving restraint and the use of harsh drugs. So the new method of treatment for which the Retreat became famous was a product of Tuke's humanitarianism and Fowler's empiricism.

In 1797, William Tuke relinquished the day-to-day control of administration, and a male superintendent was appointed. This was George Jepson, who later married the female superintendent, Katharine Allen; together, they shared the responsibility for the immediate care of the patients until 1823. There was a staff of five in addition to the Jepsons— two men and three women. The ratio of staff to patients (7 : 30) was thus very much higher than at any other existing institution for the care of the insane.

*The Work of the Tuke Family.*

William Tuke continued to act as secretary and treasurer,[1] and still found time to know the patients individually, and to supervise the details of their treatment in many cases. His work has been commemorated by a

[1] All the early bills preserved at the Retreat are directed to him—'Mr. Tuke, for the Retreat'.

minor poet of his time in lines which compensate for their lack of literary merit by the sincerity of their sentiment:

> On a fair hill, where York in prospect lies
> Her towers and steeples pointing to the skies,
> A goodly structure rears its modest head;
> Thither my walk the worthy founder led.
> Thither with Tuke my willing footsteps prest,
> Who, oft the subject pondering in his breast,
> Went forth alone, and weigh'd the growing plan,
> Big with the lasting help of suffering Man.[1]

The inscription on the foundation stone at the Retreat does not bear his name, stating simply, 'Hoc fecit amicorum caritas in humanitatis argumentum'; but his portrait, painted by a descendant,[2] still has the place of honour in the board room.

The philanthropic work of the Tuke family was not confined to the Retreat. William Tuke and his second wife, Esther, were co-founders of the Friends' Girls' School at York; his son Henry (1755–1814) was associated with the educational work of the British and Foreign Bible Society; Henry's son was Samuel Tuke, the author of the *Description of the Retreat*. When William became totally blind—some years before his death in 1822 —it was Samuel who took his place as unofficial supervisor and general counsellor at the Retreat. Both William and Samuel Tuke were among the body of citizens who finally achieved the reform of the old York Asylum in 1814–15,[3] and William, then over eighty, gave evidence before the Select Committee on Madhouses which was appointed in 1815.

Although Samuel Tuke studied medicine, he eventually entered the family business in deference to his grandfather's wishes.[4] The first of the family to qualify as a medical practitioner was Daniel Hack Tuke, who only overcame the family prejudice against that profession in 1852 after refusing to enter Tuke, Son & Co., giving up a legal career in its early stages, and failing lamentably to become a poet.[5]

### 'Moral' Treatment at the Retreat.

'People in general,' noted Samuel Tuke in his *Description of the Retreat*, 'have the most outrageous notions of the constantly outrageous behaviour

---

[1] Thomas Wilkinson, friend of Wordsworth. Hunt, op. cit., p. 52.
[2] The artist H. S. Tuke, son of D. H. Tuke.
[3] See p. 86.
[4] *D.N.B.* Samuel Tuke, 1784–1857.
[5] *D.N.B.* Daniel Hack Tuke, 1827–95.

or malicious dispositions of deranged persons: and it has in too many instances been found convenient to encourage these false sentiments to apologize for the treatment of the unhappy sufferer, or to admit the vicious neglect of their keepers.' The Tukes believed that many patients could be rational and controllable, provided that they were not aggravated by cruelty, hostility, or harsh methods of restraint. 'Vous voyez,' wrote Delarive in the 'Visiter's Book',

'que dans le traitement moral, on ne considère pas les fous comme absolument privés de raison, c'est-à-dire, comme inaccessibles aux motifs de crainte, d'éspérance, de sentiment, et d'honneur. On les considère plutôt, ce semble, comme les enfans qui ont un superflu de force, et qui en faisoient un emploi dangereux.'

The patients were never punished for failure to control their behaviour, but certain amenities were given to them in order to foster self-control by a show of trust. The female superintendent gave tea-parties, to which the patients were invited, and for which they were encouraged to wear their best clothes. There was an airing-court in the grounds for each class of patients, and each court was supplied with a number of small animals— rabbits, poultry, and others—so that the patients might learn self-control by having dependent upon them creatures weaker than themselves.

'These creatures are generally very familiar with the patients, and it is believed that they are not only the means of innocent pleasure, but that the intercourse with them sometimes tends to awaken the social and benevolent feelings,' commented Samuel Tuke.

Every attempt was made to occupy the patients suitably. Some cared for the animals, some helped in the garden, the women knitted or sewed. Writing materials were provided, and books were carefully chosen to form a patients' library. Samuel Tuke stated that this did not contain 'works of the imagination'—probably a wise choice in view of the popularity at that time of horrific novels such as *The Castle of Otranto, Vathek* and *The Monk*. It may be said that members of the Society of Friends were not at this period given to novel-reading. Books on mathematics and the natural sciences were recommended as 'the most useful class of subjects on which to employ the minds of the insane'.

The Friends believed firmly in the integrating influence of religion in cases of mental disorder; religious meetings were held at the Retreat, and parties of patients were taken from time to time to share in the common worship of the city Quakers. In short, the patient was given no excuse for feeling that his mental condition precluded participation in normal human activity, or cut him off from the outside world.

An account by Samuel Tuke of the reception of a violent patient illustrates the complete antithesis between the old system and the new:

'Some years ago, a man of Herculean size and figure was brought to the house . . . so constantly during the present attack had he been kept chained, that his clothes were contrived to be taken off and put on by means of strings, without removing his manacles. They were . . . taken off when he entered the Retreat, and he was ushered into the apartment where the superintendents were supping. He was calm. His attention appeared to be arrested by his new situation. He was desired to join in the repast, during which he behaved with tolerable propriety . . . the maniac was sensible of the kindness of his treatment. He promised to restrain himself, and he so completely succeeded that during his stay no coercive means were ever employed towards him . . . in about four months, he was discharged, perfectly recovered.'

*Mechanical Restraint.*

'Point de barreau, point de grillages aux fenêtres,' wrote Delarive. The windows of the Retreat were specially designed to look like ordinary windows, the iron sashes being painted to look like wooden ones. Restraint was seldom used, except to prevent a patient from injuring himself or his fellows. Chains were never used as a method of restraint, and the strait waistcoat only as a last resort. Extracts from the case-history (preserved at the Retreat) of a patient named Wilson Sutton give a vivid picture of the degree of forbearance which this system demanded of the keepers:

'1814. 12th August. To-day, after a walk in the country and eating a good dinner, while the attendants were at theirs he became quarrelsome—struck Josh. Whiting hurt Saml. Lays head and neck. After this he was shut up in a room to get calm.

'1815. 15th January. When S.L. has come into sight, he has fallen on him furiously with his fists.

'. . . 20th February . . . seized Saml. Smith his attendant and threatened to throw him downstairs, breaking his watch and chain and straining his thumb.

. . . 16th September. Fecht him (Smith) a blow betwixt the eyes.'

Sutton was then placed in the strait waistcoat for a few hours, but when freed, seized an iron fender, and felled the unfortunate Smith with it.

'. . . 11th October. He has since conducted himself in a peaceable manner, but has not deigned to speak to S. S.'

Mortification of the extremities through prolonged cold and physical restraint was frequently met with in institutions for the insane at this time. Reference has already been made to the practice of wrapping the patients' feet in flannel as a preventive measure. This was done not only at the Manchester Lunatic Hospital, but also, according to Samuel Tuke, at Bethlem. He goes on to say that Dr. Pinel, himself a pioneer in the humane treatment of the insane, admitted that 'seldom has a whole year elapsed during which no fatal accident has taken place in the Hôpital de Bicêtre (Paris) from the action of cold on the extremities'. Yet Tuke was able to write of the Retreat,

'Happily, this calamity is hardly known, and no instance of mortification has occurred . . . connected with cold or confinement. Indeed, the patients are never found to require such a degree of restraint as to prevent the use of considerable exercise, or to render it at all necessary to keep their feet wrapped in flannel.'

*Medical Treatment.*

'The physician,' wrote Samuel Tuke, 'plainly perceived how much was to be done by moral, and how little by any known medical, means.' Accordingly, medical treatment took a subordinate place at the Retreat. Drugs were seldom used to quiet elated patients. Dr. Fowler stressed the curative and soothing effects of warm baths, especially in cases of melancholia, and Jepson believed that an abundant diet of 'meat, bread and good porter' was more effective than a policy of semi-starvation. He thought porter as successful as opium in inducing sound sleep, and less detrimental to the constitution. Good food, air, exercise and occupation took the place of drastic medical methods practised in other institutions for the insane.

*Diet.*

There were different dietaries for the different classes of patients, but food was plentiful, and all patients were encouraged to eat freely. The following diet is that for the patients 'on the charity':

Breakfast: Milk and bread, or milk porridge.

Dinner: Pudding and animal food five days a week, fruit pudding and broth or soup on two days.

In the afternoon, bread and beer for the men, and tea or coffee for the women.

Supper: Generally the same as breakfast, or bread, cheese and beer.

It will be seen that this diet contained a generous amount of milk and meat, regular supplies of fruit, and an extra small meal in the afternoon, when the women were supplied with the relatively expensive products of tea and coffee.[1] The 'patients of the higher class' dined at the superintendents' table, and shared their meals. The household bills of this period show frequent expenditure on porter, and on such luxury items as wines, oranges and figs.

*Household Items.*

Samuel Tuke frequently referred to the community of staff and patients as 'the family', and indeed the accounts preserved at the Retreat show that the expenditure was far more like that of an ordinary household than of a charitable institution. William Tuke bought pots and pans, tin trays, beer jugs, coffee mugs, cream jugs, cutlery, cruets; great emphasis was placed on the steadying effect of properly served and attractive meals.

Bills for the year 1796, when the Retreat was originally furnished, show that beds and bedding were supplied for all the patients, including paupers. These beds were made of wood, and a special design was devised for those suffering from enuresis—patients who in other institutions for the insane would have been relegated to bundles of straw. The beds of 'those who are not of the lowest class' were of better quality, but all patients were provided with sheets, blankets, bags of goose feathers, and counterpanes.

*Visitation.*

While the Tuke family exercised a regular supervision over the affairs of the Retreat, representatives of the Quarterly Meeting of the Society of Friends were sent regularly to make independent reports,[2] and from 1796, three women Friends were appointed to carry out additional visits.[3] The 'Visiter's Book' shows that from the earliest days, the Retreat re-

---

[1] Provided by Tuke, Son & Co.
[2] *Report of Select Committee on Madhouses*, 1815, p. 160.
[3] Ibid. Cp. the activities of Catherine Cappe at the York Asylum. See pp. 125–6.

ceived distinguished visitors—English philanthropists such as Robert Owen and Elizabeth Fry; medical men such as Dr. Delarive and a Dr. Duncan from Dublin who described the Retreat as 'the best-regulated establishment in Europe'; writers and thinkers such as Sydney Smith, who wrote his famous article 'Mad Quakers' for the *Edinburgh Review* of 1813, immediately after reading Samuel Tuke's *Description of the Retreat.* No less than three parties were sent over by the Russian royal family— the first, early in 1814, including Alexander I's Physician and Chamberlain, the second, later in the same year, consisting of the Grand Duke Nicholas and his entourage, and the third, in 1818, headed by the Grand Duke Michael. It is interesting to speculate whether these visits had any connection with the mental instability of the Romanovs in general, and of Alexander I in particular. Perhaps the most picturesque visitors of all were the seven Red Indian braves who had been brought over to England to appear in a London theatre. After they had seen all that was to be seen, their Chief offered up a short prayer of thanks, and friends and warriors remained for some few minutes in prayerful silence.[1]

It would be unfair to compare the conditions at the Retreat during this period with those at St. Luke's and the Manchester Lunatic Hospital. The Retreat catered only for a restricted section of society. It was small enough for the community to be referred to as 'the family', and sufficiently well-endowed to be run on the lines of a comfortable guest-house. The treasurer was not a salaried official whose duty lay in managing as economically as possible, but a wealthy philanthropist who was one of the chief benefactors. The staff, though it lacked formal qualifications, was drawn from the Society of Friends, and had at least the qualification of unimpeachable moral integrity. The Retreat was thus spared the troubles which were likely to beset other institutions for the insane—problems of financial peculation, of apathetic visitors, and untrustworthy staff.

To say all this is not to minimize the extent of the achievement, but merely to point out that conditions were particularly favourable to success. The influence of the experiment at the Retreat on the subsequent conduct of less-favoured institutions was immense. It removed the final justification for neglect, brutality and crude medical methods. It proved that kindness was more effective than rigorous confinement; and it threw a startling light on the activities of private madhouse keepers, many of whom charged large fees for keeping patients in conditions as miserable as those of the parish workhouse.

[1] H. C. Hunt, *A Retired Habitation*, pp. 49–50.

# Chapter Five

## THE FOUNDATION OF COUNTY ASYLUMS

L UNACY reform began on a national scale with the foundation of the
county asylums, following the Act of 1808; but no reform takes
place in a vacuum, and it is necessary to refer briefly to the movements in thought and philanthropic practice which bridge the gap between the small local reforms of the late eighteenth century, and the parliamentary reform movement of the early nineteenth.

Somervell writes that the nineteenth century started in 1789;[1] and certainly the ideas and ideals of the 1790's form an immense contrast to those
of fifty years earlier. Reasoned apathy had been replaced by violent
emotion. 'Cosmic Toryism' was challenged on all sides—by Paine, by
Godwin, by Paley, by Malthus, by Bentham. Changes in agricultural
and industrial methods now affected the lives of the whole population,
virtually abolishing the traditional pattern of English living. The working classes began to feel their power, and to be aware of wrongs accen-
tuated by the pressure of industrialization. There was a considerable shift
of population, as workers from the south moved to the new industrial
towns of the north. It is no mere generalization to say that a curious kind
of unrest seized the whole country in these years. The Americans had
rejected George III, France rejected the Bourbons; the religious became
converted, the literary wrote lyrical poetry, the politically-minded talked
of revolution; and gradually the word 'revolution' became applicable to
almost every sphere of systematized thought, so that ideas and habits of
thought which had gone unchallenged for centuries were examined in a
new and searching light. Out of this intellectual and social ferment arose
two movements which were to have a decisive effect on lunacy reform:
Evangelicalism and Radicalism.

[1] D. C. Somervell, *English Thought in the Nineteenth Century*, p. 1.

The Evangelical movement in the Church of England was, to quote Halévy, 'a species of Anglican Methodism'[1] which owed much to the example of the Wesleys; and, like Wesley's followers, the Clapham Sect —that group of lay 'Saints' which gathered round Wilberforce in the years 1795–1808—made use of experience gained in the world of politics and business to develop a concrete policy for social action. The individual activities of the earlier philanthropists—Howard, John Wesley, Elizabeth Fry and the Tukes—were now replaced to a large extent by group activities. Societies for the reform of particular abuses became the fashion, and each cause had its small group of parliamentary adherents who were ready to press for legislative action. In the years which preceded the passing of the County Asylums Act, the influence of the Clapham Sect was at its peak. Wilberforce and Hannah More were its prophets, and lunacy reform was only one of the many avenues explored.

Evangelical humanism stemmed from an emotional appreciation of the plight of the poor and oppressed. It may be said to have started with the Wesleys, and to have reached fruition in the person of the seventh Earl of Shaftesbury; but Radicalism came from cold reason, from a fundamental love of order, a hatred of administrative confusion. Its dominant figure was Jeremy Bentham, whose thought was to have so great an influence on Chadwick and J. S. Mill. Round Bentham, as round Wilberforce, gathered a group of disciples. The Benthamites were both a philosophical school and a political party, and their thought can in some ways be traced back to Hume's associationism: the belief that all complex ideas could be reduced to show their dependence on simple sensations led inevitably to the 'pleasure-pain principle', and thus to the belief in 'the greatest happiness of the greatest number'; but for the Benthamites, any connection with the past was purely accidental. They were without a sense of history, being characterized by 'a volcanic desire for utter, organic, sweeping change'.[2] They were not concerned with the plight of the insane from any sense of pity. Bentham himself considered it right and proper that lunatics should be kept under constant surveillance and in perpetual solitude,[3] apparently thinking both medical and 'moral' treatment useless. It is unlikely that he ever gave the matter much thought; but because he taught his followers to detest legal anomalies, because they

[1] E. Halévy, *A History of the English People in the Nineteenth Century*. Vol. I—England in 1815, p. 433.
[2] S. Finer, *Life and Times of Sir Edwin Chadwick*, p. 14.
[3] See a discussion of the relevant sections of the 'Panopticon' in Appendix II.

thought in terms of legal action and public institutions, his disciples are to be found among those who worked and planned for the reform of the conditions of the insane.

## Sir George Onesiphorus Paul.

In 1806, the new train of events was set in motion by a Benthamite, the High Sheriff of Gloucestershire, who addressed a letter to the Secretary of State urging him to take action concerning the condition of criminal and pauper lunatics.[1]

Paul was a prison reformer who had known John Howard,[2] and who had also absorbed something of the Howard tradition. He had personally designed the new county gaol and Bridewells erected at Gloucester, being:

'the head and heart of the committee, the draftsman of the Bill, the financier who raised the funds . . . the author of the reformed system of discipline, and the scapegoat on whose head were laid all the stupid anathemas that the scheme provoked.'[3]

This energetic man, then sixty years old,[4] was also the president of the Stroud Society for providing medical attention for the poor, and his practical experience led him to consider criminal lunatics and pauper lunatics as two components of a single problem which might be dealt with in a uniform way.

Of pauper lunatics, he wrote in his letter:

'I believe there is hardly a parish of any considerable size in which there may not be found some unfortunate human creature of this description, who, if his ill-treatment has made him phrenetic, is chained in the cellar or garret of a workhouse, fastened to the leg of a table, tied to a post in an outhouse, or perhaps shut up in an uninhabited ruin.'

He added in a footnote, 'I have witnessed instances of each of these methods of securing under 17 George II.'[5]

The condition of pauper lunatics at this time has been partially misrepresented by the Webbs, who state that 'right down to 1835, the typical method of dealing with pauper lunatics was to place them out under con-

---

[1] *Suggestions of Sir George Onesiphorus Paul, Bart., to the Secretary of State*, 1806. Published as an appendix to the 1807 *Report on Criminal and Pauper Lunatics.*
[2] W. L. Clay, *Memoir of the Rev. John Clay, B.D.,* p. 63.
[3] D.N.B.
[4] 1746–1820.
[5] The Act of 1744.

# THE FOUNDATION OF COUNTY ASYLUMS

tract',[1] that is, to place them in private madhouses. While this statement was true of the large metropolitan parishes, where the workhouse was a highly-organized institution, it did not apply in the provinces; parishes outside London were generally too small, too poor, and too remote to avail themselves of this method of ridding themselves of their most troublesome inmates.

In the prisons, the position had been complicated by the Criminal Lunatics Act of 1800,[2] which provided for the first time for the detention of criminal lunatics 'during His Majesty's pleasure'. This Act applied not only to persons tried for treason, murder and felony, who were found to have been insane at the time of the commission of the offence, but also to those found insane on arraignment, and to any person 'discovered or apprehended under circumstances that denote a derangement of mind and a purpose of committing some crime'. The Act had not directed where these different classes of the criminally insane were to be housed, nor had it provided any machinery by which they might ultimately be released. Sir George Onesiphorus Paul referred in his letter to two cases personally known to him in which prisoners had been detained under this Act.

Charles Roberts had been tried on a charge of felony in 1800, and James Need on a charge of assault in 1803. Both had been declared insane, and were detained 'during His Majesty's pleasure' in the county gaol. In the first case, Paul thought that the plea of insanity was a false one, since Roberts was 'uniformly quiet and well-behaved'; but the man had already in effect served six years' imprisonment—probably more than the sentence he would have received if his sanity had never been held in question—and there was no way of securing his release. Paul thought that the other man, Need, was a genuine case of insanity, but that he was not troublesome, and that it would be safe to let him go free. He pointed out that both these men had to be maintained in the county gaol, and that the 1800 Act had given no directions as to where the cost of maintenance should fall. Housing such prisoners in the county gaol presented almost insuperable problems, since solitary confinement would aggravate the malady, while to keep a lunatic in company with the other prisoners resulted in a situation 'pregnant with disturbance'.

From Paul's evidence, there was clearly a case for the construction of a new type of institution where pauper and criminal lunatics could be treated as insane persons, and not primarily as paupers or criminals.

Paul's letter arrived at an opportune moment. The long tradition of

[1] S. and B. Webb, *English Poor Law History*. Part I—The Old Poor Law, p. 304.
[2] A more detailed consideration of this Act and its consequences is given in Appendix C1

Tory rule had at last been broken, and the Whigs who had followed Burke in accepting office in 1792 were reunited with the Foxite remnant. The Secretary of State in the new Ministry of All the Talents was the second Earl Spencer (1758–1834) the father of that Viscount Althorp whose name was later to be associated with factory reform. Lord Grenville headed the administration after the death of Fox in 1806; Sheridan was Treasurer of the Navy, and the Solicitor-General was Samuel Romilly. Although Romilly achieved no outstanding reform of the penal code during this brief period in office, he was both a Benthamite and a personal friend of Wilberforce. He would certainly have known of Paul's work at Gloucester, and it seems probable that he would have welcomed this attempt to mitigate the harshness of the penal code.

*The Select Committee of 1807.*

A select committee 'to inquire into the State of Criminal and Pauper Lunatics in England, and the Laws relating thereto' was appointed in January, 1807.[1] The prime mover was Charles Williams-Wynn, then Under-Secretary of State for the Home Department, and a nephew of Lord Grenville.[2]

Wynn was at that time thirty-one years of age, and had been in parliament for nine years. He remained intimately connected with lunacy reform until 1850, the year of his death, and was actually present in the House to hear Lord Ashley introduce the Lunatics Bill of 1845.[3] Wynn was not a brilliant man; his later career failed to fulfil its early promise, for he never became a major parliamentary figure. Canning described him as 'The worst man of business I ever saw', and even Southey, his life-long friend, thought him 'One of the most impracticable persons to deal with, taking crotchets in his head, and holding to them with invincible pertinacity.'[4] This latter characteristic may have been an advantage in the circumstances. Wynn, with his lack of gifts of oratory or parliamentary vision, his capacity for detail and his single-track mind, was in some ways the ideal person to undertake the wearisome task of compiling a parliamentary report on an unpopular subject.

George Rose was also a member of the Committee of 1807.[5] He was

---

[1] The date is given in Wilson's *Biographical Index to the House of Commons* (article on Wynn) as January 23rd, 1807. H.C.J. has no reference to the first appointment of this committee.

[2] Charles Watkin Williams-Wynn, 1775–1850. Brother of Sir Watkin Williams-Wynn. See *D.N.B.*

[3] His presence was mentioned in debate by Sir James Graham. Hansard, June 6th, 1845.

[4] *D.N.B.*

[5] Rt. Hon. George Rose, 1744–1818.

considerably older than Wynn, but of a similar temperament. 'His whole life was active, laborious and useful' stated his obituary in the *Gentleman's Magazine*; it 'presented an instance of what may be accomplished by industry and integrity'. Rose's integrity was sometimes questioned by his contemporaries—he was accused by his Whig adversaries of intriguing to obtain posts with large material rewards[1]—but his industry was irrefutable. The use made of his patient, meticulous mind by successive Tory administrations is well known. Seldom has one man held so many exacting offices in a life-time. He was Keeper of the Records at Westminster, Secretary to the Board of Taxes, Clerk of the Parliaments, a Privy Counsellor, a Trustee of the British Museum, an Elder Brother of Trinity House; he was a close friend of Pitt, and the originator of the story, derided by the Whigs, that the dying premier's last words were, 'My country—save my country!'[2] He was also a close friend of George III, who stayed more than once at Cuffnells, Rose's country house in Hampshire. He patiently accumulated power and influence in an unspectacular way which led his friends to describe him as a power behind the Tory party, and his enemies to consider him a political jobber.

Rose was not the sort of person whom one would expect to become closely associated with social reform; but there was another side to his character which has generally received less attention. He showed an unexpected but continuous interest in the problems of poverty. He was a county magistrate for many years, and applied the same unflagging energy to local administration as to the machinations of the Tory Party. He was the chief sponsor of the Act for encouraging Friendly Societies which was passed in 1793, and the author of a pamphlet entitled 'Observations on the Poor Laws' in which he wrote, 'The relief of the poor, so strongly recommended by religion and humanity, is no less obviously required by the plainest dictates of good policy. It is impossible that multitudes should perish or suffer from hunger . . . without endangering the safety and destroying the comfort of the rest of the community.'—and again, 'Few matters of higher importance' (than Poor Law reform) 'can occupy the deliberations of parliament.'

Rose's view of poverty, and his experience as a magistrate, explain his interest in lunacy problems. In 1807, he followed Wynn's lead, though

---

[1] D.N.B. See also Aspinall, *Politics and the Press, 1780–1850*. Canning stated that it was 'not easy to remain long in politics without making the acquaintance of George Rose'. Aspinall, op. cit., p. 163.

[2] Lord Holland's *Memoirs*, vol. I, pp. 207–8.

he was later to emerge for a short time as the leader of the parliamentary group.

Three members of this Committee are better-known for their connection with social reform in other spheres—Romilly, Wilberforce, and Whitbread. Wilberforce's main preoccupation at this time was with the slave trade—the Bill for the abolition of slavery having been passed in the preceding session—but any movement for social amelioration was assured of his help. Romilly was primarily a prison reformer, but was closely associated with Wilberforce in many of his activities. He served with the committee in his official capacity as Solicitor-General. Whitbread, described by Romilly as 'the promoter of every liberal scheme for improving the condition of mankind, the zealous advocate of the oppressed, and the undaunted opposer of every species of corruption and ill-administration'[1] was at this time busy with his Poor Law Bill—an elaborate document providing for the equalization of the county rates, the partial abolition of the laws of settlement, a national system of education, and a method of differentiating between the worthy and the unworthy poor. This was destined to rejection.

In addition to Romilly, two other members represented the legal interest—Charles Shaw-Lefevre, who was a barrister and a county magistrate,[2] and Charles Dundas, a barrister.

The committee thus included members of both political parties, and both groups of reformers. The terms of reference 'to enquire into the State of Criminal and Pauper Lunatics in England' reflect the double interest in penal and Poor Law reform. The Committee also included barristers and county magistrates—the people who were most closely concerned with a change in the existing state of the law—but as far as can be ascertained, no member adequately represented the medical interest in insanity—partly because a medical interest in insanity had yet to be aroused, and partly because parliament was still thinking primarily in terms of confinement.

*The 1807 Report.*

The report consisted of a brief survey of existing conditions, together with several appendices containing valuable evidence. The Committee

---

[1] Holland's *Memoirs*, vol. II, p. 237. Whitbread was related to John Howard—see Clay, *Memoirs of Rev. John Clay*, p. 49.
[2] 'He spares no trouble as a magistrate in the discharge of the multifarious but important duties of that station.' (Wilson's *Biographical Index to the House of Commons*, article on Charles Shaw-Lefevre.)

found that the only law which might be construed to affect pauper lunatics was the Vagrancy Act of 1744, and referred to the evidence of Sir
George Onesiphorus Paul in stating that the condition of those in workhouses was 'revolting to humanity'. It recommended that an asylum
should be set up in each county, to which both pauper and criminal lunatics might be sent. Each asylum should have a committee of governors
nominated by the local justices of the peace, and should be financed by
means of a county rate.

'To this the public opinion appears so favourable that it may be sufficient at least in the first instance rather to recommend and assist than to
enforce the execution of such a plan.'

The first appendix to the report comprised the returns of pauper and
criminal lunatics made to parliament in 1806. The Select Committee commented that these returns were 'so evidently deficient in several instances,
that a very large addition must be made in any computation of the whole
number'. This was one reason why it was necessary to make the new Act
a permissive one: the total dimensions of the need could only be guessed at,
and it was necessary for the scheme for county asylums to pass through an
experimental stage.

The total number of lunatics in pauper institutions in England was
given as 1,755,[1] but as the committee perceived, the omissions were considerable. Hampshire ignored the request for information. The authorities of the counties of Hereford, Stafford, Warwick, Hertford, Bedford,
Cumberland and Cambridge replied that there were no pauper lunatics in
their boundaries, though two of these counties—Staffordshire and Bedfordshire—were to find it necessary to construct county asylums only a
few years later. The East Riding of Yorkshire found only three pauper
lunatics, while the West Riding by contrast made a return of 424.

On behalf of the committee, Dr. Andrew Halliday[2] personally investigated the position in Norfolk and Suffolk, in order to arrive at an approximate estimate of the proportion of pauper lunatics to population. In the
workhouses of Suffolk, which had made a total return of 92, he found
47 'lunatics' and 67 'idiots', confined to 'damp, dark cells'. Thus there
were 22 persons who had been overlooked by the county authorities in
their return. In Norfolk, the position was worse. The official figure was
22; Halliday's figure was 112.

The same inaccuracies were apparent in the returns for criminal

[1] 1807 *Report*, Appendix I. The total figure of 1765 included ten in Wales.
[2] See p. 131.

lunatics. It was clear that no one had any idea of the actual number of criminal and pauper lunatics in the country, and that under the existing administrative framework, it would be impossible to obtain an accurate picture of the situation.

The deficiencies of these returns might be explained in several ways. The most obvious cause is administrative inefficiency; when each parish controlled its own pauper institution, it was not easy to obtain information over the area of a whole county. Few counties possessed men of the calibre of John Howard or Sir George Onesiphorus Paul—men who would be willing to make protracted journeys by coach or on horseback, to risk the contagion of typhus or gaol-fever, solely in order to verify their facts. The desire for concealment may also have been an operative factor; if pauper lunatics were being kept in conditions 'revolting to humanity', parish overseers and local magistrates would have no desire to see those conditions publicized—especially when the only practicable alternative was to send all lunatics to expensive private madhouses. Probably many local officials had only the most elementary idea of what constituted insanity, and included in their returns only those in a state of ungovernable mania or complete idiocy. Some counties may have experienced a curious sort of local pride in proclaiming that all their inhabitants were in full possession of their faculties; but it seems likely that the chief cause of the inadequacy of these returns was a characteristic apathy concerning the condition of the insane.

### The County Asylum Act, 1808.[1]

The Ministry of All the Talents fell in 1807—partly, it is alleged, as a result of the Whigs' refusal to follow George Rose's system of paying 'hireling scribes' to praise the ministry in the Press[2]—and the Act of 1808 'for the better Care and Maintenance of Lunatics, being Paupers or Criminals, in England' was passed under the ægis of the Portland admistration.[3] The measure was piloted through both Commons and Lords without difficulty, and became known as 'Wynn's Act'. It implemented the recommendations of the committee of the previous year by laying down detailed specifications for the construction and maintenance of county asylums.

In the first twenty years of its operation, only nine counties proceeded

---

[1] 48 Geo. III, c. 96.
[2] A. Aspinall, *Politics and the Press, 1780–1850*, p. 163.
[3] June 23rd, 1808. See Holland's *Memoirs*, vol. 1, p. 22 for an estimate of Portland's political affiliations.

to erect asylums. This slow beginning might be attributed partly to the prevalent apathy, partly to flaws in the framing of the Act, and partly to a reluctance on the part of local magistrates to become involved in expenditure to an unforeseeable extent; but, in spite of its limited application, the Act was of considerable importance in the progress of reform. The county asylums so set up were the forerunners of the mental hospitals of to-day—some of which still occupy the original premises constructed under Wynn's Act. The importance of the Act lies primarily in the conception of treatment of a non-deterrent type as a public responsibility, and in the attempt to deal with the root cause—insanity—rather than with the symptoms of anti-social behaviour.

The preamble of the Act stated:

'. . . the Practice of confining such Lunatics and other insane Persons as are chargeable to their respective Parishes in Gaols, Houses of Correction, Poor Houses and Houses of Industry is highly dangerous and inconvenient . . . it is expedient that further Provision should be made for the Care and Maintenance of such Persons, and for the erecting (sic) proper Houses for their Reception . . . it is also expedient that further Provision should be made for the Custody of insane Persons who shall commit Criminal Offences . . .'

(i) Initiation (sections 1–7).

Justices of the Peace might give notice at the Quarter Session of their intention to erect an asylum; two or more counties might combine for this purpose. A committee of visiting justices was to be appointed at the Quarter Sessions to be responsible both for the erection of the asylum, and for periodical inspection. They were authorized to contract, to purchase land, and to appoint a Clerk and a Surveyor.

(ii) Finance (sections 4, 7, 8, 13 and 22).

The justices were empowered to raise a county rate for the purpose of building the asylum, and were given power to mortgage the rates for a period not exceeding fourteen years. No justice was to derive individual advantage from any asylum contract. Where two or more counties combined to erect an asylum, a calculation of the expense to be incurred by each was to be made on a population basis. An appeal for voluntary contributions might be made to meet part of the initial cost of the buildings.

(iii) Site and Accommodation (sections 16 and 26).

'The said Visiting Justices, as well in the Choice of Ground and Situation as in determining on the Plans for building or for purchasing and altering Buildings for such Lunatic Asylums, shall as far as conveniently may be, fix upon an Airy and Healthy Situation, with a good Supply of Water, and which may afford a Probability of constant Medical Assistance, and pursue such Measures and adopt such Plans as shall provide separate and distinct Wards for Male and Female Lunatics, and also for the Convalescents and Incurables, and also separate and distinct Day Rooms and Airing Grounds for the Male and Female Convalescents, and dry and airy Cells for Lunatics of every Description.'

The buildings were to be exempt from the window-tax.

*(iv) Admission (sections 17–19).*

Patients were to be admitted as 'dangerous to be at large' under the 1744 Act—on a warrant from two justices—or as criminal lunatics by the varied procedures outlined in the Criminal Lunatics Act of 1800. Furthermore,

'the Justices are hereby authorized and directed to issue Warrants on the Application of the Overseers of the Poor . . . for the Conveyance of any Lunatic, Insane Person, or dangerous Idiot who may be chargeable to such Parish, to such Asylum.'

The parish was to pay a charge laid down by the justices, this charge not to exceed 14s. weekly per patient.[1] If the overseer did not apply to the justices for a warrant to convey within seven days of receiving notice that there was an insane or mentally deficient person in his parish, he became liable to a penalty of not less than 40s., and not more than £10.

*(v) Discharge (section 23).*

Patients were to be discharged by the committee of visiting justices upon recovery. A penalty of from 40s. to £10 was prescribed for any officer or servant of the asylum who made possible, either through neglect or connivance, the unauthorized departure of any patient.

*(vi) Appointment of Staff (section 24).*

The visiting justices were to appoint a Treasurer, and 'such other Officers and Servants together with such Numbers of Assistants as they shall from Time to Time find necessary in Proportion to the Numbers of Persons confined in such Asylum'—and were to fix the weekly rate of

---

[1] Section 17. This limit was removed in 1815 (section 7 of amending Act).

payment at a sum which would defray 'the whole Expence of the Maintenance and Care, Medicines and Clothing, requisite for such Person, and
the Salaries of the Officers and Attendants.'

Experience was to show that this first experiment in the public care of
the insane was far from adequate. A mere comparison in length between
the Act of 1808 and that of 1890 shows that the framers of the latter were
aware of many possible abuses which Wynn and his associates did not
envisage.

*Amendments to the 1808 Act.*

The first asylum to be constructed under the new Act was that at
Nottingham, which received patients from 1810, and was formally
opened in 1811.[1] According to the returns of 1806, the county had only
35 pauper lunatics for whom provision was needed, and no criminal
lunatics whatever. The asylum was built to accommodate 76–80 patients
and yet this accommodation was found at once to be totally inadequate.[2]
By the terms of the Act, there was no way in which the asylum staff or the
visiting justices could exercise their discretion in admitting patients.
Parish overseers were bound, on pain of heavy fines, to give information
of all insane persons in the area, and the justices were equally bound to
send those who were in poverty, or who exhibited criminal propensities,
to the asylum. The new institution had already cost over £21,000,[3] and
was badly overcrowded in the first year. An amendment passed in 1811
(51 Geo. III, c. 79) remedied this situation, which not only severely
handicapped the one asylum in operation, but also deterred justices in
other counties from using their powers under the Act. Justices were
given

'discretionary power as to issuing or not issuing warrants . . . particularly in cases where it shall be found that the number of applications
on behalf of persons having just cause to be admitted does at any time
exceed the number of those who can be properly accommodated in such
an asylum, with a view to cure, comfort and safe custody.'

An Amending Act of 1815 (55 Geo. III, c. 46) dealt with questions of
admission, certification and discharge of patients. Overseers of the poor
were required to furnish returns of all lunatics and idiots within their

[1] *Nottingham Evening Post*, October 10th, 1811.
[2] Sir G. O. Paul, *Doubts Concerning the Expediency . . . of immediately proceeding to provide
a Lunatic Asylum for the County of Gloucester*, p. 14.
[3] *1815 Report*, p. 152.

parishes to the justices on request, and to provide a medical certificate[1]
for each, whether admission to the county asylum was sought on behalf
of the patient or not. This provided some guarantee that the overseers
were carrying out their duties adequately. No attempt was made to
define the status of the 'medical person' who was to give a certificate,
nor was any provision made that he should receive payment for the exercise of this duty. The question of discharge arose out of the apathy of the
visiting justices, and the difficulty of inducing a quorum to be present at
their meetings. Under the 1808 Act, patients could be discharged only by
the visiting committee as a whole. In order to obviate any delay in procedure, the 1815 amendment carried a clause enabling any two visiting
justices to discharge patients on their own responsibility at any time.

The 'Small Act' of 1819 (59 Geo. III, c. 127) returned to the problem of
certification; until this date, certificates stating merely that 'Mr. —— is a
suitable Object for your Place'[2] or, to quote a well-known example, that
'Hey Broadway, a Pot Carey' thought that 'A Blister and Bleeding and
Meddeson' would be suitable for a gentleman who 'Wold not A Gree to
be Done at Home'[3] were quite common. The new prescribed form of
certification was as follows:

'I do hereby certify that by the direction of L.M. and N.O., Justices of
the Peace for the County of H., I have personally examined C.D., and
that the said C.D. appears to me to be of insane mind.'

The 1819 Act also gave the justices power to send patients to the county
asylum on their own initiative, without the concurrence of the parish
overseer.

The total effect of these three amending Acts was to place the responsibility for the admission of patients with the magistrates rather than with
the overseers, thus weakening the connection of the county asylums with
the Poor Law authorities.

[1] The new importance attached to the medical certificate at this stage is a reflection of the
rise in professional standards in the medical world. The Company of Barber-Surgeons had
split in 1750, the Surgeons forming their own company. In 1800, they were granted a Crown
Charter, and the College of Surgeons was established. The apothecaries—who were in effect
the forerunners of the general practitioners of to-day—regularized their position in 1815, an
Act of that year defining their status and qualifications.
[2] Hunt. *A Retired Habitation*, p. 27. Certificate of a patient admitted to the Retreat.
[3] *1815 Report*, p. 317. Certificate delivered to the Select Committee by Mr. Finch, of
Laverstock. Broadway was a local druggist without qualifications.

# Chapter Six

## THE SELECT COMMITTEES OF 1815–16[1]

*Public Opinion in 1815.*

WHILE the first developments in theory and practice were taking place in connection with the county asylums, the parliamentary group considered less satisfactory aspects of the lunacy problem. On April 28th, 1815, parliament again proceeded to appoint a select committee on the subject, and this time public opinion was actively and vocally on the side of the reformers.

Samuel Tuke had published his *Description of the Retreat*—a book which told of the success of the new system of 'moral' management—in 1813, and the impact of the work of the Tukes on the national consciousness dates from that time. The book elevated the Retreat in the public estimation from a local experiment to something very like a national monument.

In the same year, a county magistrate named Godfrey Higgins uncovered a series of abuses at the York Asylum. Failing to obtain satisfaction from the authorities, he communicated his findings to the Press. When an investigation seemed imminent, the staff resorted to panic-stricken measures, burning down part of the building in order to conceal the appalling conditions in which some of the patients were kept, and destroying records to remove the evidence of financial peculation. This not unnaturally had the effect of rousing rather than allaying public indignation, and Higgins sent his evidence to Earl FitzWilliam, one of the leaders of the Whig party, who was then lord-lieutenant of the county.[2]

---

[1] Material in this chapter is taken from the report of these Committees unless otherwise stated.

[2] Higgins, *Letter to Earl FitzWilliam*. The incidents at York Asylum are discussed in detail later in this chapter.

Another notable case of abuse which became public knowledge at this time was the discovery at Bethlem of William Norris, a patient who had been confined in a special apparatus of iron for nine years without respite. An iron collar several inches wide encircled his neck, and was fastened to a wall behind his head; his feet were manacled, and a harness fitted over his shoulders, pinioning his arms to his sides. It was just possible for him to stand, or lie on his back, but he was unable to shift his position when lying down, or to move more than one step away from the wall.[1] Six members of parliament visited Norris before his release; they found him quiet and rational, able to hold intelligent conversation on political matters, and to read with comprehension any matter which was put before him. He was in an advanced stage of tuberculosis, and died shortly after being set free.

*The Select Committee of 1815.*

Armed with the evidence of these two cases, and strengthened by public opinion, the parliamentary group was able to press for the appointment of a new select committee with wider terms of reference. The committee set up in April, 1815, represented a powerful body of parliamentary opinion. Wynn, George Rose, Lord Robert Seymour, the younger Peel, Sir William Curtis, Sir James Shaw, William Smith, William Sturges-Bourne and George Tierney were among its members. Wynn was out of office, hovering uncertainly between the Whigs and the Tories. Between 1815 and 1819, he made an unsuccessful attempt to form a third party, and failing, joined the Tories.[2] Rose was over seventy, and had only three more years to live. The editor of his diaries states that 'during these three years, Mr. Rose's activity was subsiding into the grave',[3] but the account in the 1815 report of the sessions at which he took the chair shows that he was still mentally alert, and an extremely competent chairman. Shaw-Lefevre and Whitbread were again appointed. A new name was that of Lord Robert Seymour, who emerges as one of the leaders of the group at this time. Lord Robert was a younger son of the first Marquis of Hertford, and thus a member of a family which was in the early nineteenth century notorious rather than celebrated. His sister-in-law, the wife of the second Marquis, was widely supposed to be the mistress of the Prince Regent, and his nephew, the third Marquis, became the model for Thackeray's 'Lord Steyne'; of Lord Robert himself,

---

[1] See illustration in O'Donoghue, *Story of Bethlehem Hospital*, facing p. 320.
[2] *D.N.B.*
[3] *Diaries of the Rt. Hon. George Rose*, vol. II, p. 517.

little was apparently known even by his contemporaries. He was a back-bencher who seldom took his place in the House, and hardly ever made a speech.[1] His death on November 23rd, 1831, at the age of eighty-three, occasioned only the most perfunctory mention in the newspapers and periodicals of the day. In 1815, he was already a quiet, elderly man, apparently of a lethargic temperament; yet Lord Robert, like Rose, showed an unexpected interest in social reform. He was a vice-president of the London Society for Promoting Christianity among the Jews—one of Wilberforce's many societies; from this fact we may infer that he was associated to some extent with the Clapham Sect. He was also a guardian of the poor for the parish of St. Marylebone, in which parish Hertford House was situated; and he was a county magistrate for the county of Middlesex. Lord Robert shared with Wynn and Rose the task of taking the chair at the meetings of the select committee, and showed in his questions to witnesses an intimate knowledge of the abuses practised in private madhouses.

Robert Peel—not yet a baronet, for his father was still alive—was at that time Secretary of State for Ireland. His interest in the reform of the penal code, which found expression later in the reforms he carried out as Home Secretary, brought him into touch with Romilly and Whitbread; but the Peels had another and more direct link with lunacy reform. They lived at Drayton Park in Staffordshire, and the memorial tablet in the Stafford Asylum (built in 1818 and now St. George's Hospital, Stafford), shows that the elder Peel was one of the original benefactors of that institution. The Peels may therefore have been concerned in 1815 in the plans already in preparation to erect this asylum. Sir William Curtis and Sir James Shaw were aldermen of the City of London, and therefore *ex officio* Governors of Bethlem. William Smith was a Whig, a member of the Clapham Sect, and a close friend of Wilberforce. He was renowned both for the strength of his religious convictions and the length of his speeches, being apt, in the words of a then current political satire, to entertain a weary House with his religious opinions at inopportune moments:

> At length, when the candles burn low in their sockets,
> Up gets William Smith, with both hands in his pockets,
> On a course of morality fearlessly enters
> With all the opinions of all the Dissenters.

Two other members should be briefly mentioned: Sturges-Bourne, a

---

[1] See Wilson's *Biographical Index of the House of Commons.*

barrister, chairman of the Malthusian Committee of 1817, and later Home Secretary for a short period in 1827, and George Tierney, the brilliant and ambitious Whig politician—'an old rogue, the very focus of intrigue, descending to all sorts of tricks'.[1] Tierney was unpopular in the House, partly because of his sarcastic tongue, and partly because the great Whig landowners thought him a parvenu.

This, then, was the group which proceeded throughout 1815 and 1816 to issue a series of reports on the conditions of the insane in institutions of various kinds. There is one connecting link between them which may have a certain significance: nearly all of them were in some way connected with the developing London hospitals. Lord Robert Seymour and Whitbread were vice-presidents of the Middlesex Hospital. Whitbread and Shaw-Lefevre were vice-presidents of St. Luke's, the lunatic hospital which rivalled Bethlem. Sir James Shaw was president of St. Bartholomew's Hospital. William Smith was associated with the London Dispensary, Tierney with the Surrey Dispensary in Southwark, Sir William Curtis with the London Hospital and the Universal Medical Institution. The acceptance of the position of president or vice-president of a medical institution did not, of course, necessarily imply a strong interest in medical progress, since such a position was a merely formal honour; but in this case, the coincidence seems too strong to be ignored. We may at least conclude that some members of the Select Committee were interested in medical reform, and therefore that the medical aspects of insanity were considered by an official body for the first time, though the medical profession was not represented.

Thus the interest-groups represented on this Committee were largely the same as those represented on that of 1807—barristers, county magistrates, and those interested in Poor Law and penal reform; but the emergence of a new group—those interested in the public provision of medical services—has a certain significance.

The Committee produced a voluminous series of reports of evidence received.[2] It dealt with the York Asylum and with Bethlem, St. Luke's, the new county asylum at Nottingham, the Retreat, and with the condition of pauper lunatics in workhouses. Upon being reappointed in 1816, it proceeded to consider private madhouses. The condition of criminal lunatics was no longer a separate consideration, since their numbers were very small, and they could usually be accommodated in

[1] Herries to Lord Hardinge, quoted in Aspinall's *Politics and the Press*, 1780–1850, p. 218.
[2] These were laid before parliament on several occasions, but published together as the 1815 *Report on Madhouses*.

one of the new county asylums, or in Bethlem. The reports thus covered all the main types of institutions in which the insane were then confined. This was the first attempt to provide a comprehensive survey of the situation.

It showed that both law and practice were in a state of unbelievable chaos. There were two types of lunacy law—that relating to county asylums, and that relating to private madhouses; in the latter case, the defective 1774 Act was still unamended. Subscription hospitals operated untrammelled by any considerations of legal powers and duties, and the thousands of pauper lunatics who remained in workhouses came under the Poor Law authorities. As a result, enormous varieties in practice were possible, from the humane treatment of the Retreat at one end of the scale to the inhumanity of Bethlem and the worst of the private madhouses at the other.

The rest of this chapter is based on the evidence given before the 1815–16 Committee. It has been amplified here in some respects, but was in itself enough to give a fairly comprehensive picture of the position.

## I. YORK ASYLUM

In order to understand the full story of the events of 1813, it is necessary to go back to the early history of the Asylum.

An advertisement in the *York Courant* of August 7th, 1772, first drew the attention of the citizens of York to 'the deplorable situation of many poor lunatics of the county, who have no support except what a needy parent can bestow, or a thrifty parish officer provide. An appeal was made on the 27th of the same month for donations from 'such Noblemen, Gentlemen and Ladies as are desirous of promoting an Institution for the Relief of an Unhappy Part of the Community'. Unfortunately the institution built with such high ideals and excellent motives never lived up to its early promise. By 1790, when Hannah Mills died, its conditions were as bad as those of many a private madhouse, where the only motive involved was that of personal profit for the proprietor.

A local historian reports that 'the building, as an edifice, was worthy of the architects',[1] and the Asylum possessed an imposing list of Governors headed by the Archbishop of York;[2] but it appears that, as with Bethlem,

---

[1] E. Baines, *History of the County of York*, 1823, p. 55.
[2] Higgins, *Letter to Earl FitzWilliam*, etc. (This volume contains, in addition to the original letter, a collection of letters and reports relevant to the reform of York Asylum.) Appendix, p. 19.

the magnificence of the frontage and the social status of the Governors bore little relation to the conditions inside. A later Medical Superintendent of the Retreat, Dr. Thurnam, tells us in his *Statistics of Insanity* (1845) that the building was originally designed for fifty-four inmates, and by 1815, it held 103. The patients were verminous and filthy, herded together in cells with an utter disregard for cleanliness or ventilation. The first physician, Dr. Hunter, had his 'secret insane powders, green and grey' which were nothing more than powerful emetics and purges. 'Flogging and cudgelling were systematically resorted to,' writes Thurnam.

'. . . this indeed was denied at the time, but . . . several cases which were brought forward leave little doubt that these cruel practices of the Middle Ages, during which other methods of managing maniacal patients were unknown, were continued in the asylum with the concurrence of its officers.'[1]

All this was suspected, but there was no concrete proof. After 1792, the Retreat provided an alternative system for the care of the insane, but only on a small and restricted scale. Those who had no connection with the Society of Friends, and these were of course the majority, still went to the Asylum, where Dr. Hunter and his successor, Dr. Best, received patients, discouraged inquisitive visitors, and succeeded in evading public condemnation until 1813. In that year, Godfrey Higgins joined forces with the Tukes.

Higgins was then forty years of age, a quiet country gentleman who possessed a considerable estate, and who had a passion for the more abstruse forms of religion. He wrote a number of privately-printed pamphlets—'The Celtic Druids', 'An Apology for Mohammed' and others of a like nature, was a member of several learned societies, and dabbled in archæology. Yet he also had a keen interest in contemporary events; he favoured the abolition of the Corn Laws and the disestablishment of the Irish Church, and he was a member of the African and Asiatic Society, which may have brought him into contact not only with Wilberforce, its prime mover, but also with Charles Williams-Wynn.[2] Finally, he had a knowledge of law, having studied in London, though he was not called to the Bar. We are told that he 'acted with great energy as a justice of the peace',[3] and it was in this capacity that he became associated with

---

[1] Thurnam, op. cit., Appendix I, p. 3.
[2] See *D.N.B.* articles on Wynn and Higgins, and *Gent. Mag.* obit. of Higgins (1833, vol. 2, p. 371).
[3] *Gent. Mag.* obit. (1833, vol. 2, p. 371).

lunacy reform. A man of independent means, considerable leisure, with an objective and inquiring mind, he was admirably suited for the role which his judicial duties thrust upon him.

## The Vickers Case.[1]

In the summer of 1813, a pauper named William Vickers or Vicars was brought before Higgins, being charged with assault. Higgins 'presently discovered he was insane', ordered the overseer of the parish to obtain the proper certificates, and issued a warrant to convey Vickers to the Asylum.

In October of the same year, the man's wife, Sarah Vickers, appeared before Higgins to ask for relief, and alleged that her husband, now discharged, had been ill-treated at the Asylum. Higgins sent the surgeon responsible for the paupers of the district to examine the man, and received the following report:

'He had the Itch very bad, was also extremely filthy, for I saw his wife not only comb several lice from his head, but take them from the folds of his shirt neck; his health was so much impaired that he was not able to stand by himself; his legs were very much swelled, and one of them in a state of mortification.'

There were lash marks on Vickers' back, and he told Higgins that he had been flogged. His friends and relatives had been denied an opportunity of visiting him in the Asylum, being told on the occasion of one visit that he was 'insensible in an apoplexy'. Higgins commented, 'No doubt it must have disturbed him very much to be looked at in a state of insensibility.'

Higgins found on inquiry that it was the general belief that conditions at the Asylum were very bad, and that a previous attempt had been made to achieve reform. He corresponded with the physician, Dr. Best, but obtained no satisfaction from him, and at length, on November 27th, 1813, he published a statement in the York Herald, together with extracts from the correspondence.

## Attitude of the Asylum Authorities.

Dr. Best's defence against the charges made by Higgins had consisted of a complete and unequivocal denial. He stated that Vickers' condition was 'the unavoidable consequence of the lamentable and dangerous illness under which he had recently laboured, and from which he was but then in an early stage of convalescence'. Vickers had had a fire in his

[1] See Higgins, Letter to Earl Fitz William, pp. 3–9 and Appendix.

room, a special attendant, 'assiduous medical treatment . . . nutritious food . . . mulled ale . . . everything conducive to his recovery'. Best urged Higgins to consider 'whether you are not lending your name as a magistrate to a purpose most foreign to your office as a magistrate, and giving effect . . . to a malicious conspiracy against myself and the Asylum'.

Best sustained this air of injured innocence throughout the subsequent revelations. When the Quarterly Court, or Governors' Meeting, was convened a week later, its members accepted his statement at its face value. A statement signed by Archbishop Venables-Vernon was issued:

'The Governors, having taken into consideration the statement published in the York and other newspapers respecting the condition of William Vickers, lately a patient in this Asylum, and having examined upon oath such witnesses as were competent to afford information of the same, are unanimously of the opinion that during the time the said William Vickers remained in the Asylum, he was treated with all possible care, attention and humanity.'[1]

Higgins was less easily convinced:

'The Archbishop, the last minute before I came away, told me very politely that they would detain me no longer, they had no further occasion for me . . . I am very far from satisfied with what has been done.'

The Quarterly Court had been adjourned for a week, and when it met again on December 10th, it had forty-six new members. The foundation rule was that any person subscribing £20 to the work of the Asylum became a Governor, and forty-six citizens of York, including Godfrey Higgins, William Tuke and Samuel Tuke, had availed themselves of this opportunity.[3] The old Governors, if not out-voted, were certainly out flanked. The Archbishop bowed to the inevitable after what Higgins called 'a warm debate',[4] and a committee of investigation was formed.

*The Fire.*

On December 26th, the Asylum caught fire. A letter to the *York Herald* of April 4th, 1814, signed 'A Governor of the Asylum' gives these detail

---

[1] Higgins, *Letter to Earl FitzWilliam*, pp. 16-17.
[2] *York Herald*, December 9th, 1813.
[3] Higgins, *Letter to Earl Fitz William*, p. 12, and (lists of Governors before and after December 10th respectively) Appendix, pp. 16 and 18.
[4] Higgins, op. cit., p. 12.

of the occurrence: conditions were unusually propitious for the flames, for most of the staff were absent. Dr. Best was thirty miles away, attending a private patient, the apothecary and the housekeeper had 'gone out to keep Christmas'; two of the four male keepers had Christmas leave, and of the two that remained, one was asthmatic, and could not bear the smoke. Thus one keeper was left to deal with the outbreak.

'Before the flames could be extinguished, damage was done to the building and property amounting to £2392, and four patients perished in the conflagration. This served to shut out from all mortal eyes proofs of maladministration at which the imagination shudders.'[1]

A plausible explanation was again forthcoming from Dr. Best. The fire was said to have been caused by sparks falling down a chimney from an adjoining one, and 'setting fire to some flocks laid there to dry in a room locked up'.[2]

Godfrey Higgins, in his new capacity as a Governor of the Asylum, demanded to see the chimney in question, and found that it was 'built in a direction so far from the perpendicular' that it was almost impossible for the outbreak to have originated in this way.[3]

The next turn of events is obscure. It appears that the old Governors succeeded temporarily in their efforts to stifle criticism. By some means, pressure was exerted on Higgins to induce him to withdraw from further investigation, for the *York Herald* of January 10th, 1814, contained a letter in which he expressed himself satisfied with conditions at the Asylum, and added unexpectedly, 'It gives me great pleasure to be able to second a motion of thanks to his Grace the Archbishop'; but if promises of reform were made, they were not carried out. Nine weeks later, Higgins launched his second attack through the medium of the Press.

*The Second Investigation.*

'Having suspicions in my mind that there were some parts of the Asylum which had not yet been seen, I went early in the morning, determined to examine every place. After ordering a great number of doors to be opened, I came to one which was in a retired situation in the kitchen apartments, and which was almost hid. I ordered this door to be opened . . . the keepers hesitated . . . I grew angry, and told them that I insisted on (the key) being found; and that, if they would not find it, I

---

[1] Baines, *Hist. of the County of York*, 1823, p. 55.
[2] Higgins, *Letter to Earl FitzWilliam*, p. 13.
[3] Ibid.

could find a key at the kitchen fireside, namely, the poker; upon that, the key was immediately brought.'[1]

Higgins unlocked the door, and went in. He found a series of cells about eight feet square,

'. . . in a very horrid and filthy condition . . . the walls were daubed with excrement; the air-holes, of which there was one in each cell, were partly filled with it . . . I then went upstairs, and (the keeper) showed me into a room . . . twelve feet by seven feet ten inches, in which there were thirteen women who, he told me, had all come out of those cells that morning. . . . I became very sick, and could not remain longer in the room. I vomited.'

Higgins expressed in his letter to the Press the hope that 'the public will never rest until this Augean stable is swept clean from top to bottom'. Five months were to elapse before this wish became realized—five months of urbane explanations, recriminations, and constant pressure to induce the reformers to give way. In a letter published in the *York Herald* on March 30th, Dr. Best complained that 'Mr. Higgins' attack is personally and particularly levelled at me'. He behaved throughout as though he were the victim of a monstrous conspiracy. The cells mentioned by Higgins were, he stated, reserved for women of unclean habits. They were cleaned out every morning, and it was an extremely offensive undertaking. Chains and handcuffs found in the Asylum had been examined by the Governors, and found to be covered with rust, which proved that they had not been in use for a considerable time. He then shifted to a defensive position. The place was damp and low-lying, half the building had been destroyed by fire, there were too few staff, and too many patients.

'If the servants neglect to perform their duties . . . if the laws and constitution are defective . . . I do not consider myself as responsible for any of these circumstances, or for the evils which may naturally be expected to result from them'.

The *York Herald* of April 4th contained the first letter on the subject written by anyone other than Higgins and Best. It was signed 'A Governor of the Asylum' and contained a detailed point-by-point refutation of Best's letter of the previous week. The writer may have been one of the

[1] *York Herald*, March 21st, 1814. The evidence given by Higgins before the 1815 Committee was slightly more detailed than the newspaper version, and is quoted here.

Tuke family, who would not wish his identity generally known, since the family was responsible for what was in some sense a rival establishment.

Best had stated that the women in the cells seen by Higgins had 'straw beds'. 'The expression,' commented 'A Governor of the Asylum' acidly, 'is scarcely applicable to loose straw covering the floor as in a stable.' On the question of the fire: 'It would certainly be unjust to blame any individual connected with the Asylum as answerable for the fire'; yet it was, to say the least, 'an unfortunate coincidence' that all the staff save one were absent or incapacitated. 'Thus it came about that four patients were burned to death—or, as the Steward's book records it, they died.' On Best's disclaimer of responsibility, the writer retorted that he was well paid for taking responsibility, since he received a large salary, and was permitted to take private patients in addition. The letter concluded:

'The public are convinced that if there be any prospect of a reformation of the defects and abuses which are now admitted to exist, they are chiefly indebted for it to the independent exertions and the firmness of Mr. Godfrey Higgins.'

Mr. Higgins' exertions continued. He had discovered other cases of cruelty, in which patients had been flogged or otherwise ill-treated by the keepers.

Some of these had been exposed at the first inquiry, but without result. One such was the case of 'the Rev. Mr. Skorey', an elderly cleric suffering from a mild disorder, and having frequent lucid intervals. He had been 'inhumanly kicked downstairs' by the keepers, and told in the presence of his wife that he was 'no better than a dog'. To this complaint, Best made a typical reply:

'Mrs. Skorey stated in evidence that she heard him kicked downstairs, which I conceive to be impossible . . . I mean, impossible that she could have distinguished by the ear alone whether her husband had been kicked downstairs or not.'

The male side of the Asylum was not completely separated from the female side. Two female patients had become pregnant while in the Asylum—one by a male patient, and one by a keeper named Backhouse. The latter openly admitted paternity, and paid regular sums to the overseers of the poor for the parish of Louth to maintain the child in the poorhouse. The keeper subsequently retired from the Asylum after twenty-six years' service, received a handsome present from the Governors—and

LUNACY, LAW, AND CONSCIENCE

opened a private madhouse. Higgins stated that he did not think the Governors knew of Backhouse's defection, but that Dr. Hunter certainly knew, and kept silence.

Samuel Tuke also made use of his status as a Governor in order to investigate conditions. On one occasion, he found a mental defective in the wash-house:

'He was standing on a wet stone floor, apparently in the last stages of decay; he was a mere skeleton; his thighs were covered with excrement in a dry state, and those parts which were not so appeared excoriated . . . he was spoken of by all the attendants as a dying man.'

This patient was removed from the Asylum, and Higgins reported that he eventually made a physical recovery.

The reformers then turned their attention to the records, and found that they were false in many particulars. The number of deaths for 1813 was given as 11, but comparison with the parish registers showed that there had been 24 funerals. The inference was that 13 patients had died during the year, whose existence in the Asylum had never been recorded. When the fire took place, it was stated that four patients died in the flames; but the records were so inadequate that it would have been possible for several more to have died without trace.

Higgins went through the accounts, such as they were, and mercilessly exposed their discrepancies.

'One quarter's account was missing; of another quarter, two statements were transmitted, both apparently complete documents, but each in fact essentially differing from the other.'[1]

He proved that large sums of money had been appropriated by Dr. Best and his predecessor; but again, the conspiracy of silence came into operation. The steward, when asked to produce the books for the inspection of the Quarterly Court, said lamely that he had burned then 'in a moment of irritation'.[2] It is difficult to ascertain exactly what happened, since the Court adopted a resolution against making the matter public. 'Another Y.Z.', in a letter to the *York Herald*, on December 12th, 1814, wrote, 'The movers of the resolution against the freedom of the press discovered a fearful apprehension lest the burning of the books should find its way into the papers.'

---

[1] Letter from S. W. Nicol, a Governor, in Higgins' *Letter to Earl Fitz William*.
[2] Letters in *York Herald*. December 12th and 19th, 1814.

*Reform of Conditions, 1814.*

The abuses came to an end in August, 1814—nearly a year after the release of William Vickers. The Quarterly Court finally dismissed all the servants and officers of the Asylum. Dr. Best was either asked or permitted to resign, though this of course did not affect his private practice, which was considerable.[1] He apparently did not consider himself either condemned or defeated, since the *York Herald* published on December 28th of the same year a letter written by him to the editor:

'I merely write this to give you notice, that if ONE SYLLABLE shall appear in any of your future papers in allusion to me, which may admit of an INJURIOUS or even an OFFENSIVE construction, my next communication with you will take place through my attorney.'

The editor's comment on this letter was apt:

'It was . . . sent to intimidate me from that course which it is my duty as the Editor of a Public Paper to pursue. I give it, therefore, to the world.'

When the new staff was appointed, the Asylum was given a new constitution. The Quarterly Court of August, 1814, laid down that two Governors were to visit the Asylum each month; that three ladies were to be asked to undertake the visitation of the female wards; that the physician was to receive £300 a year, but was not to undertake private practice or to receive gratuities; that a resident apothecary was to be appointed, whose duties would be those of superintending the issue of medicines, and also of supervising the work and conduct of the keepers; that the diet was to be revised regularly by the Committee; and that an annual report was to be issued.[2]

A postscript was supplied by the declaration of the Quarterly Court of August, 1815, from which the Archbishop of York was absent. The chairman was Earl FitzWilliam, to whom Higgins' long letter of protest had been sent. It was resolved unanimously

'that this Court feels with the highest degree of satisfaction the very great improvement which has taken place in every department of this institution, since the general meeting in August last, by which they have no doubt that in point of humane treatment of patients, and the general

---

[1] 1815 *Report*, p. 28. Rose in questioning Best, spoke of 'The Asylum of which you *were* physician.'

[2] Higgins, *Letter to Earl FitzWilliam*, Appendix, pp. 37-44.

order and cleanliness of the house, the York Lunatic Asylum is scarcely excelled by any similar institution in the Kingdom. . . . This Court, contemplating the great improvement made in the state of the house, feels a pleasure in acknowledging its great obligation to Godfrey Higgins, Esq., to whose zeal and perseverance the origin of these improvements must in great measure be ascribed.'[1]

The scandal was ended, as far as the city of York was concerned. From that time, the York Asylum stood comparison with any county asylum; but in 1815, the affair had repercussions on a national scale. Wynn, Rose and Seymour revived the Vickers case, the circumstances of the fire, the financial peculations, the destruction of the records. Higgins gave evidence, and so—less happily—did Dr. Best. The attitude of the Committee left no doubt as to which they believed to be telling the truth.

### 2. BETHLEM

The course of events at Bethlem in the years 1814-15 was in outline similar to that at York. Again a philanthropist visited the hospital in connection with a special case; again the circumstances of that case were sufficient to arouse public indignation; again, the medical and lay administrative officers did their best to excuse the inexcusable, and failing, tried each to shift the blame on to the shoulders of the others. It is probable that, since Bethlem was in London, the facts concerning the standards of treatment there were well known to the parliamentary reformers, but it was not until Edward Wakefield[2] visited the hospital in April, 1814, and made known the condition of William Norris, that an opportunity presented itself for attacking the entire system.

*Administration and Medical Treatment at Bethlem.*

The apothecary of Bethlem at that time was Mr. John Haslam, and the physician Dr. Thomas Monro. Haslam was responsible for administering medicines and directing the control of patients, and Monro for prescribing medicines and the form of treatment. The surgeon to both Bridewell and Bethlem until 1815—in which year he died—was Dr. Bryan Crowther. This member of the College of Surgeons published in 1811 a

---

[1] Higgins, *Letter to Earl FitzWilliam*, Appendix to the Letter to the Committee, p. 14.
[2] Father of Edward Gibbon Wakefield and a notable Quaker philanthropist. 'Mr. Wakefield's circumstances were by no means prosperous: he was, however, an active, zealous advocate for any thing likely, in his opinion, to be useful to mankind . . .'—Francis Place, quoted in R. Garnett's *Edward Gibbon Wakefield*, 1898 edition, pp. 6-7.

treatise entitled 'Practical Remarks on Insanity', in which he described in detail the method of treatment employed at Bethlem.[1]

'The curable patients at Bethlem Hospital are regularly bled about the commencement of June, and the latter end of July.'

'. . . the lancet has been found a very communicative sort of instrument . . . I have bled a hundred and fifty patients at one time, and have never found it requisite to adopt any other method of security against hæmorrhage than that of sending the patient back to his *accustomed confinement.*'

The last two words here reveal clearly Crowther's attitude to mechanical restraint. He believed firmly in the efficacy of purges and vomits in all cases of insanity. 'The servants at Bethlem have told me repeatedly of the quantity of phlegm evacuated.' He still believed in the cold bath, and used a notorious device known as the 'circular swing', in which the patient was rotated rapidly until he lost consciousness. His section on 'Management' has nothing to say about diet, clothing, occupations, or remedial measures of any kind, being solely concerned with the necessity for obtaining 'ascendancy' over the patients. It was the patient who was to be managed, not the institution.

It is easy to discredit Crowther, whose methods, even for his own time, were harsh. At best, he belonged to the old school of 'mad-doctors' and knew nothing of more enlightened methods of treating the insane. At worst, if Haslam's evidence before the 1815 Committee is to be believed, he was totally unfitted to have charge of patients. Haslam succeeded in discrediting Crowther most effectively when, less than a month after his death, he described him to the Select Committee as having been

'for ten years . . . generally insane and mostly drunk. . . . He was so insane as to have a strait waistcoat . . . he was so insane, that his hand was not obedient to his will.'

How far these charges were based on fact it is not easy to ascertain, for the dead man made a convenient scapegoat; searching cross-examination by Rose forced both Monro and Haslam into hesitation, contradiction and evasion. Haslam blamed Monro, Monro blamed Haslam, and both blamed Crowther. They were charged repeatedly with having ordered indiscriminate bleeding and purging of all patients at certain times in the year, and repeatedly, in the face of all evidence to the contrary, they

[1] See Crowther, op. cit., pp. 102–9. Patients at Bethlem had, on admission, to be certified as 'strong enough to undergo a course of treatment' See also Appendix to the 1815 Report.

denied it.[1] The following dialogue between Rose and Monro illustrates clearly the physician's attitude towards his Bethlem patients:

'Would you treat a private individual patient in your own house in the same way as has been described in respect of Bethlem?
'—No, certainly not.
'What is the difference of management?
'—In Bethlem, the restraint is by chains; there is no such thing as chains in my house.
'What are your objections to chains and fetters as a mode of restraint?
'—They are fit only for pauper lunatics; if a gentleman was put in irons, he would not like it.'

The apothecary visited the hospital usually only for half an hour a day, and was sometimes absent for days at a time. Monro admitted that he 'seldom' went round the galleries to see the patients, but stated that they were sent to him if they were physically ill. Thus the patients—who at that time numbered nearly 150—were left almost entirely to the care of the keepers. There were five keepers—three men and two women: a ratio of one to thirty.

*The Norris Case.*

Both Monro and Haslam were called upon to account for the condition of William Norris. Haslam admitted the truth of the facts—that the man had been chained continually for nine years with his (Haslam's) knowledge and consent.

'Do you mean he was never out of those irons for the whole nine years?
'—They were never taken off, I believe. I do not know that they were ever taken off. If the keeper took them off, it was unknown to me.'

Having made these admissions, Haslam put forward a series of statements in his own defence. He stated—and this was not contested—that Norris had at one time been homicidal, and had attacked a keeper and another patient with a knife. 'He was the most malignant and mischievous lunatic I ever saw.' Norris was, he said, a powerful man, who could free himself from any normal method of confinement, and could burst open a strait jacket with ease. He could not be secured by manacles, since his hands had an unusual bone formation, the circumference at the widest part being less than that of his wrists.

The Select Committee never attempted to prove that Norris had been

[1] Though Monro was forced into an admission which he subsequently retracted.

wrongfully sent to Bethlem. He had undoubtedly been violently insane at one time; but the length of his period of confinement, its method, and the fact that, when he was discovered, he was so physically weak from tuberculosis that he would have been unable to escape or to harm others even had he so desired—all these things far outweighed any explanation which Haslam could make. Accordingly, he fell back on his last line of defence—shifting the responsibility to others. He declared that the device had been constructed in accordance with the orders of a committee of the Governors, and that he himself would have preferred to have kept Norris in solitary confinement. This statement he partially contradicted by another—that Norris in his lucid moments had thanked him for restraining him from further crimes.

The Norris case at Bethlem was the equivalent of the Vickers case at York; it was not that either case was exceptional—rather that the ill-treatment involved was taken for granted by those concerned in the administration of the respective asylums. In each instance, it was only one case of cruelty among many.

*The 'Blanket Patients'.*

Edward Wakefield, in his initial visit to Bethlem, found a number of female patients chained to the wall by an arm or a leg, and completely unclothed save for a blanket apiece. Some of these women were quiet and coherent when he visited them, and fully able to comprehend the degradation to which they were being subjected.

By the time the Select Committee received evidence, the old matron had been pensioned off, and a younger woman named Mrs. Forbes appointed. She obtained clothes for these women, freed all those who were not violent, washed and cleaned them, cut their hair. She related to the parliamentary reformers a typical response—that of a patient named Ann Stone.

'I asked the reason for her being always confined to the wall. I was told she was very troublesome, and tore her clothes; that she had a good many things sent her, but they were all torn. I said I would try to walk her about . . . I gave her a couple of caps, and she did not tear them. She looks better, and very comfortable and tidy; and every time I go round the gallery, she says, "Accept my real thanks for allowing me my liberty."'

*The Steward's Evidence.*

A new steward was appointed at the same time as Mrs. Forbes, to replace an elderly and incompetent official.[1] He gave guarded evidence concerning the administration and general conditions at Bethlem. He admitted that there was no system of classification, violent and dirty patients being allowed to mingle with those in a state of convalescence. The beds were 'tolerably good ones; they are what they call Hessian beds; a flock bed, three blankets, and a cover lid.' The violent patients slept on straw which was changed once a week, or more often if it was wet. The windows were unglazed, and the upper galleries unheated. He was asked:

'Have you ever been there during the winter?
'—It was February when I took possession.
'Have you ever seen in the morning in the cells that the wood of the walls has been crystallized over with hoar frost?
'—No. There has been but little frost since I went there.'

The same guarded note of partial admission was evident when he gave evidence concerning the activities of Haslam:

'Where does Mr. Haslam reside?
'—At Islington . . . He generally comes at about eleven o'clock and stays half an hour, or sometimes longer than that.
'In case any person should be taken with a fit, what medical or surgical attendance have you?
'None but Mr. Haslam; if he has leave of absence for a day or two, he generally leaves word, if an accident happens, to send for a person.'

He agreed that, during the six months he had been at Bethlem, no other medical man had been called in during Haslam's absence.

It appears that the new steward was a man who wished to keep his post; his evidence gives the impression that he wished to satisfy the Select Committee while at the same time remaining on good terms with his employers, the Governors of the Hospital—in the circumstances, an extremely difficult task.

### 3. ST. LUKE'S

St. Luke's Hospital had been briefly considered by the 1807 Committee. Since that inquiry was not concerned with subscription hospitals, and

[1] 1815 *Report*, p. 131. The old steward was 'gradually declining. He was at the age of eighty-one'. The new steward's name was Nathaniel Nicholls.

made no attempt to collect evidence concerning any other, it may be inferred that the object of that investigation was to assess the suitability of St. Luke's as a model for the projected county asylum. Whitbread and Shaw-Lefevre, who were members of this Committee and also of that of 1815, were vice-presidents of St. Luke's. We might reasonably expect from these considerations to find that this hospital presented a picture of asylum administration at its best. In fact, the issue is in considerable doubt. In some ways, the system was excellent, and gave added force to the criticisms against Bethlem. Master, matron and apothecary were all resident. The apothecary made a round every day, the physician visited three times a week, and the surgeon as required. There were sixteen servants or keepers, six men and ten women, for three hundred patients— roughly one to nineteen. The diet was ample, and of good quality; every patient had a proper wooden bed.

The master, Thomas Dunston, was not a medical practitioner but an ex-attendant, having served in this capacity at Bethlem for seven or eight years prior to his appointment. He believed that patients could best be cured by a system of rewards for good behaviour and punishment for the reverse—that is, by treating them as irresponsible children. Dunston stated in 1807 that coercion was only used on three patients in every twenty—

'They are patients disposed to injure themselves or others, and are seldom or never to be trusted with confidence; much is certainly to be done by management, but it is impossible on this head to lay down a general rule; each effort must be adapted to the general indisposition. It is necessary to check some, to encourage others, and to animate all with the hope of recovery.'

In 1815, Dunston said that only five out of three hundred patients were under restraint at the time of the inquiry. Restraint was imposed only by order of the master, and the keepers had no power to continue restraint on their own authority.

The only major criticism of the hospital voiced before the 1815 Committee was that of Edward Wakefield, who had given evidence on Bethlem. He stated that the premises were highly unsuitable, and that the hospital was both overcrowded and cheerless. The site was particularly undesirable in view of the fact that the patients' windows overlooked a burial ground where dead patients were often interred.

There was nothing in this evidence to confirm Samuel Tuke's statement that 'on the whole . . . St. Luke's stands in need of radical re-

dress',[1] or Sir Andrew Halliday's comment, made some years later, that
St. Luke's was 'only fit to become a prison for confirmed idiots'.[2] It is
possible that the knowledge that the vice-presidents were members of
their group induced the parliamentary reformers to take a more benevolent view than they might otherwise have done. St. Luke's was undoubtedly very much better than Bethlem or the York Asylum; and it
would have been impossible, within the limits set by financial considerations, for a large asylum containing a high proportion of pauper patients
to be administered on the lines of the Retreat. Nevertheless, the impression remains that St. Luke's had not developed as it might have done.
It was an early example of a phenomenon which was to become common
in the development of mental hospitals, and which is to be found in the
development of most kinds of social institutions—the establishment which,
having done pioneer work, rests on its laurels and fails to keep abreast of
later developments. The administration was more or less as it had been in
1752, the year of foundation, and it had then been found good; but the
public idea of what constituted adequate treatment of the insane was
leading to a demand for a higher standard.

### 4. NOTTINGHAM COUNTY ASYLUM

By 1815, three county asylums were in operation—those at Nottingham, Bedford and Thorpe (Norfolk). These had been opened in 1811,
1812 and 1814 respectively, but were not yet sufficiently well established
to be fairly judged. Evidence was given on the principles on which
Nottingham Asylum had been founded by the Rev. J. T. Becher, a
prominent member of the penal reform movement, who was also a
member of the visiting committee of that asylum.[3]

Mr. Becher was questioned by the members of the Select Committee
about the cost of the Asylum, the maintenance charges for paupers, the
system of classification of patients, the staff, the use of mechanical restraint
in connection with violent or dangerous patients, and the amenities provided for those patients who were capable of appreciating them. The
form which these questions took showed that the parliamentary group
had evolved a series of criteria by which the administration of any institution for the insane could usefully be judged. This was a distinct step

[1] Quoted by D. H. Tuke, *Hist. of Insane*, p. 89.
[2] Halliday, *General View of Lunatics*, 1828, p. 18.
[3] See W. L. Clay, *Memoirs of the Rev. John Clay, B.D.*, p. 76.

forward, for one of the great difficulties in the earlier days of reform had been the lack of definite standards.

The Asylum had been built by the county magistrates, and financed by a county rate and voluntary subscriptions. The total cost was £21,686, of which £16,651 was spent on the actual buildings, and the rest on the purchase of the site, furnishings and other considerations. The patients were divided into three groups, as at the Manchester Lunatic Hospital and the Retreat—the first and second classes being supported by their relatives, and the third, the pauper class, being paid for by the overseer of the parish concerned in each case. There were 16 patients of the first and most privileged class, 20 of the second class, and 40 paupers, for each of whom the charge was 9s. per week.

There was a rudimentary scheme of classification. Male and female patients were completely separated, and there was a special ward for the refractory cases of each sex.

Six keepers had charge of the patients—a male and female keeper for each class. This meant that each keeper had sole charge of a group of patients, though the others could be summoned, if needed, to quell an outbreak of violence.

The parliamentary reformers, considering this provision inadequate, inquired of Becher:

'Do you conceive that a keeper under any circumstances is equal to the due care of 20 patients?

'The reply was "20 patients are seldom found without some in a state nearly advancing to recovery, and with a disposition in the case of any emergency to assist the keeper." '

The system of restraint used was very mild, and it is significant that the medical director, Dr. Storey, had been sent to the Retreat to study the system in use there before taking up office. This is the first recorded instance of an attempt to equip members of what was in reality a new profession by giving them a knowledge of asylum administration. Previously any medical practitioner had been considered capable of dealing with the insane; now it was necessary that he should become acquainted with the work already done in the field.

The rules of Nottingham Asylum contained the provision that

'the assistants and servants . . . abstain from unnecessary acts of violence . . . that they do not use chains unless with the knowledge and consent of the director; and that they inflict neither blows nor stripes, but on the contrary that they behave with the utmost forbearance, tenderness, patience and humanity towards the unfortunate sufferers entrusted to their care and protection.'

Some attempt was made to occupy the patients; there were gardens and airing-courts for each class, and those patients who were sufficiently rational were encouraged to take up various forms of useful occupation. The whole picture, as given by Becher, affords an interesting glimpse into the early development of county asylums. The old idea of deterrence had not quite been eliminated, but a real effort was being made to develop the new experiment on humanitarian lines. Comparison with the conditions in workhouses and private madhouses was to show how urgent was the necessity for extending the provision of county asylums.

## 5. WORKHOUSES

Both Sir William Curtis and William Smith were bankers by profession, and one or both of them may have been responsible for bringing before the Select Committee a banker named Henry Alexander, who had undertaken a self-imposed tour of forty-seven workhouses in order to discover the conditions under which pauper lunatics were confined.

Most of these workhouses were in the West Country. Nine had insane inmates, and of these only three had separate accommodation for them. One of the three was St. Peter's, Bristol, where the inmates were 'comfortable' on the whole; but even there, Alexander found four incurable patients in wooden cells 'like pig-styes'—dark and lacking in ventilation and sanitation.

At Liskeard in Cornwall, Alexander found two women confined in the workhouse.

'In a fit place for them?

'—Very far from it. Indeed, I hardly know what to term the places, they were no better than dungeons.

'Were they underground?

'—No; they were buildings, but they were very damp and very low. In one of them, there was no light admitted through the door; neither light nor air. Both of them were chained down to the damp stone floor, and one of them had only a little dirty straw, which appeared to have been there for many weeks . . . we asked if she was allowed water to wash herself, and found she was not . . . the whole place was very filthy.

'Filled with excrements and very offensive?
'—Yes.'

One of these women was apparently confined under section 20 of the Act of 1744.

'We enquired the reason of her confinement from the mistress of the workhouse; and it appeared she had been confined many months, both winter and summer; and the only cause they assigned was, that she was troublesome, they could not keep her within; she was roving about the country, and they had complaints lodged against her from different persons.
'Not of any act of violence?
'—Not at all; we enquired particularly, and they gave us no other reason than her being troublesome.'

At Tavistock, Alexander and his companions experienced difficulty in gaining admission.

'I am sorry my information will not be altogether satisfactory, as we did not see the insane poor themselves . . . the situation . . . was dreadful, indeed I could not stand up at all in some of the lower rooms; the rooms were very small, and in one of the bedrooms, 17 people slept; one man and his wife slept in the room with 15 other people.
'We enquired if there were any insane persons; and upon expressing a desire to see them, we were at first refused on the ground that the place was not fit for us to go into; but we persisted in our intreaties to see them, and went up the yard where we understood the cells were, and upon entering them, we found that the inmates had been removed. There were three of them . . . they had been removed out that morning.
'For what purpose?
'—The cells had been washed and cleaned out.
'Who refused you?
'—The master of the house. He did not do it in a peremptory manner at all, but told us it was unfit for us to go, and indeed we found it so.
'What was the state of the cells?
'—I never smelt such a stench in my life, and it was so bad that a friend who went with us said he could not enter the other. After having entered one, I said I would go into the other; that if they could survive there the night through, I could at least inspect them . . . the stench was so great I felt almost suffocated; and for hours after, if I ate anything, I still retained the same smell; I could not get rid of it; and it should be remem-

bered that these cells had been washed out that morning, and the doors had been opened some hours previous.'

Alexander's further evidence reiterated the same story—filth, neglect, and unthinking brutality. Evidence on conditions in workhouses was also given by Thomas Bakewell, keeper of a private asylum in Staffordshire.

'I know parishes where they keep lunatics, and I have every evidence I can have that they are very improperly treated . . . there was a glaring instance of a person being taken from me before he could be perfectly recovered, although in a convalescent state, and carried to a workhouse; where I afterwards learned that he met with improper treatment, and he died under it very soon.'

Bakewell was asked whether the parishes in his locality normally sent patients to his house under contract, or whether they were sent to the workhouse in order to save the expense. His reply was:

'They never bring them to me, but under two considerations; one, when the Magistrate will not permit their remaining in the workhouse, and next, when they feel it an object to have them cured.'

The inference from the evidence of Alexander and Bakewell was quite clear—that the Poor Law authorities would not or could not make adequate provision for pauper lunatics, and that any hope of bettering the condition of this class lay in removing them to institutions of the county asylum type.

### 6. PRIVATE MADHOUSES

In 1816, the Select Committee was reappointed to consider the condition of private madhouses, and the parliamentary reformers continued their accumulation of evidence of the abuses which were possible under the 1774 Madhouses Act.

#### 'Naval Maniacs' at Hoxton.

Mentally deranged seamen were commonly sent by the Navy to a large private madhouse kept by Sir Jonathan Miles at Hoxton. In 1814, the house contained 14 officers and 136 seamen, together with other patients. Lengthy evidence was given by Dr. John Weir, the Inspector of Naval Hospitals, and other independent physicians, who stated that the conditions there were extremely bad, but that, although they were responsible for inspection, they had no power to effect any improvements. The mortality rate was extremely high, and there appeared to be no attempt at classification. Dr. Weir was particularly indignant because in one case a naval captain shared a room with a civilian grocer; but the confusion was not merely a matter of social caste; clean and dirty patients, violent and peaceable, incurable and convalescent officers and men—all were thrust together without regard for their mental or physical condition. Male patients slept together two in a bed; the food consisted almost entirely of beef and beer—a diet which Weir thought 'too stimulating'—and there was no medical treatment.

Sir Jonathan Miles was cross-questioned by Rose, as chairman of the Committee:

'You do not consider yourself responsible for the medical treatment of the Government patients?
'—Yes, I am.
'Do the Government patients receive any medical treatment for the cure of their insanity?
'—I cannot say that they do, exactly.
'Is any medical attention particularly directed in your establishment to the cure of insanity?
'—None. Our house is open to all medical gentlemen who care to visit it.
'That is at the expense of the patient?
'—It is.
'How many are visited by their own medical men?
'—I cannot tell. . . .
'Do you suppose that there are twenty?
'—Yes, from twenty to thirty, probably.
'Is it your opinion, then, that there are above three hundred persons in your house, who receive no attention on account of the particular complaint for which they are confined?
'—Certainly.'

Here was the policy of confinement at its worst.

There were in all 486 patients in this house, and the Commissioners had inspected it in the space of about two and a half hours. Dr. Richard Powell[1] admitted that on this visit, he had not checked the number of patients, and that some might have been concealed in hidden rooms or cells. He had not seen samples of the patient's food, and he saw nothing

[1] Secretary to the Metropolitan Commissioners.

H

harmful in male patients sleeping two in a bed—'it cannot be expected that a man who pays only ten shillings a week should have a separate bed'. He considered the house 'in very excellent order'.

*Warburton's Houses.*

Thomas Warburton was the proprietor of four madhouses in the metropolitan area—Talbot's, the White House and Rhodes', all at Bethnal Green, and Whitmore House at Hackney. Pauper lunatics from the parishes of Marylebone, St. George, Hanover Square, and St. Pancras were regularly sent to these houses, and in 1815, there were 300 patients in the White House alone.

Warbuton was related by marriage to the master of St. Luke's, Dunston's son John having married Warburton's daughter. The younger Dunston was visiting surgeon to the three Bethnal Green houses; 'he is his son-in-law,' said Warburton's apothecary, 'and consequently they put everything in Mr. Dunston's way.'

Lord Robert Seymour, as chairman, questioned John Rogers, the apothecary at the White House, and his sister, Mrs. Humières, who was the housekeeper. They both gave overwhelming evidence of cruelty and neglect. Rogers alleged that two patients—Captain Dickinson, R.N., and Mr. Driver, 'a respectable farmer', had died as a direct result of having been beaten by the keepers at the White House. Rogers' evidence consisted of a reiteration of acts of brutality of a type now becoming unpleasantly familiar. He made the following statement on the forcing of patients to take medicine or food:

'I have known sundry instances where the mouth has been lacerated and the teeth forced out, and I have known patients suffocate. I recollect Mrs. Hodges, wife of the vestry clerk of St. Andrew's, Holborn, dying in this way. I do not suppose there is a keeper who has been in these houses four or five years who has not had patients die under their (*sic*) hand in the act of forcing.'

Mechanical restraint was used frequently, and Rogers had known a patient have both feet amputated as a result of mortification.

Rogers was questioned about a structure in the White House known as 'Bella's Hole'. This consisted of a box with a base three or four feet square; Rogers alleged that a patient named Charles Green had been confined there for 'several months' naked and in the dark, with only a few holes bored in the top to allow the passage of air. He further alleged that the White House was infested with bugs and rats, and that over 100 patients had died of typhus in the Bethnal Green Houses during the winter of 1810–11.

Mrs. Humières gave additional evidence of the more domestic abuses. She stated that the pauper patients were frequently kept naked in cribs without straw, and that no heating of any kind was provided. She produced before the Committee bills showing that patients' clothes had been sold by the keepers in many cases.

The allegations were sufficiently clear; on the other hand, they were specifically denied not only by Warburton, who sweepingly contradicted them all, stating, 'I never knew an instance of an injury so much as any boy has received at school from a chilblain, or not more', but also by Thomas Dunston, who was a man of some standing in his profession. 'I say they live very well, and are well taken care of, for anything I know.' Dunston was connected with Warburton both professionally and privately, and had a motive for concealment in wishing to shield his son; but even so, it is difficult to disregard his evidence. His opinion, whether justified or otherwise, was bound to carry weight with the Select Committee in view of his official connection with Whitbread and Shaw-Lefevre.

*Other Private Madhouses: Evidence of Edward Wakefield.*

Wakefield, who, it will be remembered, was responsible for the discovery of William Norris at Bethlem, explained in answer to the Committee's inquiry that his work as a land agent[1] took him to various parts of the country, and that he made a point, at each place he visited, of asking to see the gaols, Bridewells and madhouses in the vicinity. He was in the true tradition of the early nineteenth-century reformers. He knew the Retreat, and his standards, as far as madhouses were concerned, were roughly those of the Tukes. At Miles' house at Hoxton, he had been refused admission, a keeper telling him that 'an inspection of that house would be signing my death-warrant'. At Gore House, Kensington, he was also refused admission. At Thomas Monro's house at Hackney, he was told by the physician of Bethlem that he was welcome to visit—if he could secure the consent of the relatives of every patient; and he was refused a list of the names of the patients, which made an improbable task impossible.

There were a few private madhouses in which conditions were good, as far as Wakefield could tell. As an unofficial visitor, he had of course no

---

[1] Edward Wakefield set up as a land agent from offices at 42 Pall Mall, after an unsuccessful farming venture, in 1814.

power to make a thorough inspection, and had to base his opinion on what the individual proprietor allowed him to see. At Talfourd's house at Fulham, there were fourteen ladies who appeared to be treated with the greatest kindness. They went to the local church, and were allowed out for walks—Wakefield met two who had just 'walked to Walham Green to see Louis XVIII'. London House, Hackney, also appeared to be excellently conducted. There

'One lady, who conceives herself to be Mary, Queen of Scots, acts as preceptress to Mrs. Fox's little children, and takes great pains in teaching them French'.

*Powers and Duties of the Commissioners, 1816.*

It is significant that, while evidence of abuses had been forthcoming from other sources, the evidence of the Commissioners was almost entirely concerned with their own position. Dr. Powell had been the secretary of the Metropolitan Commissioners since 1808. He testified that they visited all madhouses in the area, inquiring into the administration and the condition of the patients, but not into the form of medical treatment, which they considered outside their province—despite the fact that all the Commissioners were members of the College of Physicians.[1] The visitation lasted six days in the year; Powell himself had personally visited thirty-four houses—'some days, perhaps two; other days, six or eight'—over an area covering all central London, and as far out as Lewisham, Stockwell, Walham Green, Enfield and Plaistow. They suspected that some houses made false returns, but did not check the number of patients returned against those actually seen in the houses. The following scrap of dialogue concerning one house visited is illuminating:

'How many patients were there?
'—Three.
'Men or women?
'Women, I think, but I am hardly certain.'

In defence of the Commissioners, it may further be said that the state of the law was so defective that even had they applied themselves conscientiously to their duties, they could still have achieved very little in the way of reform. They had no power to refuse licences, and no power to liberate those whom they considered sane; the certificates of confinement could be signed by any 'medical man'—who need not even have examined

[1] Under 14 Geo. III, c. 9 (1774).

106

the patient, but could give a certificate on what he had heard by repute. No medical certificate at all was necessary for pauper patients. A licence was issued for each separate madhouse, but without regard to the number of patients in it; the holder of the licence was not required to be resident in the house, so that it was possible for Warburton and others to own several houses and leave them largely in the hands of untrained and un-supervised keepers. No licence was needed for single lunatics, and con-sequently it was perfectly possible for a madhouse proprietor to keep a number of small separate houses, or even single rooms in houses next door to each other, each containing one patient, and to evade the attention of the statutory authority completely.

The Select Committee presented its evidence to Parliament, but it drew no conclusions, and made no recommendations. In this respect, it departed from the usual procedure of select committees. The 1807 Committee had, more conventionally, drawn up a brief report embody-ing concrete proposals, and included only what evidence was necessary to establish the point of Wynn's argument; but the reports of 1815–16 are simply verbatim accounts of evidence received, with no attempt to sift the true from the false, or the salient points from a mass of irrelevancies. The inference is that the Committee did not expect immediate legislative action to be taken. Perhaps, also, they thought that the facts spoke for themselves. All they could do was to publish the evidence, and to con-tinue their agitation in Parliament for a system 'of administration which would remedy the appalling conditions they had uncovered.

# Chapter Seven

## THE REFORM MOVEMENT, 1815-27

FROM 1815 to 1819, repeated efforts were made by Wynn and his associates to introduce new and effective legislation. The reports of 1815-16 had shown clearly that a comprehensive lunacy law covering all types of institutions was necessary; but for that, the time was not yet ripe. The parliamentary group concentrated instead on a limited objective—that of reforming the private madhouses. The most pressing need was for a competent and powerful inspectorate; had this been achieved, it would have been a comparatively simple matter to extend the scope of its activities at a later date, and thus bring all the insane under a central control.

Bills designed to set up such an inspectorate were three times steered through the Commons—in 1816, 1817 and 1819. On each occasion the Bill was rejected by the Lords after many deferments. It was apparent that, even after the lapse of more than fifty years, the Upper House retained the stubborn opposition to lunacy reform which had characterized its approach to the subject in 1773.

The first Bill was ordered on July 11th, 1815, and a small group including Rose, Wynn and Charles Shaw-Lefevre was commissioned to prepare it. This draft apparently never came to fruition, possibly because of continued revelations which brought to light fresh abuses needing correction.

A second Bill was ordered on May 28th of the following year, and was subsequently introduced into the House of Commons by Lord Robert Seymour in one of his rare speeches. The intention was to repeal the Act of 1774 and to appoint eight full-time Commissioners under the jurisdiction of the Secretary of State for the Home Department. These Commissioners were to be responsible not merely for the metropolitan area, but for the inspection of all private madhouses in the country. They were to be given power to direct such alterations in the accommodation as they saw fit, and to lay down requirements as to the management and treatment of patients.

'When parliament in 1774 passed the Bill for the regulation of private madhouses,' said Lord Robert,

'it must have meant to do three things—in the first place, to secure all persons against unnecessary confinement; in the second, to better the chance of recovery for all such persons confined as being insane . . . and thirdly, to insure the restoration of all such of the last persons as might become again of sound mind to society, to their friends, and to their employment. The Madhouse Act does none of these three things . . . it was not surprising that with (the) limited powers of the Commissioners, the greatest abuses should have been found to prevail in some of these houses, and that medicine should have been seldom, if ever, applied to the correction and cure of mental disease. The duty imposed on the Commissioners was prodigious, and the remuneration allowed them so pitifully small, that it would scarcely satisfy the coachman who drove them from house to house, each Commissioner receiving only one guinea for every house he inspects. Under these circumstances, it was natural that the visits of the Commissioners should become short and hurried. . . . He was ready to admit that the Commissioners devoted as much time to the service of the madhouses as could reasonably be expected for the paltry remuneration they received, but he contended that the visits could render no service whatever to the maniacs, and that it was injurious to them, as giving sanction to the abuses which prevailed in those houses, and furnishing a plausible excuse to the friends of these sufferers for not themselves seeing them.'[1]

The 1816 Bill in its final form included provision for the inspection of single lunatics,[2] and it was known that the House of Lords was still strongly opposed to this measure; accordingly, after the rejection of the Bill, a new proposal was produced in the Bill of the following year.[3] Returns of single lunatics were to be made in confidence to the Secretary of State for the Home Department; but, as Wynn commented later, since no authority had the power to inquire as to the whereabouts of

---

[1] Hansard, June 17th, 1816.
[2] The amended form was presented on June 18th, 1816. The original draft of May 28th specifically excluded single lunatics. (Section 39.)
[3] Madhouse Bill, 1817, sections 31-3.

# LUNACY, LAW, AND CONSCIENCE

these people, the clause was useless. 'To whom was the Court of Chancery to address a Habeas Corpus to bring up any lunatic or alleged lunatic for examination?'[1]

The Bill met the same fate as its predecessor, and a third Bill was introduced in 1819. Wynn, making the speech of introduction on this occasion, threw out a challenge to the House of Lords. The Lower House

'had done its duty by repeatedly sending up a Bill to the other House of Parliament, which that House thought proper to reject . . . he could not forbear from remarking that no reason was at any time publicly stated in that House for rejecting the Bills attended to. He was indeed at a loss to divine the grounds upon which such rejections took place.'[2]

This Bill was the most stringent of the three. It proposed a general Board of Inspection which was to visit all houses 'at different and uncertain times', to act upon the information of private individuals concerning cases of alleged ill-treatment and neglect, and to have power to enforce the correction of abuses. It stipulated that inquiries should be made by the Commissioners concerning the treatment and management of patients, and that the intervals between the Commissioners' visits to any one house should not exceed eight months. Penalties were to be enforced for persistent ill-treatment or for making false returns.

The Bill was passed by the Commons on May 19th, 1819, and was considered by the Lords on June 12th. It was moved in rather lukewarm tones by the Marquis of Lansdowne, and immediately opposed by Lord Eldon, the Lord Chancellor.[3]

'He said it was impossible for him to give his support to the present Bill, because he conscientiously believed that its regulations would tend to aggravate the malady with which the unfortunate victims were affected. The Bill gave a number of penalties, half of which were to go to the informer, and it was evident that the informer would be found amongst the attendants and servants in receptacles for lunatics, who would thus be made the judges of the conduct of the physicians.'

It was at this juncture, and in this context, that Lord Eldon made the famous remark which summed up the illiberal attitude of the House of Lords: .

[1] Hansard, March 10th, 1819.
[2] Ibid.
[3] John Scott, Lord Eldon, 1751–1838. See Foss, *The Judges of England*, vol. 8, and *D.N.B.*

'There could not be a more false humanity than an over-humanity with regard to persons afflicted with insanity.'

Lord Eldon was a staunch believer in the old methods of secrecy and restraint. His was the chief influence exerted against any attempts to increase public control over the private madhouses; he was the spokesman of those High Tories who believed that any attempt to improve the conditions of the insane was but one more aspect of the social unrest and the growth of liberal sentiments which they so greatly deplored. In the resulting division, fourteen peers voted in favour of the Bill, and thirty-five against it.[1]

After this final defeat of the reformers' hopes, there was no major parliamentary activity for some years.[2] The small group of reformers began to disintegrate. George Rose died in 1818; Wynn abandoned the Whigs and took office under the Liverpool administration in 1822; William Smith was out of parliament from 1820 to 1826; Romilly and Whitbread were dead—the latter dying while the Select Committee was still sitting, and the former committing suicide in 1818. Lord Robert Seymour was now too old to rouse himself from his habitual lethargy in order to take single-handed action. Perhaps he, like those of his colleagues who remained, recognized that under existing conditions, the battle was a hopeless one; but although the parliamentary group was temporarily inactive, the wider reform movement was gathering force. The Governors of Bethlem, shaken out of complacency by the revelations of 1815, took immediate action with regard to the management of that institution; as the county asylum movement developed, a distinct pattern of asylum administration gradually became apparent; and for the first time, new ideas on the treatment and care of the insane became widely current through the medium of the written word. Newspapers, periodicals and specialist publications spread the concepts of the small group of philanthropists and reformers to a larger public. All these factors facilitated the passage of the Bill when it was reintroduced in 1828. The earlier attempts to provide adequate legislation were part of the slow but necessary process of convincing the general public of the need for reform.

---

[1] Hansard, June 12th, 1819.
[2] Halliday, *General View of Lunatics*, 1828, p. 12: 'The Bill . . . was uniformly rejected by the Lords, and after that it got into Chancery, and there it has slept for the past nine years.' (A reference to the obstructive tactics of Lord Eldon.)

# LUNACY, LAW, AND CONSCIENCE

## 2. REFORM AT BETHLEM

The publication of the Norris case and other evidence given before the Select Committee had a salutary effect on the Governors of Bethlem. While the inquiry was still pending, they dismissed the old steward and matron, appointing younger and more competent people to their posts. In 1816, with the full evidence of the Committee before them, they met to consider the future of their apothecary and their physician. Haslam was dismissed,[1] and returned to private practice until his death in 1844. His dismissal did not apparently cloud his reputation, for his biographer described him as 'long distinguished in private practice by his prudent treatment of the insane'.[2] The obituary notice in the *Gentleman's Magazine* more discreetly noted only his capabilities as 'reviewer, critic, epigrammatist, and author of witty and comic papers'.[3]

Dr. Thomas Monro was also called before the Governors to justify himself, but he was more fortunate than Haslam. There was a long tradition of Monros at Bethlem, and the Governors seem to have been unwilling to proceed to extreme measures in his case. Moreover, he had taken the precaution of preparing an attempted rebuttal of the charges made against him, which he read aloud and subsequently had printed.[4]

In this address, he disposed of the Norris case by the simple method of saying that he had no wish 'to agitate it anew'. Of the case of Miss Stone, the blanket patient released by the matron, he said,

'The crowded state of the hospital afforded no means of classification . . . although one may deeply lament that an individual with such attainments as she possessed should be so degraded, it was difficult consistently with the general attention due to the other patients to place her in any other situation but that which she occupied.'

Concerning the accusations levelled against him on the score of medical treatment, he stated baldly,

'With respect to the merits of the mode of treatment which I have practised, consisting chiefly of evacuants, as a general rule, I know no better.'

[1] O'Donoghue, *Story of Bethlehem Hospital*, p. 324. 'He was turned out of the hospital at the age of fifty-two without a pension.'
[2] *D.N.B.*
[3] *Gent. Mag.*, 1844, vol. 22, p. 322.
[4] *The Observations of Dr. Monro*, read before the Governors at Bethlem, April 30th, 1816.

There is no record of the Governors' reaction to this defence, but it is significant that Monro resigned in July, 1816—nominally of his own accord. He was replaced by his son, Dr. Edward Thomas Monro, who seems from later evidence to have been more humane in the performance of his duties.[1]

Although it was many years before public control could be established over Bethlem, there was undoubtedly a considerable degree of reform in conditions after the disclosures made by the 1815 Committee. An anonymous publication which appeared in 1823[2] gave a detailed account of the state of the hospital in that year. The author styled himself 'A Constant Observer'; it would appear from the subject matter that the book was inspired by the Bethlem authorities in an attempt to convince the general public that all was now well with the administration. It bears the unmistakable stamp of propaganda.

The hospital had moved at the end of 1815 to new premises so designed as to permit a scheme of classification.[3] By 1823, according to 'A Constant Observer', male and female patients were housed in separate wings, and there were four galleries to each wing. Number 4 gallery, the top floor, was reserved for chronic patients, number 3 for curable patients, number 2, the ground floor, for recently admitted cases awaiting diagnosis and classification, and number 1, the basement, for the noisy and unclean. There was also a criminal wing, in which male and female patients were housed separately. Airing courts, known as the 'Green Yards', had been constructed for male, female and criminal lunatics separately.

The regulations provided that the patients should rise at six o'clock in the summer and seven in the winter; breakfast was served at eight, dinner at one, and supper at six. The patients were locked up for the night at eight o'clock in the evening. 'Each patient has a separate room,' wrote 'A Constant Observer'. All had beds and linen, except those in the basement, who still slept on straw. The linen was changed weekly, and baths were 'in constant use'.

The scheme of classification marked a definite improvement in conditions, except where violent or unclean patients were concerned. The arrangements in the basement seem to have been no better than those described in *Jack Sheppard*. There was still apparently no attempt to train the dirty patient or to calm the noisy by a calm and compassionate approach such as that practised at the Retreat. Confinement in the base-

---

[1] See p. 115.
[2] *Sketches in Bedlam*, by a Constant Observer, 1823.
[3] The reasons for the move were primarily financial. See D. H. Tuke, *Hist. of Insane*, p. 83.

ment may well have meant for many patients the loss of the last vestiges of self-respect.

The regulations concerning the hours of rising and going to bed marked the end of an abuse. One of the charges made against the keepers in 1815 was that they left physically healthy patients in bed all day to save themselves the trouble of dressing them and supervising their activities.[1] The result over a long period was often a deterioration in both mental and physical capacity. By 1823, the keepers were obliged to have their fit patients up for a thirteen- or fourteen-hour day.

'Each patient has a separate room' is a sentence of doubtful implication. It may have meant only 'Each patient is subject to solitary confinement at night'; but the regulations concerning the hours of rising safeguarded most patients against long periods of solitary confinement.

On the matter of treatment, 'A Constant Observer' wrote,

'The grand principle of this establishment is mildness, for it is now generally acknowledged that this mode of treating the maniac is much better calculated to restore reason than harshness or severity'.

While mechanical restraint was still used, each occasion of use had to be recorded, and the record book was read to a sub-committee of the Board of Governors once a week. No mention was made in this publication of the system of medical treatment.

The diet was a light one, not much above workhouse standards. Breakfast consisted of 'wholesome gruel, mixed with milk' and bread; supper of bread and butter. The main midday meal was of meat and bread on three days, with such substitutes as 'soup', 'broth', and rice milk on the other four. Beer was apparently plentiful—

'Table beer is served without any stint . . . some drink more, some less, but the average quantity does not exceed 2 pints each patient per day'.

Patients were allowed to be visited by their relatives once a week for a period of two hours. The medical staff consisted of two physicians, a surgeon, and a resident apothecary, the last-named being responsible for keeping case-books, record books, admission and discharge books, and for reporting to the physicians on the condition of the patients. This was a distinct improvement from the days of Haslam, whose duties were so ill-defined that he was able to comply with the minimum expected of him in half an hour a day, and to plead that other responsibilities were not his.

[1] 1815 *Report*, p. 72.

Of Dr. Edward Thomas Monro, one of the two physicians, the writer stated,

'Too much praise cannot be conferred on Dr. Monro for his human attention and the kind feeling he at all times evinces for the unhappy persons under his care'.

The second half of *Sketches in Bedlam* justified the title, for it consisted of case-histories of individual patients—a fact which strengthens the presumption that the author was officially connected with the administration of the hospital.[1]

The most interesting point about these case-histories is the principle on which they seem to have been selected. They provide neither a typical cross-section of patients nor a random sample taken from one ward—unless indeed they were all taken from the basement. They exhibit all the most unpleasant aspects of mental disorder—physical violence, blasphemy and indecency. Patrick Walsh, a 'ferocious maniac', had served on the frigate *Hermione*, whose crew mutinied and massacred the officers in 1797. He admitted to 'nine or ten murders', and since being admitted to Bethlem, had murdered two patients and broken over seventy panes of glass, in spite of being subject to the most rigorous forms of confinement.

'Any topic of murder or bloodshed is his delight . . . he presents a hideous and appalling specimen of the human savage deprived of reason'.

Francis Mardin thought that he was the Archangel Gabriel, and that the medical staff were respectively Pontius Pilate, Judas Iscariot, and the Devil. George Woods told a party of ladies of 'rank and distinction' that he had been castrated.

Publication of cases of this nature served two purposes: it discouraged visitors, and it was calculated to rouse all the old moral prejudices against the insane, to erect again the barriers of fear and apathy which had been slowly broken down by the reformers.

It seems clear that a certain amount of reform had indeed taken place in Bethlem; but it was a grudging reform, proceeding less from conviction than from social pressure. The principles on which material was selected for this publication, the defensive nature of its presentation, and the anonymity of its author suggest that its statements should be treated with caution.

'Bedlam is well-conducted,' wrote Sir Andrew Halliday in 1828, 'and

[1] The author may have been the apothecary who took Haslam's place—and who was responsible for keeping case-records.

the patients are humanely and judiciously treated; but it has still too much of the leaven of the dark ages . . . for it ever to prove an efficient hospital'.[1] There was some truth in this statement; the name of Bethlem continued to be associated with the reign of Haslam and Thomas Monro, and several generations of improved administration failed subsequently to eradicate 'Bedlam' from the English language as a derogatory term.

### 3. THE COUNTY ASYLUMS

By 1827, there were nine county asylums in operation. Nottingham, Bedford and Norfolk were followed by Lancaster (1816), Stafford (1818), the West Riding of Yorkshire (at Wakefield, 1818), Cornwall (at Bodmin, 1820), Lincoln (1820), and Gloucester (1823). The cost of these asylums in relation to the accommodation provided was as follows:

| Asylum | Approx. Total Cost £ | Accommodation | Initial Cost per Head £ |
|---|---|---|---|
| Nottingham . . | 21,000 | 80 | 262 |
| Bedford. . . | 10,000 | 52 | 192 |
| Norfolk. . . | 35,000 | 102 | 343 |
| Lancaster . . | 60,000 | 170 | 353 |
| Stafford . . . | 36,000 | 120 | 300 |
| West Riding . . | 55,000 | 250 | 220 |
| Cornwall . . | 15,000 | 102 | 147 |
| Lincoln . . . | 12,000 | 50 | 240 |
| Gloucester . . | 44,000 | 120 | 367[2] |

*Sites of County Asylums.*

Wynn's Act had specified that the new asylums were to be 'in an airy and healthy situation, with a good supply of water, and which may afford a probability of the vicinity of constant medical assistance'.[3] This implied a contradiction, since the only sites satisfying the last requirement were those in large towns, which at that period were neither healthy nor airy, and frequently had no public water supply.

[1] Halliday, *General View of Lunatics*, p. 17.
[2] Figures of total cost and accommodation are taken from Halliday's *General View of Lunatics*, p. 25. Wages and prices fluctuated considerably during the period 1810–23, due to the economic effects of the Napoleonic Wars, and the figures are therefore not strictly comparable. For wage-fluctuations in the building trade at this period, see A. L. Bowley, *Wages in the Nineteenth Century*, pp. 82–4.
[3] 1808 Act, section 16.

In Lancashire, the magistrates met in 1810, and issued a statement proposing the erection of the new asylum at Liverpool for the rather curious reason that the patients would be able to enjoy 'the beneficial effects of sea air and sea bathing'.[1] The doctors of Liverpool, led by Dr. James Gerard, protested strongly against this proposal. They reminded the magistrates that the Liverpool Royal Infirmary already had an asylum attached to it;[2] that, although they had not been consulted about the proposal prior to its publication, they would undoubtedly be expected to assume the responsibility for the extra work involved in prescribing care and treatment for the lunatics of the whole county; and they stated that, in their opinion, the situation should be 'exceedingly retired, and quite in the country'. This was an understandable sentiment. While admitting the necessity for an asylum, they were not pleased at the prospect of having it built in their own immediate vicinity. Another reason was more cogent. Patients would be sent to the new asylum from all parts of the county, and it was therefore advisable that transportation costs should be equalized as far as possible by building the asylum in a central position. Some thirty or forty doctors wrote in support of Dr. Gerard, many of them advancing Chorley or Wigan as suitably 'retired positions'.[3] The asylum was eventually constructed in the northern part of the county, about a mile from Lancaster. It had five acres of grounds and a dairy farm extending over a further ten acres.

In Stafford, the asylum was built next to the County Gaol.[4] This arrangement permitted of some degree of common administration between the two institutions, thus minimizing expense. The Society for the Improvement of Prison Discipline reported in 1823 that 'as a source of hard labour, the treadmill is in full operation; it grinds corn for the consumption of the prison and the lunatic asylum, and also for sale.'[5] Stafford Asylum, in spite of its proximity to the prison, had an almost ideal site. It was built on rising ground, and although within a few minutes' walk of the centre of the town, was so enclosed in acres of park and woodland that the situation was both 'retired' and 'airy'.

The asylum at Wakefield was built within easy reach of the centre of the town, and enclosed in twenty-five acres of woodland.

The Cornwall Asylum was erected at Bodmin, on a low-lying and badly-drained site which caused dissatisfaction to the Lunacy Com-

[1] Address to the Magistrates of the County of Lancaster. James Gerard, M.D., et al., 1810
[2] Opened in 1792. See T. H. Bickerton, A Medical History of Liverpool, pp. 28–30.
[3] Gerard et al., op. cit.
[4] They are still (1954) contiguous.
[5] Report of the Society for the Improvement of Prison Discipline, 1823, p. 100.

missioners in the 1840's.[1] The view was 'cheerful' and the grounds were 'extensive', according to Halliday,[2] though a visiting Frenchman later in the century recorded 'les cours sont humides et sombres'.[3] Most authorities settled the problem by building on the edge of a large town, or two or three miles out into the country. In the days before suburban living became popular, the boundary between the town and the surrounding country was usually sufficiently distinct for a building to be constructed in the latter while still within relatively easy reach of the former. The subsequent spread of the towns has meant that, where the buildings of the old asylums are still in use, they are generally well within the town boundaries.

*Problems of Administration.*

Since the visiting justices had no reliable precedents to follow, they inevitably made mistakes in these early days.

A frequent practice at this time was to appoint a superintendent who was paid on a capitation basis, and to leave him to provide out of that sum for the complete upkeep of the establishment. This practice was followed at Nottingham, where Dr. Storey was also allowed to accept gratuities from grateful relatives, and to take private patients.[4] At Bodmin, a study of the first Minute Book of the Cornwall Asylum shows that a particularly difficult series of situations arose. The first superintendent was a surgeon named James Duck, who received 14s. a week for each patient. There were constant disagreements with the visiting justices over matters of finance, he contending that the amount was inadequate, and they, that he was not providing necessities for the patients. Before the Asylum was fully established, Duck resigned, and claimed a large sum of money which he alleged he had spent on furnishing and provisions. The justices refused to meet his claims, and in February, 1820, they appointed a Mr. Kingdon on the same basis, with the title of 'Governor and Contractor'. This appears to have been a lay appointment. Within four years he too had found the tasks of satisfying the justices and making a profit irreconcilable. In June, 1824, a third Governor was appointed, and the financial arrangements were reconsidered. He and his wife, who acted as matron, were given a joint salary of £200 a year, together with accommodation, full board, and all amenities. They were requested to visit Bethlem before

---

[1] Report of Metropolitan Commissioners in Lunacy—recorded in Visitors' Book of the Cornwall Asylum, 1842.
[2] Halliday, *General View of Lunatics*, p. 23.
[3] Battelle, *Rapport sur les établissements aliénés d'Angleterre*, 1851, p. 22.
[4] 1815 *Report*, p. 158.

taking up office in order to familiarize themselves with the nature of their duties.[1] The justices then proceeded to make five other appointments:

'One Head Keeper (Baker & Shaver) . . . £25
One Keeper and Shoemaker . . . . . £20
One Female Head Keeper . . . . . £10
One Kitchenmaid . . . . . . £6
One Labourer by the Week to work in the Garden.'

This meant that the Governor was relieved of the responsibilities of engaging staff and of handling the duties usually assigned to a steward. It suggests that former Governors had either appointed no staff except for their own personal domestics, or that the justices had dismissed the previous holders of these posts.

Three years later, in 1827, the visiting justices became aware of another flaw in the terms of appointment of their chief officer. Since they visited the Asylum only at infrequent intervals, they had no real means of supervision, and it was possible for the Governor to absent himself from his duties without leave. On August 8th, 1827, the third Governor appeared before the Committee, charged with being absent for ten days. He was allowed to resume his duties on giving a promise of better behaviour in the future, but apparently the humiliation involved was too much for him, as he resigned a few months afterwards.

The justices were then faced with the task of appointing their fourth Governor in seven years. Their experiences appeared to have taught them four things about the office of Governor; that the man appointed should have a medical qualification; that he should have some knowledge of work among mental patients; that it was necessary to ensure at the outset that he would remain at his post; and that it was unwise to confuse clinical work with financial administration. Dr. L. K. Potts of Bethlem was appointed, and paid a salary for his own use only. He was requested to sign a declaration to the effect that he would abide by the rules drawn up by the Committee, including the proviso that he would not absent himself without leave.[2] It would seem that Dr. Potts' rule was a beneficent one, since he stayed for some years, and subsequent resolutions concerning the welfare of the patients frequently bore the clause 'at the discretion of Dr. Potts'.

At Stafford, the original Minute Book of the Visiting Justices shows that the arrangements with regard to senior staff were somewhat different.

[1] This was after the reform of conditions at Bethlem.
[2] This declaration, signed by Potts, is incorporated in the Minute Book.

A physician was appointed on a part-time basis at a salary of £200 a year, and a lay administrative superintendent, who was to be resident, at a salary of £200 and maintenance. The other staff were:

'One Matron at £40 and Maintenance.
One Porter with a Suit of Clothes and a Hat, £15.
One Keeper £25.
One Female Keeper £25.'

The matron originally appointed was a Mrs. White, but her term of office lasted only a few weeks. As soon as he was installed, the superintendent, Mr. Garrett, asked permission to house his elderly mother in the asylum. This permission was granted on condition that she should provide all her own fuel and food; the condition was short-lived, for within a very short period Mrs. White was dismissed, and the elderly Mrs. Garrett installed in her stead. If there was any reason for the abrupt dismissal, apart from the discreet pressure of the superintendent, it was not noted in the Minute Book.

These cases are quoted as examples of incidents which were typical of many in the early history of the county asylums. They arose partly out of the inexperience of the visiting justices, and partly out of the fact that senior administrative officers were appointed without prescribed experience, qualifications, or a guarantee as to personal integrity.

There is no generic term, apart from the inaccurate and slightly invidious 'asylum doctors' which may be used to describe the small body of men experienced in the treatment of mental disease at this time. They were not even necessarily medical practitioners. Their views and methods varied from those of Thomas Monro to those of William Tuke. Some of them were quacks, and some of them were highly enlightened men; and the people with whom their work brought them into contact—magistrates, Poor Law officials, clergy, general practitioners and others—rarely had sufficient knowledge to distinguish the one from the other.

These new specialists frequently published books in which they expounded their own systems, but showed no acquaintance with work being done in the same field in other parts of the country. This accounts in part for the extremely uneven development of the new methods.

*Mechanical Restraint.*

Since the staff of the average county asylum was so small, it is hardly surprising that both keepers and doctors tended to rely on mechanical restraint as the one method of keeping patients quiet and orderly.

The Act of 1808 laid down no regulations concerning treatment, but it provided statutory penalties against the keepers if patients escaped.[1] These penalties were high, being equivalent to at least one month's wages. The maximum penalty of £10 was a keeper's total wages for five months. As a result, the staffs of county asylums were unwilling to take the slightest risk in allowing a patient liberty of movement; mechanical restraint provided a way of preventing escapes without exercising unremitting supervision. At Bodmin, the visiting justices in 1819 requested one of their number, the Right Hon. Reginald Pole Carew, to apply to the Governors of Bethlem for 'patterns of the different securities necessary for patients' and subsequently ordered '12 padlocks for patients' belts'.[2] At Lancaster, which was a large asylum by contemporary standards, accommodating 150–200 patients,[3] the resident surgeon, Dr. Paul Slade Knight, had his own methods of restraint. These he described in his treatise entitled, 'Observations on the Causes, Symptoms and Treatment of Derangement of the Mind', which was illustrated with diagrams of the apparatus involved. One illustration shows a leather muff with iron wrist locks at each side in which a patient's hands could be confined, and a variant called the 'pocket muff' in which each hand could be encased separately. A more strict form of coercion was a device consisting of two strong leather sleeves terminating in 'pocket muffs'; the sleeves were fastened across the shoulders by a strap and a lock, and the whole apparatus was connected to leg-locks on the thighs, a chain joining the ankles. It is not known to what extent this crippling device was actually used, but Dr. Knight advanced it in his treatise as being considerably more humane than the methods generally employed in asylums and madhouses.

Mention has already been made of the provisions concerning restraint laid down in the rules of the Nottingham Asylum.[4] Restraint at Stafford was also apparently kept to a minimum, since there are few records in the Apothecary's Day Book of its being employed. When the Lunacy Commissioners made their first official visit to this establishment in 1842, they were gratified to find the patients 'tranquil and comfortable, and free from all restraint'.[5]

---

[1] 48 Geo. III, c. 96, section 23.

[2] 1st Minute Book, Cornwall Asylum.

[3] Cash-book of the Lancaster Asylum, 1828, where the figures for each quarter of the foregoing year are given as 176–180–181–198. Halliday (*General View of Lunatics*, p. 25) gave the figure for the same year as 300, but was evidently mistaken.

[4] See pp. 99–100.

[5] Report of the Metropolitan Commissioners in Lunacy, recorded in the Visitors' Book of the Stafford Asylum, 1842.

*Diet.*

The food provided in the early county asylums was very much better than that in gaols and workhouses. A weekly order given at Stafford during this period for a total of sixty-nine persons has these items:

| | |
|---|---|
| Meat, 264 lb. . . . . . . | £7 3s. 0d. |
| Cheese, 64 lb. . . . . . . | £2 2s. 8d. |
| Milk, 119 quarts . . . . . . | £1 9s. 9d. |
| Beer, 126 gallons, Ale, 5 gallons . . . | £5 0s. 3d. |

Bread was made at the County Gaol, and therefore does not appear as an item of expenditure. This list of provisions—which was approximately repeated each week—would have supplied each patient and member of staff with a little less than 4 lb. of meat, 1 lb. of cheese, 2 pints of milk and 2 gallons of beer, at a cost of approximately 4s. 8d. per week.

At Bodmin, it seems that the patients installed during the brief superintendency of Mr. Duck did not receive adequate food, for when his successor was appointed in February, 1820, a diet sheet was formulated by the visiting justices, and the 'Governor and Contractor' was required to purchase the necessary provisions. This diet resembled the common workhouse diet of meat and soup on alternate days, but was enlivened by such additional items as seed cake, treacle, and best cuts of beef for roasting.

The picture at Lancaster is less encouraging; though, since this asylum had its own farm, it is not possible to reconstruct a true picture of the actual diet from the account books; but the chief expenditure on food at this asylum was that on potatoes, which were ordered so frequently, and in such large quantities, that they must have formed the staple article of diet.

Dr. Knight noted in his account book that the total cost of maintaining 176 patients in the first quarter of 1820 was £349—roughly 3s. 1d. a week per head.

*Amenities.*

The patients at Lancaster slept on straw. There is no record of the purchase of beds and bedding prior to the year 1842, when the frequent indents for straw came to an end shortly before the first statutory visit made by the Metropolitan Commissioners in Lunacy.[1] The account books show occasional entries for tobacco or snuff, but in fairly small quantities. These may have been purchased for the keepers. Dr. Knight's

[1] See pp. 174-5.

views on the management of patients coincided in the main with those of the Monros at Bethlem:

'I am quite of the opinion that one person only should have undivided authority over the lunatic . . . and that superior person should be his physician.'[1]

Patients were required to help in the kitchen or the garden when fit enough to do so;[2] Halliday noted that Lancaster did not possess a 'manufactory' for the occupation of the patients;[3] they were allowed in their spare time to play ninepins or knit, according to sex.[4]

At Wakefield, Halliday found that the patients were employed at various trades, approximating where possible to their trades in normal life. At Nottingham, Stafford and Gloucester, they worked in kitchen and garden, being 'useful to themselves, and beneficial to the establishment'. At Bodmin, the patients were 'not much employed in any regular manner', but in other respects, the general conditions appeared to Halliday to be above the average. Beds were supplied for all but the 'foul patients', who went to the 'straw room'. The bedsteads were three feet wide for men, and four feet wide for the women, who slept two in a bed. Blankets and sheets were supplied. This asylum, unlike most, had a form of central heating. In January, 1817, when the building was in the course of construction, the surveyor was sent to London, 'to ascertain the best means of warming the asylum for £30'. Three years later, there is an entry in the Minute Book which refers to repairs to the pipes 'which circulate hot and cold air to regulate the temperature of the building'. These pipes seem to have been frequently in need of repair, and caused constant concern to the Committee in the early days.

*Visitation.*

*(i) by the visiting justices.*

A study of the Visitors' Books of these asylums leaves the impression that official visitation was cursory in the extreme. The main criteria of the justices were cleanliness and quietude. 'Visited the asylum and found all in good order' . . . 'all going on well' . . . 'behaviour satisfactory' . . . 'everything regular and very cleanly'—phrases such as these recur constantly, and criticism or constructive suggestions are very rare. The jus-

---

[1] *Knight on Insanity*, p. 95.
[2] *Knight on Insanity.* There is a chapter on the management and occupation of patients.
[3] Halliday, *General View of Lunatics*, pp. 19–23: a survey of conditions in the various county asylums.
[4] *Knight on Insanity*, p. 91.

tices had no complaints to make, provided only that the patients were kept quiet, washed and fed. They did not inquire into methods of treatment, and seem only belatedly to have become aware of deficiencies in such matters as ventilation, bedding, heating, clothing, diet and occupation for the patients when the Act of 1842 made inspection by an independent authority imminent. 'October 17 I saw the Asylum in Desent Order by me J. Hicks'[1] is a typical entry. The phrases used by the justices quickly developed into clichés which meant very little except that they were easily satisfied.

### (ii) by relatives and casual visitors.

Other visitors were generally admitted only by permission of the medical attendant or the visiting justices. At Stafford, the next of kin of patients were admitted freely, but other visitors were refused admission for 'a security against improper and intrusive curiosity'. The memory of the public entertainment provided by Bethlem was sufficiently strong to prejudice asylum authorities against visitation by the general public.

### (iii) by distinguished visitors.

The Visitors' Books of the better asylums show that there was a constant stream of aristocratic visitors sponsored by the visiting justices. This constituted a valuable means of propaganda for the new methods of treatment and administration. It seemed that lunacy reform was at last attracting public attention.

The Visitors' Book of Stafford Asylum records two visits from Augustus Frederick, Duke of Sussex, and sixth son of George III:

'Introduced by Lord Talbot and Lord Anson and I have been through the different wards of the Asylum I have admired the Order Cleanliness and Regularity of the Establishment, witnessing with Pleasure the Care and Attention paid to the Comfort of the unfortunate Patients.'

The Duke may well have been astonished at the difference between the treatment of paupers at Stafford and that suffered by his father the King only a few years earlier.

Thomas Mottershaw, a member of the Stafford Committee, took a succession of local gentry—churchwardens, magistrates and others, together with their wives and adult children, to see the asylum in parties of five or six.

---

[1] 1st Visitors' Book of the Cornwall Asylum.

Another visitor at Stafford was Dr. Galret, an associate of Pinel, who wrote:

'J'ai visité avec le plus grand interêt l'établissement de Stafford, et il m'est agréable de pouvoir donner les plus grands éloges à l'administration.'

Visitors at Bodmin included Lord de Dunstanville and Basset; Charles Lamb's friend, C. V. Le Grice—who, like the Duke of Sussex, had a personal interest in the treatment of insanity; and the staff of the Marquis of Hertford:[1] 'Rbt. Womersley, suisse valet de chambre de milord hertford' and Robert Partridge, footman.

While there was no legislative provision for inspection by a national authority, probably visitation of this kind was the best guarantee against the ill-treatment of patients; but distinguished visitors tended to go to the best asylums, not the worst. They went to see the best points of asylum administration, and were not primarily interested in investigating possible cases of abuse. Moreover, the asylum authorities were almost certainly forewarned of the advent of a distinguished visitor, and would generally open for inspection only the best-equipped wards containing the quietest patients. Such visits were no real substitute for official inspection, the proper purpose of the latter being to discover the points at which the administrative system fails, and to suggest remedies.

*(iv) Catherine Cappe and the 'Lady Visitors' of York.*

In this connection, mention should be made of the method of asylum-visiting initiated by Catherine Cappe, wife of the physician at the Retreat, who published her 'Thoughts on the Desirableness and Utility of Ladies Visiting the Female Wards of Hospitals and Lunatic Asylums' in 1816. Her system was in many ways analogous to the prison-visiting of Elizabeth Fry. After the reforms of 1814, she tells us, she began to visit the female patients of the York Asylum regularly, and she came to believe that such visits were a valuable safeguard against maladministration in asylums. Her standards were high:—

'A lady visitor in an asylum or hospital should be to that institution what the kind, judicious Mistress of a family is to her household—the careful inspector of the economy, the integrity and the good moral conduct of the housekeeper and the other inferior servants.'

Mrs. Cappe evidently had a low opinion of the capabilities and stan-

[1] The Marquis was related to Lord Robert Seymour. See p. 80.

125

dards of asylum staff; but she had also a wide experience. She complained that the masters and matrons of institutions for the insane were often unsuited for the office which they held; that they were frequently appointed as a result of wire-pulling and nepotism. She pointed out that physicians and surgeons frequently served only in a part-time capacity, and that the 'father' of the 'family'—here we have the exact terminology used at the Retreat—was usually the resident apothecary, generally an unmarried man since the post carried with it limited accommodation in rooms on the premises. Consequently, unless the matron was an exceptional woman, there was often no woman to whom the female patients could turn.

'May there not be a variety of minute circumstances which may occasion great distress, and may retard, if not wholly prevent, recovery, but which could be communicated only to a female ear?'

We have no means of knowing how far Mrs. Cappe's ideas were generally adopted, but the Visitors' Books of several county asylums mention frequent visits by the wives and adult daughters of the visiting justices; this suggests that these ladies may have attempted something more constructive than a mere sight-seeing tour: personal contact with the female patients, and supervision of the domestic arrangements of the asylums concerned.

The early county asylums were experimental. Since their only precedents for administration and treatment were those of the prisons and workhouses, it was not to be expected that they would at once reach the status of hospitals. They were understaffed, overcrowded, and run by unqualified staffs under the guidance of generally apathetic and frequently inept local authorities. Nevertheless, they made possible an immense improvement in the conditions of the insane who came under their care, and indirectly influenced the administration of private madhouses, in many of which conditions were still far worse. Legislation did not as yet provide adequate safeguards for the well-being of the patients, and much depended on the ability and integrity of the chief medical officer; but the experiment had been abundantly justified. The principles of non-deterrent treatment and public responsibility had been conclusively established.

4. PUBLIC OPINION

Catherine Cappe, in dealing briefly with the wider problems of lunacy reform, had come to a not uncommon conclusion: that the only remedy for a manifestly unsatisfactory situation lay in the increased pressure of public opinion on the legislature. The pressure of public opinion at any time—and particularly in the past—is extremely difficult to assess. It involves diverse movements and contradictions, the reactions not only of the vociferous few, but also of the apathetic and silent majority. It must take into account not only what people said, but also what they did not say. For these reasons, any assessment of public opinion which relates to a period over a century ago is inevitably imperfect. It is proposed here to deal briefly with the evidence of the written word as shown in the Press, periodicals, and medical works on insanity. The picture of public opinion is incomplete; but it cannot on that account be omitted, since it contributes something to an understanding of later developments in this field.

(i) *The Press.*

London newspapers neither reflected nor developed public opinion to any great extent before 1830, and they therefore had little effect on lunacy reform. They contained only a small space devoted to news, most of their columns being filled with advertisements and trade notices. Their circulation was restricted; the stamp duty of 4d. imposed by the younger Pitt's government was raised in 1826 to 6d.;[1] but though the newspapers played so insignificant a part in the national life, their potentialities were feared by the ruling classes on the grounds that free circulation of information among the uneducated would lead to radicalism and demagogy. Cobbett, in his Tory days, stigmatized the daily journals as 'vehicles of falsehood and bad principles'.[2] Wynn seldom read them, and thought them of no importance.[3] George Rose paid them some attention, but only to ensure that they said what he wanted them to say. Reference has already been made to his employment of 'hireling scribes' in the interests of the Tory party.

The London newspapers were virtually controlled by the two political parties until the third decade of the nineteenth century; favoured papers, such as the *London Evening Post* or *The Times* received subsidies of £200 or £300 a year from the Tories.[4] The Whigs, who theoretically believed in a free Press, retaliated by bribing the editor of the *Morning Post.*[5]

---

[1] A. Aspinall, *Politics and the Press, 1780-1850*, pp. 23 and 31.
[2] A. Aspinall, op. cit., p. 10.
[3] Aspinall, op. cit., p. 247.
[4] *The Times* lost its subsidy from the Tory party in 1799 as a result of an alleged libel in a report of parliamentary proceedings, and was thereafter relatively independent.
[5] Aspinall, op. cit., p. 271.

In the provinces, in spite of restrictive taxes and the mental limitations of the editors, local newspapers had a greater influence. They provided a forum for the debating of controversial issues, such as the site of a new county asylum, or the discovery of alleged abuses. The most outstanding example of the way in which the Press could be used to mould public opinion is that shown in the controversy concerning York Asylum in 1813–15. The *York Herald*, even at a time of national crisis, when every inch of its columns could have been filled twice over with news of the war with France, opened its columns to Best and Higgins, printing the salient arguments on each side without comment and without bias. This was in the highest tradition of responsible journalism. Only once was the editor stung into personal comment—when Best threatened him with an action for libel. On that occasion, his attitude showed that he was proud of his independent position.[1]

The position taken up by the editor of the *York Herald* was typical of a new trend in journalism. Editors realized gradually that they held a special position in the community—that they could influence the course of public action. Even *The Times*—that most conservative of all newspapers in its adherence to the eighteenth-century format—introduced a leading article. Moreover, it regularly printed reports of parliamentary proceedings and legal cases, thus making the facts known to a wider public.

## (ii) Periodicals.

The foundation of the great nineteenth-century monthly and quarterly reviews provided a more direct means for the dissemination of facts and ideas connected with lunacy reform. Periodicals which dealt from time to time with topics of this nature included the *Gentleman's Magazine*, founded in 1731, the *Edinburgh Review* (1802), the *Quarterly Review* (1809), and the *Westminster Review* (1827). The *Edinburgh Review* in August, 1817, published a lengthy article dealing with the progress of reform in the four previous years, concluding,

'It is the duty of every publication that has honestly obtained a great circulation on all occasions to give notoriety to these truths which are in danger of remaining unknown because they are . . . distressing in their details.'

These journals, although catering for a responsible and informed public, tended to stress revelations of neglect and cruelty rather than giving publicity to the unsensational and steady work of improvement. They

[1] See p. 91.

contained much information about the worst of the private madhouses, but generally ignored the county asylums, where a social experiment of considerable importance was being carried out. The *Lancet* was founded in 1823 by Thomas Wakley,[1] a member of the Royal College of Surgeons, who later became a member of parliament and Coroner for West Middlesex. Although Wakley later took some interest in lunacy questions, the columns of the *Lancet* in its early years were confined to subjects concerning physical sickness and disease. There was no periodical publication which could be used for discussion and for the dissemination of information about mental treatment on a professional basis.

*(iii) Medical Works on Insanity.*

Works on the nature and treatment of insanity written during this period by members of the medical profession were many in number. John Ferriar's *Medical Histories and Reflections* was published in 1792, Haslam's *Observations on Insanity*—which presented a somewhat idealized version of the treatment given at Bethlem—in 1794, and his *Considerations on the Moral Management of Insane Persons* in 1817. Bryan Crowther's *Practical Remarks on Insanity* appeared in 1811, and Paul Slade Knight's *Observations on the Causes, Treatment, etc., of Derangement of the Mind,* in 1827; but of these and many other works, as Pinel commented, 'A careful, impartial examination discloses nothing but vague dissertations, repetitions, compilations, scholastic formality'.[2] The material presented followed a stereotyped pattern, the ideas put forward had an unmistakable air of being second-hand. The publications which contributed most to the progress of mental treatment in the first quarter of the nineteenth century were those which were concerned with the human rather than the medical approach—Samuel Tuke's *Description of the Retreat* and Godfrey Higgins' *Letter to Earl FitzWilliam.*

Three works written by members of the medical profession which in some degree combined the two approaches deserve special mention—the *Letter to Thomas Thompson, M.P.*[3] written in 1815 by William Ellis, Sir Andrew Halliday's *General View of Lunatics* published in 1828, and

---

[1] Thomas Wakley, 1795-1852. See *D.N.B* and *Gent. Mag.* obit. (1862, vol. II, p. 364).

[2] P. Pinel, *Traité Medico-Philosophique,* quoted in translation by Zilboorg and Henrey, *Hist. of Medical Psychology,* p. 334.

[3] Thomas Thompson, M.P. for Midhurst, 1807-18, was a merchant from Hull, a friend of Wilberforce, and a member of the Clapham Sect. See *D.N.B.* article on his son, General Thomas Perronet Thompson (1783-1869) and Halévy, *Hist. of the English People in the Nineteenth Century,* vol. I.—England in 1815, p. 436.

# LUNACY, LAW, AND CONSCIENCE

George Man Burrows' *Commentary on the Causes, etc., of Insanity*, which appeared in the same year.

Ellis devoted some space in his letter to a consideration of the different forms taken by insanity, recognizing that all mental patients did not exhibit the same symptoms, nor did they necessarily all require the same type of treatment. He also listed some of the factors which impeded the progress of mental treatment: the quackery of some medical men, who specialized in mental cases because the work was lucrative and unexacting; the helplessness of the patients, who were unable to fight their own battles; the insistence of wealthy friends and relatives upon secrecy, and their indifference to the mode of treatment, as long as the patient was kept closely confined; above all, the general belief that insanity necessarily involved an impairment of all the mental faculties:

'It must be observed that patients may be insane on one subject and perfectly sane on all others.'

He recommended occupation, fresh air and exercise as the most beneficent factors in curative treatment, and warmly endorsed the system at the Retreat.

Burrows (1771–1846) held an M.D. from St. Andrew's, and was the prime mover in the passing of the Apothecaries' Act of 1815. He kept a private asylum at Clapham, significantly named 'The Retreat', at which the standards of care and treatment were high.[1] Though there is an echo of Burton in his statement 'Madness is one of the curses imposed by the wrath of Almighty God on his people for their sins',[2] his attempt to chart the interaction of mental and bodily symptoms was one of the first tentative approaches to psychosomatic medicine. Like Ellis, he deprecated the low standards and high pretensions of certain sections of the medical profession in relation to insanity, and issued a stern injunction to the profession not to be led away by 'psychological disquisitions,[3] German mystifications,[4] and Bedlam sketches . . . calculated to gratify a romantic and prurient taste'.[5]

Burrows divided the causes of insanity into two groups—the 'moral'

---

[1] See Statutory Reports of the Metropolitan Commissioners in Lunacy, 1830 (unpublished, handwritten. P.R.O., London).

[2] Burrows, *Commentaries on the Causes of Insanity*, p. 1.

[3] Probably a reference to Herbart's *Text-book of Psychology*, published in 1816, in which the writer contended that psychology was a separate study allied to philosophy rather than to medicine. Herbart was Kant's successor in the Chair of Philosophy at Konigsberg.

[4] A reference to Mesmerism, then in vogue on the Continent.

[5] Burrows, op. cit., p. 7.

and the 'physical', and it becomes clear in his work that the former term, as used by some writers on insanity at this time, had a specialized meaning. 'Moral' causes were emotional or affective causes, and 'moral treatment' was treatment through the emotions.[1] This was probably not the sense in which the Tukes used the word, since their method of treatment was indispensably bound up with religious and ethical teaching; but the two possible meanings should be borne in mind.

It will be remembered that Sir Andrew Halliday had undertaken an exhaustive statistical compilation on behalf of the Select Committee of 1807. His *General View of Lunatics*, written twenty years later, thus had the backing of a long semi-official association with the cause of lunacy reform, and had a great influence both in his own life-time and after. Halliday, despite his medical qualifications,[2] was associated rather with the parliamentary reformers than with the independent philanthropists or the asylum doctors; as he said of himself:

'I am neither the keeper of a madhouse nor do I practise this branch of the profession. . . . I have followed this inquiry from a desire to do all the good I could in my humble sphere. Accident brought me acquainted with some of the horrors of insanity when I had only commenced my medical studies . . . the impression made on my mind can never be obliterated.'[3]

The fact that Halliday was possessed of high medical qualifications and had no financial association with the treatment of insanity strengthened his authority with the medical profession. Like Ellis, he wanted to break down the barriers of fear and secrecy which still separated the insane from the rest of society.

'Why should we be ashamed to think or have it known that we have a brother or a sister afflicted with insanity? It is neither so loathsome as the smallpox, nor so dangerous as a typhus fever. There is, therefore, no more reason for mystery in the one case than in the other.'[4]

He denied that insanity was necessarily hereditary—

'I am convinced that danger can never arise to the offspring of a healthy

---

[1] This corresponds to the French use of 'moral', and may have originated with Pinel.
[2] Halliday was M.D., F.R.S., and L.R.C.P. He held the post of domestic physician to the Duke of Clarence, later William IV. See *D.N.B.*
[3] Halliday, op. cit., p. 74.
[4] Halliday, op. cit., p. 75.

mother and a healthy father merely because the one or the other may have been insane from a casual circumstance.'[1]

These three works struck a new note: an interest in insanity not merely from the clinical point of view, but as a social problem. They served to direct the attention of the medical profession away from 'vague dissertations' and 'repetitions', helping to establish a new and constructive approach to the subject.

[1] Halliday, op. cit., p. 81.

# Chapter Eight

## THE METROPOLITAN COMMISSIONERS

### I. THE SELECT COMMITTEE OF 1827

O N June 13th, 1827, the lunacy question came to the fore again, when a select committee was appointed to consider the state of pauper lunatics from the metropolitan parishes. The immediate cause of this action was the renewed investigation by Lord Robert Seymour of the conditions of Warburton's madhouses.

Lord Robert was not a member of the Committee, having retired from parliamentary life some years previously. An old and sick man, he was unable to give evidence in person, but he submitted a written statement to which considerable importance was attached.

The Committee had thirty members, but a quorum of only five. The chairman was a Dorsetshire magistrate named Robert Gordon, who was renowned for his financial acumen,[1] and who appears to have been politically allied to Peel at this time. Gordon enjoyed a brief period of parliamentary prominence in 1827–8, when he was responsible not only for this Committee, and for the two Acts resulting from its report, but also for a committee on the ill-treatment of horses and cattle at Smithfield, which excited great public interest. He became a Lunacy Commissioner after the passing of the 1828 Act, and retained that office until his death in 1864;[2] but after 1828, he appears to have faded from the parliamentary scene, and the leadership of the parliamentary group devolved upon that capable and indefatigable reformer, Lord Ashley.[3]  Gordon's speeches

---

[1] *Gent. Mag.* obit., May, 1864, which states that Gordon was known as 'the Dorsetshire Joseph Hume'.

[2] D. H. Tuke, *Hist. of Insane*, p. 203.

[3] Anthony Ashley Cooper, Lord Ashley, later 7th Earl of Shaftesbury.  See Hodder's *Life*, Hammond's *Lord Shaftesbury*, *D.N.B.*, etc. 1801–85.

show him to have been a man of wide sympathies and a considerable command of language.

Though inexplicably brief, Gordon's period of leadership fulfilled a need. Wynn and Seymour were too old, Ashley too young, to lead the new group. Gordon bridged the gap. His purpose achieved, he seems to have returned after 1828 to less spectacular activities.

Ashley was only twenty-six years of age when he was appointed to this Committee, and had been in parliament for a mere matter of months. This was the first avenue of social reform which engaged his interest, and one in which he continued to work throughout his long life. As a member of the Marlborough family and the heir to an earldom, he was to possess a far greater influence than Gordon had at his command; but during this period of his inexperience, Gordon led, and Ashley followed.

Charles Williams-Wynn served again in 1827, but took a comparatively passive role. Another member was Sir George Henry Rose,[1] son of the George Rose who died in 1818. Sir George is better known for his career as a diplomat, but he left the diplomatic service after his father's death to become his successor in the Christchurch (Hants) constituency. He seems also to have inherited his father's interest in lunacy reform. Lord Granville Somerset,[2] a younger son of the sixth Duke of Beaufort, and Charles Wood,[3] later to become the first Viscount Halifax, were other prominent and active members of this Committee. Somerset was a Peelite in his thirties, and Wood only a year older than Ashley.

This Select Committee thus provided a remarkable meeting-place for the old reformers and the new—the ageing men of experience and the young men of enthusiasm. For a few brief weeks, Lord Robert Seymour, one of the leaders in the first wave of reform, worked with the young Ashley, who was to bring about the second.

Other members of the Committee included several prominent politicians not specially distinguished for their interest in the subject, but willing to lend their political support to it: Viscount Althorp,[4] the son of that Earl Spencer to whom Sir George Onesiphorus Paul addressed his letter of 1806; Sir John Newport, a Whig banker known as 'the political

---

[1] Sir George Henry Rose, 1771–1855. See *D.N.B.*
[1] Lord Granville Somerset, 1792–1848. See *Burke's Peerage* and *D.N.B.*
[3] Charles Wood (1800–85) was a contemporary of Ashley's. *D.N.B.* dates the beginning of his official career from 1832, when he became Joint Secretary of the Treasury, but it appears that his first major parliamentary activity was in fact connected with this committee, five years earlier.
[4] John Charles Spencer, Viscount Althorp, and later 3rd Earl Spencer, 1782–1845.

ferret';[1] Thomas Spring-Rice, a future Whig Chancellor of the Exchequer;[2] John Cam Hobhouse, the Radical M.P. for Westminster, who was a friend of Francis Place;[3] and Michaelangelo Taylor, the current 'Father of the House', who had legal qualifications.[4]

The fact that the Committee was officially approved may be deduced from the inclusion among its members of Sturges-Bourne, then Secretary of State for the Home Department. It will be remembered that Sturges-Bourne was a member of the Select Committee of 1815-16.

The constitution of this Committee was thus similar to that of previous committees on lunacy: it was supported by prominent politicians from both sides of the House, but most of the active work was done by backbenchers who were prepared to make a special study of the questions involved. It differed from previous committees in that medical and legal interests were not well represented. This may have been due to the fact that its terms of reference were strictly limited, and did not involve the consideration of overall problems of the nature and treatment of insanity.

The Select Committee was appointed on June 13th, and made its report on June 29th. The report contains a body of evidence concerning the state of pauper lunatics from the metropolis, a statement on the standards of inspection which the Committee thought desirable, and some concrete recommendations. It is thus a more satisfying document than the report of 1807, which contained recommendations with very little evidence, or the reports of 1815-16, which contained a wealth of evidence and no recommendations.

*Pauper Lunatics at the White House.*

Warburton had escaped definite censure in 1816; now his madhouses were investigated again, and the so-called 'crib-room cases of Bethnal Green' provided the most startling revelation of conditions since the investigations at Bethlem and York Asylum twelve years earlier.

Mr. John Hall, a Guardian of the Poor for the parish of St. Marylebone, stated that he visited the White House in order to inspect the pauper lunatics from his own parish, whom the parish was maintaining at a cost of nine or ten shillings a week per patient.

'There was a little hesitation in showing us the place . . . we found a

[1] Sir John Newport, 1756-1843.
[2] Thomas Spring-Rice, 1790-1866. Later Lord Mounteagle. Chancellor of the Exchequer, 1835-9.
[3] John Cam Hobhouse, later Baron Broughton de Gyfford, 1786-1869.
[4] Michaelangelo Taylor, 1757-1834.

considerable number of very disgusting objects, a description of pauper lunatics, I should conceive chiefly idiots, in a very small room: they were sitting on benches round the room, and several of them were chained to the wall. The air of the room was highly oppressive and offensive, insomuch that I could not draw my breath. . . .'

These were

'the description of patients called the wet patients; they were chiefly in petticoats; the room was exceedingly oppressive from the excrement and the smell which existed there'.

Hall had been told by a discharged patient named William Solomon, who gave evidence separately, that patients were confined to cribs at a very early hour. To verify this, he called at the White House in company with Lord Robert Seymour, also a Guardian, about half-past seven in the evening.

'Mr. Jennings (the keeper) refused to let us see the patients; he complained of the visit at such an unseasonable hour; he said he hoped the legislature would protect houses from visits of that sort. Lord Robert looked at his watch, and it was then a quarter before eight. Mr. Jennings was pressed three or four times by Lord Robert, and at last he turned round and said, "Surely you would not wish to see females in their beds at this time of night?", making use of the term "night". The answer of Lord Robert was, "Show us the males".'

Jennings refused, and the Guardians were forced to withdraw. The Marylebone paupers were subsequently removed from the White House, and—for want of a better alternative—sent to Sir Jonathan Miles at Hoxton, with the condition that the house should be open to inspection by day or night.

The surgeon to the parish of St. Pancras, who visited the pauper lunatics of that parish from time to time in the White House, stated that there was:

'No observance whatever as to regulation of diet . . . no observance of sending them back to bed when they are sick; I scarcely ever go there but I do not find someone that is lingering about the yard in a half-dying state that ought to be in bed. They are entirely at the mercy of the keepers; and my visit is of no use as a medical visit.'

The overseers of St. Pancras paid nine shillings per patient, and the surgeon was asked whether an increase in the amount would be likely to lead to better conditions.

'I do not think they would be a bit better off for the increase; the evil is in the system, and that evil begins in the parishes which send them off at once to a house for incurables.'

The Committee then turned its attention to the crib-room cases. Previous witnesses had heard of this room, but had not seen it; positive evidence was given by Mr. Richard Roberts, the assistant to the overseers of St. George's Hanover Square:

'A crib-room is a place where there are nothing but wooden cribs or bedsteads; cases, in fact, filled with straw and covered with a blanket, in which those unfortunate beings are placed at night; and they sleep most of them naked on the straw, covered with a blanket'.

The details of this type of accommodation were supplied by John Nettle, an ex-patient, who had personally experienced it. The unclean patients were placed in the cribs at three o'clock in the afternoon, their arms and legs secured, and left there until nine o'clock on the following morning. At the week-ends, they were secured at three o'clock on Saturday afternoon, and left there until nine o'clock on Monday. Food was brought to them, and their arms were freed just sufficiently to enable them to eat it. On Monday, they were taken out into the yard, and the accumulated excrement was washed from them with a mop dipped in cold water. When Nettle was convalescent, and freed from the crib-room, he went back to examine the cribs.

'I turned the straw out of some of the cribs, and there were maggots in the bottom of them where the sick men had laid.'

John Dunston, who had testified in 1816, was called to give evidence. He stated that he was a surgeon, and that he attended the White House every other day; Warburton stated that an apothecary lived within three or four hundred yards of the house, and had been repeatedly called in when John Dunston was not available; on closer questioning, however, he was unable to recall the apothecary's name. When he was questioned on the crib-room cases by Robert Gordon, the following dialogue ensued:

'If all the violent cases in your establishment are confined from Saturday to Monday, do you consider that an unnecessary confinement?
'—I consider it necessary to confine them.

'Do you consider it necessary to confine all violent crib patients in your establishment from Saturday night to Monday every week?
'—They were not confined under my direction, certainly.
'Do you consider it necessary?
'(The witness hesitated.)
'Do you decline answering the question?
'—I do.'

The most striking instance of evasion and falsehood was that provided by Mr. Cordell, John Dunston's 'occasional assistant', best told in Gordon's subsequent speech to the House of Commons:

'This person was asked whether any register was kept of the state of the patients. He replied, "Yes, we have the most perfect register you can conceive; it is an account of the treatment and condition of every patient, moral and medical: it is, for accuracy and neatness, a perfect . . . pattern. We can trace the illness of every patient for six or seven years, and we can find a statement of every prescription written for him, and every circumstance attending the progress of his malady." Would the House believe that there was not one word of truth in this statement? Could they believe that it was wholly false? Yet so it was.'[1]

After making the statement mentioned, Cordell was sent for by the Committee a second time.

'Are we to understand that all you have said to us is correct?
'—Yes, very probably. (A laugh.)
'Is the story of the book?
'—No.
'Which are we to believe—what you have to-day told us, or your previous statement?
'—Take your choice. (A laugh.)
'He then admitted that it was all false.'[2]

*Standards of the Commissioners, 1827.*

A footnote to the conditions at the White House is provided by the evidence of two Commissioners who were still operating under the defective Act of 1774. Dr. Grant David Yates said that he understood the mode of management to be merely for confinement, not cure. Dr.

[1] Hansard, February 19th, 1828.
[2] *The Times*, February 20th, 1828—a fuller account than that given in Hansard or the Report.

Alexander Frampton considered the White House to be 'excellently regulated . . . a very good house'. He agreed that there was no glass in the windows, but that was 'usual' in institutions of this kind. He had no objection to the establishment.

'Have you ever seen any county lunatic asylum?
'—I have not.
'You have not thought it part of your duty . . . either to examine New Bedlam or to examine any lunatic asylum in order to form a comparative view of the treatment at Mr. Warburton's and those other establishments near London?
'—I have not examined any of those asylums.
'How many visitations do you make to each (madhouse) in the course of a year?
'—Seldom more than one.'

*Standards of the Parliamentary Reformers, 1827.*

Appendix III of the Report was particularly valuable. It consisted of a detailed list of 'Inquiries relative to Lunatic Asylums and the Treatment of the Insane', tabulated by the parliamentary reformers, which showed how far the theory of lunacy administration had advanced in more enlightened circles than those frequented by the Commissioners. The suggested inquiries are here given at some length because they give a clear picture of the kind of asylum people like Gordon and Ashley had in mind as the ideal:

On accommodation:
    Is the separation of the sexes complete?
    Are the dormitories properly ventilated?
    Are the courtyards airy and dry . . . do they afford some prospect over the walls?
    Are there complete baths for hot and cold water?
On the physical care of the patients:
    What steps are taken to ensure the personal cleanliness of the patients, particularly of the most unclean?
    How often is bathing insisted on generally?
    Is the practice of daily exercise . . . insisted on with all patients able to partake of it?
On occupation:
    How far has manual labour been adopted with advantage, and with what description of patients?

Has the active engagement of the mind to the sciences, fine arts, literature or mechanical arts been attempted with patients of a superior description; and what has been the result?

Where graver studies would be unsuitable, has it been found beneficial to afford patients such employments as are calculated to engage the attention to external objects . . . such, for example, as drawing, painting, designs, models, gardening, etc.?

Where the mind is so diseased as to be evidently unfit for the foregoing exercises, has benefit been experienced by furnishing the patients in their courtyards with means of innocent amusement, from music, domestic animals, poultry, birds, flowers, and objects of a similar nature?

Is it the opinion of the superintendent that a state of entire indolence and mental inertness is decidedly prejudicial to the patient?

On moral treatment:

In the moral treatment of the patients, is it considered an object of importance to encourage their own efforts of self-restraint in every possible way, by exciting and cherishing in them feelings of self-respect, by treating them with delicacy, more especially in avoiding any improper exposure of their cases before strangers in their own presence; and generally by maintaining towards them a treatment uniformly judicious and kind, sympathizing with them, and at the same time diverting their minds from painful and injurious associations?

This questionnaire was apparently sent to asylum authorities, though there was at that time no statutory power to compel them to answer. Dr. E. P. Charlesworth's book, *Considerations on the Moral Management of Insane Persons*, published in 1828, consists largely of the answers given at the Lincoln Asylum, where he was then superintendent.

The influence of the Retreat is clearly to be seen in the formulation of these questions; however difficult it might be to universalize the Tukes' system of treatment, it was set as the ideal towards which institutions of every type must strive. The reformers were no longer concerned only with material standards of well-being—cleanliness, order, and quietude; though the second part of the Report showed that even these minimum requirements were lacking in Warburton's treatment of the lunatic poor at Bethnal Green.

*Results of the Investigation.*

The conclusions to be drawn from this mass of evidence were clear:

'If the White House is to be taken as a fair specimen of similar establish-ments, your committee cannot too strongly or too anxiously express their conviction that the greatest possible benefit will accrue to pauper patients by the erection of a County Lunatic Asylum.'

The result was the construction of the large Middlesex Asylum at Hanwell, which afterwards absorbed most of the insane poor from the metropolitan area.

It was also clearly necessary that legal provision should be made for more stringent inspection, and above all for more efficient and experienced inspectors. The parliamentary reformers were determined to remove the inspectorate from the sphere of the Royal College of Physicians, which had proved incompetent, and to assume the responsibility themselves. Clauses dealing with these matters were embodied in a Bill introduced by Gordon in the following year.

## 2. THE ACTS OF 1828

Gordon and his associates proceeded to introduce two Bills which, though designed not to alarm unduly the House of Lords, nevertheless carried the process of centralization a stage further. The Liverpool administration had fallen a few months earlier; the Tories of the Welling-ton-Peel coalition, uncertain of their position, were prepared to conciliate the Whigs in order to maintain themselves in office. Peel, Robert Gor-don's chief supporter, was now Secretary of State for the Home Depart-ment; and in the Lords, Eldon's iron rule was at last broken. The time was thus unusually propitious for the furtherance of the reform movement.

The Bills were framed by Gordon, Ashley, Wynn and Charles Wood,[1] and introduced in the Commons by Gordon, Peel and Ashley.[2] It was in this connection that Ashley made his maiden speech, and later wrote in his Diary, 'So, by God's blessing, my first effort has been for the advance-ment of human happiness'.[3] Peel, in spite of his other preoccupations, was consistent in his support. Lord Malmesbury was the chief spokesman in the House of Lords, and both Bills were passed without difficulty.

The Acts dealt respectively with private madhouses and with county asylums. The County Asylums Act (9 Geo. IV, c. 40), was largely a con-solidating measure, but it provided in addition for a certain degree of centralization. Visiting justices were to send annual returns of admissions,

[1] H.C.J., February 19th, 1828.
[2] H.C.J., February 20th, 1828. The Bills were obviously prepared before the official order for their preparation was given.
[3] Quoted Hodder's *Life*, vol. 1, p. 97.

discharges and deaths to the Secretary of State for the Home Department, who acquired the power to send any visitor he chose to inspect any asylum. Such visitors were to be paid a fee out of the asylum funds. This link with the Home Department was the first step towards bringing all institutions for the insane under one form of administration.

The Madhouse Act (9 Geo. IV, c. 41) also simplified the administrative structure, since it covered not only private madhouses, but also all subscription hospitals with the exception of Bethlem.

The Act did not abolish the distinction between metropolitan and provincial houses, but it removed the power of inspecting the former from the jurisdiction of the medical profession and placed it under that of a statutory authority. The number of Commissioners was increased to fifteen. Five of these were to be physicians who were to be paid at the rate of £1 per hour; the others were to be unpaid. All were to be appointed by the Secretary of State for the Home Department, and were to make an annual report to him. They were to visit each asylum four times a year 'between the hours of eight in the morning and six in the evening in winter and six in the morning to eight in the evening in summer, with or without notice, and for such a length of time as they think fit'. They could visit at night if malpractice had been alleged on oath. They were to meet quarterly for the purpose of granting licences, and were given power to recommend to the Secretary of State for the Home Department that certain licences should be revoked or refused. They could release any person who was in their estimation improperly confined.

Similar provisions applied to the visiting justices in the provinces, where two justices and a medical visitor appointed at Quarter Sessions were to visit each house four times yearly, and to submit a report to the Home Department.

The Act also provided for a more detailed form of certification of patients, designed to obviate the possibility of illegal detention:

'. . . and be it further enacted that every Certificate upon which any Order be given for the Confinement of any Person (not a Parish Patient) . . . shall be signed by two Medical Practitioners . . . who shall have separately visited and personally examined the Person to whom it refers, and such Certificate shall state that such Insane Person is a proper Person to be confined, and the Day on which he or she shall have been so examined, and also the Christian and Surname and Place of Abode of the Person by whose Direction or Authority such Patient is examined and the

Degree of Relationship or other Circumstance of Connection between such Person and the Insane Person, and the Name, Age, Place of Residence, and the Asylum, if any, in which such Person shall have been confined . . . provided always that no Physician, Surgeon or Apothecary shall sign any Certificate of Admission to any House for the Reception of two or more Insane Persons of which he is wholly or partly the Proprietor or the regular Professional Attendant.'

Pauper patients were to be admitted on the signature of two justices or of the parish overseer, the incumbent of the parish, and one medical practitioner.

The Act did not introduce any specific provisions with regard to treatment, save that it ensured that each house should have regular medical attention. All establishments containing more than one hundred patients were to have a resident medical officer. Those containing less than a hundred patients were to be visited by a medical practitioner not less than twice a week. Proprietors were to keep records which could be inspected by the visitors (i.e., the Commissioners or the visiting justices). Schedule B of the Act gives the details of the returns which were required. They included the number of curable patients in the house, differentiated by sex, the number of those judged to be incurable, details of those under restraint, and general remarks on patients' conditions. Restraint was only to be imposed by the order of the medical attendant, who might be a physician, a surgeon, or an apothecary.

Divine Service was to be performed every Sunday in the presence of the patients[1] and the relative or friend on whose authority the proceedings for certification had been initiated was obliged to visit the patient twice a year, or to appoint someone to carry out this duty for him. Records of certification, admission, and death or discharge of patients were to be kept, and to be forwarded annually to the Commissioners or the justices in metropolitan and provincial areas respectively.

### 3. THE NEW COMMISSIONERS AT WORK

The first Commissioners appointed under the 1828 Madhouse Act took office in the same year. Eleven of them were members or ex-members of parliament, and five were medical practitioners. The chairman was Lord Granville Somerset, and other members included Robert Gordon, Lord Ashley, Lord Robert Seymour, Charles Williams-Wynn, and Sir George Henry Rose. As might be expected, they took their duties seriously.

[1] This clause was inserted by the House of Lords.

The reports made by them to the Secretary of State in 1830 show that even in the space of two years their vigilant inspection had brought about a great change in conditions. Of the notorious White House, they were able to report that they were:

'. . . much gratified with the general condition of the House . . . Mr. Warburton has devoted much pains to the improvement of this establishment, and the result is highly creditable'.

Ashley found another of Warburton's houses 'extremely clean and well-ventilated . . . greatly improved'. Gordon complained that the kitchen and privy accommodation at Peckham House was offensive, and the proprietor immediately proceeded to have a new kitchen built. At Holly House, a statement by the Commissioners that there was only one bath produced a second by the time of their next visit, six months later. Only one house, a small madhouse at Plaistow, showed signs of flagrant maladministration. The proprietor, a Dr. Elliot, had been in debt to the local butcher and baker; his creditors had seized possession of the house, and at the time of the Commissioners' visit, were attempting to run it themselves. The capabilities and standards of the butcher and the baker were apparently of a low order, for the Commissioners immediately sent in a strong recommendation to the Secretary of State that the licence be revoked, and this was done.

A study of the Commissioners' first reports shows that they did in fact abide by the standards laid down in the 1827 Report, and that their inspection was highly effective. Madhouse proprietors who had flouted the spirit, if not the letter, of the law since 1774, seem to have recognized that they could no longer do so, and that the only alternative to compliance with the Commissioners' demands was a total loss of livelihood.

Although the system worked well, and resulted in an improvement of standards inside the metropolitan madhouses, the reformers were not satisfied that it dealt adequately with the question of possible illegal detention. Medical representation among the Commissioners had been safeguarded, but legal representation had not, and the legal aspects of insanity had been largely ignored. An Act passed in 1832 (2 and 3 Will. IV, c. 107) redressed the balance by stating that at least two of the Commissioners must be barristers, and by removing the inspectorate from the jurisdiction of the Secretary of State to that of the Lord Chancellor. This last was in some ways a retrogressive step, since it decreased the immediate possibility of a centralized and uniform control. County asylums continued to be under the supervisory authority of the Secretary of State.

# Chapter Nine

## LOCAL AND DEPARTMENTAL DEVELOPMENTS, 1832-42

A FTER 1832, there were still five separate ways in which insane people might be confined, and it may be useful at this point to recapitulate them:

1. In private madhouses under Gordon's Act and the Act of 1832. The departmental authority was the Lord Chancellor's Office.
2. In county asylums under the second of Gordon's Acts, the ultimate control being that of the Home Department.
3. In workhouses, controlled until 1834 by the local authorities, and after that date by the Poor Law Commissioners.
4. In Bethlem, which was still exempt from all legal supervision.
5. As single lunatics. The Madhouse Act of 1828 contained provision for the compilation of a list of single lunatics, but this clause was so hedged about with precautions and restrictions to ensure secrecy that it remained virtually a dead letter.

Thus, even as late as 1842, we still have to deal with five distinct systems of administration, the possible relationship between which was only dimly recognized. Before turning to the final movement which led to the establishment of a central control, it is necessary to discuss briefly the developments which took place in each category between 1832 and 1842.

### I. PRIVATE MADHOUSES

Although private madhouses in the London area had greatly improved in character, the situation, especially with regard to problems of illegal detention, was still far from satisfactory. Mention can only be made here of a few of the outstanding cases which excited the public attention during this period.

John Mitford, Esq., of London produced about 1830 two pamphlets— 'The Crimes and Horrors of Warburton's Private Madhouse' and 'The Crimes and Horrors of Kelly House'. These publications, couched in lurid and unrestrained language, clearly catered for the sensation-seeking public. It is significant that the details given by the author were almost entirely sexual in character.

A more serious publication was Richard Paternoster's 'The Madhouse System'—a series of sketches published in pamphlet form in 1841. Paternoster was a man of good education—he claimed to have been a Civil Servant in Madras—and the sketches are peppered with classical allusions. The work is bitter, sometimes abusive, and clearly biased, but it shows a vehement preoccupation with the subject of civil liberty which lifts it out of the class of merely sensational literature.

Paternoster was confined in Finch's madhouse in London in 1838 on the representation of his father, who wished to defraud him of a sum of money. Having some apprehension of this, he had taken the precaution of depositing the money with an attorney in Chancery Lane, some time before his seizure. He was captured by violence, and deprived of any contact with the outside world. The keeper in whose charge he was placed was a man who had been convicted five years previously for homosexual offences. Paternoster had journalistic connections; his friends notified the police, the Commissioners and the Press. Nevertheless, it took six full weeks for him to be freed according to the due process of law.

The picture of conditions in the London madhouses given in this pamphlet is very different from that given by the Commissioners. At Finch's House, he alleged, the linen was foul, the food revolting, restraint and cold baths were commonly used as methods of intimidation, and the answer to every complaint was, 'It's your delusion.' At Brook House, Clapham, which was owned by Thomas Monro,[1] Paternoster reported that

'. . . the coercive system is in full force, as might be expected from the cruel, brutal system of the owner, whose conduct to the patients in Bedlam has so often been a matter of enquiry and comment'.

Warburton had a thousand patients in all, and personally supervised none of them. Even George Man Burrows,[2] owner of the Clapham Retreat, was an absentee proprietor.

---

[1] Monro returned to private practice in 1816, following his dismissal from Bethlem.
[2] See pp. 130-1.

How can Paternoster's account be reconciled with the Commissioners' reports? The Commissioners were men skilled in the detection of abuse, and long experienced in the possibility of malpractice, so that it is hard to believe that they were so fully deceived as Paternoster would imply. He was, of course, a man embittered by his own experience; and he was a journalist. Moreover, having no previous experience of the subject of mental illness, he was probably unprepared for the manifestations which frequently accompany it. Nevertheless, his pamphlet pointed the need for continuous and unceasing vigilance on the part of the Commissioners.

The case of Lewis Phillips is a more fully authenticated instance of abuse, since it was recounted in the House of Commons by Thomas Duncombe,[1] and uncontested.

Phillips was a prosperous London business man, a partner in a firm of glass and lamp manufacturers. On March 16th, 1838, at the suggestion of one of his patrons (whose name is not revealed) he presented himself at Buckingham Palace in an attempt to secure the patronage of the young Queen Victoria. There had been an attempt on the life of the Queen a few weeks before, and the Palace guards were suspicious. Phillips, who was evidently a hot-tempered man, expostulated with them, and was finally arrested on a charge of attempting to force an entry to the royal quarters.

His lawyer, hastily summoned, was able to convince the authorities of his client's respectable standing, and Phillips was released; at this juncture he made the fundamental mistake of returning to the Palace in order to make trouble for the person who had caused his arrest. He was again arrested on the same charge, taken to Bow Street, and thence removed on a magistrate's warrant 'in a hackney coach, closely guarded' to one of Warburton's houses.

He remained at Bethnal Green for six months. He had no knowledge of why he had been sent to the Palace on a false pretext, who was responsible for his arrest, or why he had been sent to an asylum. Although the law required that his order of committal should be signed by at least one doctor who had no financial connection in the establishment concerned, he had been examined only by Warburton. He received no visitors, and was allowed no communication with the outside world.

---

[1] The Phillips case was recounted in full to the House in the debates preceding the Lunatics Act of 1845. See Hansard for July 11th, 1845. Duncombe (1796-1861) was well known as a champion of lost causes and a discoverer of abuses of the law. He had succeeded Wakley as M.P. for Finsbury.

The Lunacy Commissioners made their statutory round of inspection, but the patients were intimidated in advance. Phillips alleged that a woman who ventured a complaint was subsequently beaten severely by the head attendant, who afterwards reappeared with the words 'That has cured her of complaining'.

Moreover, Phillips claimed that the staff of the madhouse went to extraordinary lengths to turn his brain. On the day of the Queen's coronation, he stated,

'. . . some strange female was actually introduced to your petitioner dressed in paltry imitation of our Sovereign, to induce your petitioner to believe that it was her Gracious Majesty . . . the officers, both medical and otherwise, assisted in this nefarious scheme . . . your petitioner has suffered the torture of mind and body through the acts and filthy observations and questions, too disgusting to be mentioned . . .'

At this juncture, the motive force behind his confinement became clear. Lewis Phillips received a visit from his cousins and partners in the firm— Ralph and Samuel Phillips. They offered to secure his release, arrange his passage to Antwerp, and to provide him with a small allowance—all on condition that he signed away his interest in the family business. Evidently they had been responsible for the entire sequence of events.

Rather than remain indefinitely in the hands of Dr. Warburton, Phillips signed, and took the passage to Antwerp; but within a few days he was back in London, determined to have his legal rights. Dr. Warburton was hastily notified, and at night two keepers arrived at Phillips' house to take him back to the madhouse.

'Your petitioner, having endured so much misery, was fully prepared for any design that might show itself, and seeing the manœuvres, immediately forced his way out of the house, crying "Murder", the keepers hallooing out "Stop, thief!"'

Phillips escaped—by what means, he does not say—and succeeded eventually in indicting all the parties concerned in his detention for conspiracy. The matter was finally settled out of court for £170.

The Phillips case, more than any other, proved that in spite of the new safeguards which looked so effective on paper, cases of illegal detention could and did still occur. Both Phillips and Paternoster were men of resourcefulness and good education who succeeded in making their wrongs public knowledge; but it was disquieting to reflect that there might be many other cases in which the victim was not able to conduct his own defence. Improved methods of certification and inspection were still an urgent necessity.

## 2. COUNTY ASYLUMS

After 1828, the county asylums, which had hitherto been few in number and widely misunderstood as to purpose, gradually emerged as the most significant factor in the development of lunacy reform. Hitherto, pioneer work had been done by voluntary effort—at the Manchester Lunatic Hospital, at the Retreat. Now the impetus came from statutory institutions such as those at Lincoln and Hanwell.

### The Non-Restraint Movement

In these two asylums developed the theory and practice of non-restraint, which carried 'moral management' to the logical extreme of stating that no patient should be subject to mechanical restraint at any time, whatever his condition. The system was never adopted at the Retreat, where the Tukes always insisted on a minimum of restraint in violent cases in order to protect the patient himself and those around him; but at Lincoln and Hanwell, the system was carried out in full, and enjoyed for some years the attention of those who were seeking more enlightened methods of treatment for insanity.

During the period 1828-42, eight further county asylums were constructed in England, making a total of sixteen, as follows:

| Asylum | Accommodation |
|---|---|
| Chester | 110 |
| Dorset | 113 |
| Kent | 300 |
| Middlesex | 1000 |
| Norfolk | 470 |
| Suffolk | 591 |
| Surrey | — |
| Leicester | 104[1] |

The Middlesex Asylum at Hanwell was thus the largest in the country, being nearly twice the size of the next largest, those at Lancaster (now accommodating 600 patients) and Suffolk (591). The experiment in non-restraint began at Lincoln, which was comparatively small, having only

[1] *Report of Metropolitan Commissioners in Lunacy, 1844*, Appendix D. No figure was given for the Surrey Asylum, which was still in the course of erection.

72 patients in 1829 and 130 in 1837[1], when the total abolition of restraint
was finally achieved. The subsequent adoption of the system at Hanwell,
which served the metropolitan area and now took the majority of those
pauper patients who had formerly been confined in Warburton's madhouses, thus meant the development of the experiment on a much wider
scale, and attracted a proportionate amount of public attention.

D. H. Tuke makes the point that to speak of 'non-restraint' in this
context is terminologically inaccurate, since confinement in an asylum
is always restraint of a kind.[2] Moreover, in those asylums where 'non-
restraint' was practised, it was permissible for the attendants to hold down
violent patients with their hands, or to place them in solitary confinement.[3]
'Non-restraint' is therefore used here only in the limited sense in which it
was used at Lincoln and Hanwell—to imply the non-use of mechanical
devices which hindered the patients' bodily movements.

This policy was commenced at Lincoln by the visiting physician, Dr.
Charlesworth, who gradually reduced the instances of the use of restraint
between 1829 and 1835. Restraint was totally abolished by the house
surgeon, Mr. Robert Gardiner Hill, between 1835 and 1838. Since much
time and energy were wasted by these two officials in fruitless argument
as to which should claim the merit of having introduced the system, it is
necessary to set out here the basis on which their respective claims were
made:[4]

1829-35: *under the supervision of Dr. Charlesworth*

|  | | | Patients | No. restrained | Total instances of restraint |
|---|---|---|---|---|---|
| 1829 | . | . | 72 | 39 | 1727 |
| 1830 | . | . | 92 | 54 | 2364 |
| 1831 | . | . | 70 | 40 | 1004 |
| 1832 | . | . | 81 | 55 | 1401 |
| 1833 | . | . | 87 | 44 | 1109 |
| 1834 | . | . | 109 | 45 | 447 |
| 1835 | . | . | 108 | 28 | 323 |

These figures, taken together, show that the real move towards the
substantial reduction of the use of restraint started in 1834, when the
number of patients restrained was for the first time less than 50% of the

---

[1] R. Gardiner Hill, *The Non-Restraint System of Treatment of Lunacy*, etc., 1857, p. 184.
[2] D. H. Tuke, *Hist. of Insane*, p. 204.
[3] *Report of Metropolitan Commissioners*, 1844, pp. 137-8.
[4] Gardiner Hill, *The Non-Restraint System, passim.*

total number of patients, and the number of instances of restraint per patient restrained fell by one-half.

In the first three years of Gardiner Hill's supervision, the figures were as follows:

1836–38: *under the supervision of Mr. Gardiner Hill*

|      | Patients | No. restrained | Total instances of restraint |
|------|----------|----------------|------------------------------|
| 1836 . . | 115 | 12 | 39 |
| 1837 . . | 130 | 2 | 3 |
| 1838 . . | ——— all restraint abolished ——— | | |

Thus, within twelve months of taking up his position, Gardiner Hill improved on Charlesworth's work, and within three years he carried it to its logical, though possibly unforeseen, conclusion.

When Gardiner Hill arrived at Lincoln in 1836, the methods of restraint still in use included boot hobbles, which fastened the feet to the end of the bed and prevented the patient from shifting his position; and a belt and wristlocks similar to those designed by Dr. Slade Knight for use at Lancaster.

Gardiner Hill realized that it was impossible merely to abolish all restraint without providing other means for quieting noisy or violent patients. He induced the visiting justices to increase the staff, and also to increase the remuneration, so that it would be possible to recruit relatively intelligent and well-trained nurses. He looked especially for tall, strong attendants whose physique would in itself deter patients from violence. He instituted a continuous night watch on the dormitories, and decreed that all patients should have abundant exercise, with the object of reducing violence by the effect of sheer exhaustion. All fermented liquor was banned from the institution—in opposition to the practice at the Retreat. where copious draughts of porter were held to have a calming influence,

This system undoubtedly helped the patients. Experience at Bethlem after 1815 and at the Retreat had already shown that many patients could be restored to quietude and cleanliness by sudden freedom from restraint. Pinel found the same thing in France. Gardiner Hill's real departure from precedent lay in the fact that he openly abolished restraint even for suicidal and homicidal patients, and worked without the threat of restraint to reinforce discipline as a last resort.

One alternative to the use of mechanical restraint was, of course, the use of drugs to quiet patients, but this too was avoided at Lincoln after 1835.

L

'Every deviation from this principle should be immediately checked,' wrote Gardiner Hill, 'that neither unnecessary force nor drugs nor the douche nor the bath of surprise nor prolonged shower nor other baths be employed as substitutes . . . they form no part of the system of non-restraint.'

He published in his book a letter said to have been written by a female patient to a friend, which gave an encouraging picture of the conditions at Lincoln:

'I am in the wards up and down, where there are 33 female patients. I have not seen a strait-waistcoat nor yet leather sleeves, nor leg-locks nor muzzles nor other sorts of confinements. Say or do what you will, there is no fault found. The nurses all seem very loving and dutiful to the patients. If your finger only aches, the House Surgeon attends several times a day; and at night, if he sees any of them unruly, he orders a nurse to sit up with them. The bedrooms are carpeted (feather beds, most of them with hangings), wash-stands, basins, towels, looking-glass, comb and brush, and a nurse to attend us. We have tea twice a day, and as much toast as we can eat—milk and bread for our supper, meat dinners every day, and different sorts of puddings. The Matron of the Asylum stands at the table, and asks whether we are all satisfied; and if anyone wants more, she orders a nurse to bring it. She wishes to see us all comfortable. We go to bed at eight o'clock; we have nothing to do only to walk in the gardens twice a day, and cards to play, and other sorts of exercises. I never was better off since I left my parents.'

This system, while ideal for the average patient, imposed a tremendous strain on the attendants, who ran some physical risk and were responsible for a continuous and uninterrupted surveillance of all patients; but it had one great advantage: the removal of the pressure of fear.

*The Charlesworth-Gardiner Hill Controversy.*

It would be unnecessary to recall the facts of this unresolved and protracted argument were it not for the fact that the dispute reached far beyond the bounds of Lincoln, and thus gave the new system more publicity than it would otherwise have received. It continued until 1853, and ended in the collection of rival subscriptions for Gardiner Hill and Charlesworth. The former was presented with a silver tea-service, the centre-piece being engraved with the statement that he alone was responsible for the introduction of the system of non-restraint. Dr. Charlesworth being at that time deceased, his supporters had to content themselves with the erection in the grounds of Lincoln Asylum of a statue bearing a similar inscription.

Many medical men were involved in the controversy, and Sir Alexander Morison, physician of Bethlem, and former physician to the Surrey Asylum, earned general opprobrium by contributing to both funds. A lengthy controversy raged in the *Lancet* from 1850 to 1853; the *Medical Circular* accused the *Lancet* of receiving bribes, alleging that an article written by the Charlesworth faction had been published on receipt of a monetary payment. The *Lancet* referred to the *Medical Circular* as a 'scurrilous medical print', and stated that the charges were 'base and unfounded'. The *Medical Circular* then accused the editor of the *Lancet* of 'a career of habitual corruption'.

Most of the events here referred to fall outside the period immediately under review, but it is necessary to mention them in order to illustrate the widespread stir which the matter caused. Gardiner Hill delivered a lecture on 'The total abolition of personal restraint in the treatment of the insane' to a lay and medical audience at the Mechanics' Institute in Lincoln in June, 1838, and the lecture was afterwards published, forming the basis of his book. To quote Gardiner Hill's account of the subsequent furore:

'Public attention was soon aroused, as well it might be, to the subject . . . indeed for many years I was stigmatized as one bereft of reason myself, a speculator, peculator, and a practical breaker of the sixth commandment by exposing the lives of the attendants to the fury of the patients.'

The system was called 'a piece of contemptible quackery, a mere bait for the public ear'. Opposition grew in fact even among the Visiting Committee of the Asylum, so that Gardiner Hill was ultimately compelled to resign his appointment.

'In fact, it was impossible to remain. The attendants were encouraged in acts of disobedience, and all control was lost. Had I retained my appointment, I must have sacrificed my principles.'

Gardiner Hill seems to have returned to private practice, for he remained in the vicinity of Lincoln, and in 1852 became Mayor of the city.

*Non-Restraint at Northampton.*

The system was adopted in 1839 at the new Northampton Asylum by its first superintendent, Dr. Pritchard. This was, in the circumstances, a

hazardous undertaking, since the Asylum was as yet uncompleted. Many difficulties and apparent dangers,' wrote Dr. Pritchard,
'interposed to check our adoption of Mr. R. G. Hill's system; an unfinished building, numerous workmen employed in every direction, the inexperience and timidity of the attendants—few in number, in consequence of a prevalent disinclination to enter into our service—all contributed, during the first year, to add to the anxieties of direction and thwart my intentions, as well as to excite occasional doubts of their practicability. These impediments have long been surmounted, for they but stimulated repeated exertion and more extended enquiry; and we have the gratification of knowing that similar results have rewarded the labours of the majority of the superintendents of the largest and most celebrated hospitals in the kingdom; and that unanimity of opinion on this vital question is rapidly pervading not only our own country, but also the great continents of Europe and America.'

*Non-restraint at Hanwell.*

Dr. Pritchard wrote his report three years after the introduction of the system at Hanwell by Dr. Conolly. Though the experiment had already proved a partial success on a small scale, it was Conolly's work which drew the serious attention of medical superintendents and visiting committees to its practical application. Hanwell was by far the largest establishment for the insane in the country, and Conolly already possessed a great reputation in medical circles. He had studied in Edinburgh, practised in general medicine at Chichester and Stratford-on-Avon, becoming Mayor of Stratford. He had also been appointed Professor of the Practice of Medicine in the University of London, but relinquished this post after two years to become inspecting physician to the asylums in Warwickshire.

This unexpected action may be explained in various ways. The human reaction is that he disliked academic circles in London and preferred to live in the Stratford area, where he was well-known and appreciated. Sir George Thane, of University College Hospital, London, had another theory:[1]

'In spite of the friendship of Lord Brougham, Lord John Russell, and other very influential men, John Conolly failed in practice as a London physician, nor does it appear that his duties were performed with any distinguished ability.'

[1] Thane, *Medical Biographies.* (The lectures of Sir George Thane, Professor of Anatomy at University College Hospital, London. A student's notes in manuscript, U.C.H. Library.)

Thane judged him as 'essentially unscientific'—a good administrator, but a sentimental humanist unfitted for the detached and painstaking work of medical research.

Thane was speaking from the viewpoint of the fashionable physician and the medical research worker, so that his prejudice against Conolly, who deserted this desirable post for a branch of medicine only partially accepted and of doubtful antecedents, is perhaps only to be expected; but Conolly's interest in the treatment of the insane was not a new factor in his life, nor was it, as Thane implied, an avenue of escape from a sphere in which he had been proved a failure. Conolly's M.D. thesis, presented at Edinburgh in 1821, bore the title 'De statu mentis in Insania et Melancholia', and he had published his *Inquiry Concerning the Indications of Insanity* in 1830, the year in which he abandoned his academic post. The very qualities which made him unsuitable, in Thane's eyes, for the practice of general medicine, were admirably suited to the work of a medical administrator in a large asylum.

Conolly went to Hanwell in June, 1839. Before taking up his appointment, he visited Lincoln and undertook a thorough investigation of the methods used there, and their results.[1] This apparently convinced him that the system was workable on a large scale. In his book *On the Treatment of Insanity*, he described the steps he took to translate Lincoln's experience to Hanwell. On July 1st, he required from the officials at Hanwell a daily return of all patients kept under restraint, and within seven weeks from that time, he had totally abolished restraint.

'The coercion-chairs (forty in number),' he wrote, 'have been altogether removed from the walls . . . several patients formerly consigned to them, silent, stupid and sinking into fatuity, may now be seen cheerfully moving about the walls or airing-courts; and there can be no question that they have been happily set free from a thraldom of which one constant and lamentable consequence was the acquisition of uncleanly habits.'[2]

Conolly, like Gardiner Hill, realized that the abolition of restraint was only one factor in a new approach to the insane. If it was to be carried out successfully, it demanded a high standard of nursing and administrative staff, and the development of new ways of occupying the patients. Working in conjunction with the asylum chaplain, the Rev. John May, he established classes in reading and writing for the illiterate, and in drawing, singing and geography for the literate. This was the first experiment in

[2] Gardiner Hill, *Non-Restraint System*, p. 17.
[2] Quoted by D. H. Tuke, *Hist. of Insane*, p. 207.

England in the organized education of patients as part of their treatmen·
and rehabilitation. Unfortunately, the wishes of Conolly and May were
frustrated by the Visiting Committee, which—some forty years before the
introduction of universal education—considered such a measure an unnecessary expense.

'Many sources of happiness, of mental composure and, as I believe, o
means auxiliary to recovery, were . . . arbitrarily cut off,' wrote
Conolly.[1]

Conolly was in many ways ahead of his time. Among the suggestion
made by him to his Committee were two which have only come into
universal application in the twentieth century. These were:

(i) Clinical instruction in the treatment of mental abnormality to be
carried out in the asylum for qualified medical practitioners intending to specialize in this type of work. Instruction of this kind wa:
already carried out at St. Luke's, but the stream of St. Luke's·
trained men was totally inadequate to meet the needs of a developing
service. Most asylum doctors took up their appointments with no
more than a training in general medicine, which did not include
any work in the rapidly-developing science of psychiatry. Hanwell
with its large number of beds, would have provided an admirable
place for a training-school, especially in view of the fact tha
Conolly himself had experience in university teaching.

(ii) A 'place of education' for male and female keepers. Conolly wa
among the first to propound the view that the possession of a
powerful physique and good intentions was not enough, and tha
the nursing of the mentally ill should be a skilled profession.

The Committee negatived these suggestions, presumably on the ground
of expense, and Conolly was forced to work within the framework dic-
tated by them.

*Staff problems in county asylums.*

Not all asylums were as fortunate as Hanwell in their medical superintendent. Caleb Crowther, in his *Observations on the Management of Mad·
houses*[2] raised an important question: were the prevailing conditions o
appointment such that superintendents were encouraged to exercise thei

---

[1] On the Treatment of Insanity (1856) pp. 276-7.
[2] Published in 1838. Caleb Crowther was then the senior physician to the West Riding
Asylum at Wakefield.

powers in a responsible manner? He came to the conclusion that they were not—that in most cases the superintendents were so well paid and their duties so loosely defined that they tended to mix socially with the landed gentry and to ignore their real duties.

The election of the superintendent was in the hands of the Visiting Committee, which was of course drawn mainly from the landed gentry of the neighbourhood. It was therefore natural that they should appoint one of their own kind where possible, and that the superintendent should exert himself to remain in social contact with them. The conditions of his appointment in many cases made this only too easy. He was commonly required to be resident in the asylum, and was provided with everything he could need for normal living—food, light, fuel, servants and furniture. He could entertain on a large scale out of the asylum funds, and received in addition a generous salary. The Resident Director of the Wakefield Asylum received £550 a year for himself and his wife, plus services valued at not less than £400 a year. He was thus in receipt of a gross salary of nearly £1000 per annum at a time when a living wage was well under £1 per week.

The Visiting Committee of the Cornwall Asylum had exerted itself to prevent its chief officer from absenting himself without authority, but in other asylums, the superintendent was frequently away from duty. Crowther cited a case at the Wakefield Asylum in 1833. A suicidal patient named Ackroyd seized a razor and killed himself; it was stated at the inquest that the Director had been away at the time, and that no orders had been given to the staff for the supervision of suicidal patients. When the coroner inquired whether such absences were usual, he was told that the Director was

'. . . very often from home, sometimes for weeks together . . . sometimes on the Rhine, sometimes with the fox-hounds, and very often in the streets of Leeds or Wakefield.'

It was still the common practice for the matron to be the wife of the superintendent. While this made for simplicity of administration, it was from other points of view highly undesirable. It meant that experienced female staff were controlled by an inexperienced woman who combined a nominal post with marriage and the begetting and rearing of children, and who also shared the social round to which her husband's social position entitled her. Unless she was a very exceptional woman, she was likely to have neither the aptitude nor the inclination to exercise efficient supervision over the female side of the asylum.

Crowther wrote in 1838: it may have been partly as a result of his work that when the Surrey Asylum was opened in 1841, the Visiting Committee drew up rules which attempted to define the duties of the superintendent and the matron, and to ensure that those duties were fully carried out.[1] The superintendent was to be a qualified medical man—a surgeon or an apothecary; he was to be resident in the Asylum, and to absent himself only with the consent of the Visiting Committee. His post was to be a full-time one, and he was forbidden to undertake private practice. He was to visit all the patients (there were 350 when the Asylum opened) every day; to keep case-books; to report to the Committee on every case of the use of restraint or seclusion; to control the attendants and staff; and to read prayers without fail morning and evening. His salary was £150 a year.

No qualifications were prescribed for the matron, since there was of course no appropriate qualification that a woman might possess; but she was preserved to some extent from the pitfalls of a life of luxury by the provision that she must visit all the female wards before ten o'clock in the morning, attend prayers morning and evening, and be responsible for the employment and conduct of the female staff. Her salary was £80 a year.

The problem of ensuring that the keepers fulfilled their duties adequately was also a difficult one. Crowther stated that dysentery was general in asylums because the cleaning of dirty patients was left to other patients, who ignored the most elementary principles of hygiene. There were many ways in which the attendants could avoid the more unpleasant aspects of their duties—by employing the quieter patients to do the work for them, by using intimidation, mechanical restraint or seclusion, or by simply putting troublesome patients to bed for long periods. This last practice had been exposed in Bethlem and the private madhouses, but it apparently continued to some degree in the county asylums. Dr. Browne, in his book, *What Asylums Were, Are, and Ought to Be*, published in 1837, pointed out that the generally-accepted proportion was that of one keeper to thirty patients, and that it was impossible under such circumstances for the patients to be adequately cared for. He related a case in which a visitor inquired after a certain patient, and received from the keeper the reply, 'Oh, Mr. D. is perfectly quiet; he has been standing on his head for the last half hour.' He also made the point that while keepers were so few in number, they naturally tended to remain together for company and safety rather than walking singly about the wards. He referred to the keepers as

[1] *Rules of Surrey Asylum.* Published with Visiting Justices' Reports for 1844-6.

'. . . the unemployed of other professions . . . if they possess physical strength and a tolerable reputation for sobriety, it is enough; and the latter quality is frequently dispensed with. They enter upon their duties altogether ignorant of what insanity is.'

Again the Surrey Asylum's Committee provided detailed rules to overcome the worst of these abuses. The attendants were to rise at 6 a.m., to 'wash and comb' the patients, to report any illness, and to attend prayers. At 8 a.m., they were to serve breakfast, and to proceed to clean the sleeping-rooms, personally removing any foul straw or linen. They were to serve other meals at specified times, to attend the patients at intervals during the day, and to attend evening prayers at 9.30 p.m.

'The attendants are forbidden to strike or otherwise ill-treat the patients . . . on pain of IMMEDIATE DISMISSAL.'

In 1844, Sir Alexander Morison, the visiting physician, succeeded in instituting lectures for male and female attendants, in which he

'. . . endeavoured to communicate in a familiar and . . . intelligible manner, the principles on which our conduct towards the insane ought to be regulated.'[1]

Morison was thus the first to carry Conolly's idea into effect. Prizes were awarded to attendants whose conduct was judged meritorious, in order to provide them with an incentive for carrying out their duties well. The first steps were being taken to overcome the abuses of the existing staffing system, and to raise the status of mental nursing to that of a profession.

*Problems of Accommodation.*

The principles of classification were by now fully understood, and in some places even too stringently applied; but in many asylums, the staffs were attempting to give expression to these principles in buildings which had been erected before they were propounded. So fast had been the developments in practice that asylums built only thirty years before were already in some respects out of date. Most asylums were now too small to provide adequate beds for the areas which they served; visiting committees had to choose between piecemeal extension and acceptance of the known evils of the waiting-list.

Browne suggested a revolutionary principle designed to overcome

---

[1] Reports of Visiting Justices of Surrey Asylum, 1844–6.

these difficulties—that of housing the patients not in one large institution-type building, but in a number of cottages grouped on an estate. This system was already in operation on the continent. It had the advantage of housing all the patients in buildings only one storey high, thus lessening the risks of accidents and suicides; it provided a more home-like environment, and gave the patients a sense of belonging to a small, well-defined community, besides being infinitely more cheerful than 'an almost interminable succession of wards and corridors under one roof'.[1]

The village-system was not adopted in England during this period, and its application in this country has always been a limited one. There are certain disadvantages: the lack of centralized administration, and the rigid seclusion of those patients not fit to be allowed to go freely from one house to another; but the raising of this topic showed that the disadvantages of rigid institutionalism were also beginning to be appreciated.

The general picture of the county asylums at this time is one of continued and definite progress in both humane methods and professional standards. In the best asylums, the way was being paved for the ultimate transition from 'asylum' to 'hospital'.

### 3. LUNATICS UNDER THE POOR LAW

The position of the pauper lunatic in a workhouse was in many cases an increasingly unhappy one. After 1834, the parish poorhouse—that relic of the old Elizabethan Poor Law—was gradually superseded. With it went diversity of administration, and the last vestiges of that medieval ideal of charity which was akin to love. From the passing of the Poor Law Amendment Act of 1834, the twin watchwords were uniformity and deterrence. It is significant that the Report of the Poor Law Commissioners which preceded the framing of the Act dealt almost entirely with the problem presented by the able-bodied pauper who would not work, largely ignoring the plight of those who could not. The Commissioners complained that 'the diet of the workhouse almost always exceeds that of the cottage'[2] and claimed that 'by the means which we propose, the line between those who do and those who do not need relief is drawn perfectly'.[3] The means proposed, and carried into effect with efficiency, were those which have been summed up in the principle of 'less eligibility'.

---

[1] Browne, *What Asylums Were, Are, and Ought to Be*, pp. 142 and 185.

[2] *Report of Poor Law Commissioners* (hereafter referred to as *P.L.C. Reports*)—1834, vol. 1, p. 128.

[3] *P.L.C. Report*, 1834, vol. 1, p. 148.

The number of lunatics and idiots in workhouses in 1828 was estimated at 9000.[1] In 1845, despite the increase in the provision of county asylums and the growth of the practice of 'contracting out', there were still 4080.[2] Thus developed the anomalous position of a law framed to deter the able-bodied from seeking relief being applied in all its stringency to some thousands of people who were totally unable to support themselves, and who were in some cases subject to coercion.

*Classification of Paupers after 1834.*

Under the direction of the Poor Law Commissioners, the inmates of pauper institutions were classified as follows:

1. Aged and infirm men.
2. Able-bodied men, and boys over 13.
3. Boys from 7 to 13.
4. Aged and infirm women.
5. Able-bodied women, and girls over 13.
6. Girls from 7 to 13.
7. Children under 7.[3]

As the Webbs comment,

'. . . the modern student is struck at once by the omissions in this compulsory classification scheme. There is no class for the sick, either those suffering from infectious or contagious disease, or from others. There is no class for the lying-in cases. There is no class for the lunatics, idiots, or imbeciles. . . .'[4]

They point out that 'it was no part of the policy of the central authority that the sick should be received into the workhouse at all', but while outdoor relief was practicable in most cases of bodily illness, it was clearly not so in cases of mental illness.

The Poor Law Amendment Act of 1834 contained only one clause in which the insane were mentioned. Section 45 ran:

'. . . nothing in this Act contained shall authorise the detention in any workhouse of any dangerous Lunatic, insane Person, or Idiot for any longer period than 14 days: and every Person wilfully detaining in any

[1] D. H. Tuke, *Hist. of Insane*, p. 173.
[2] *P.L.C. Report*, 1845, pp. 186-7. The Lunacy Commissioners in the previous year gave a much higher figure—9339. See tables at end of their Report of 1844.
[3] *P.L.C. Report*, 1834, vol. I, p. 97.
[4] S. and B. Webb, *English Poor Law Policy*, pp. 61-2.

Workhouse any such Lunatic, insane Person or Idiot for more than 14 days shall be deemed guilty of a misdemeanour'.

The operative word was 'dangerous'; it became the practice for Boards of Guardians to pass on to the county asylum the violent patient, whose condition might be incurable, while retaining in the workhouse the milder or quieter cases, which were perhaps in the early stages of the disease, and more readily susceptible to treatment. The county asylum authorities were given no choice in the matter, for there was no machinery by which they might select suitable cases for treatment and reject the others. It is clear that at this time the Poor Law Commissioners regarded the county asylum as no more than a place of confinement.

In 1842, the Clerk of the Chesterton Union wrote to ask the Commissioners whether the Relieving Officer of that Union had acted rightly in sending a lunatic pauper to the workhouse until the next Board Day. He received the following reply:

'The Commissioners think, as a rule, that the workhouse is not the proper place for lunatic paupers. The 9th George IV, c. 40, s. 38[1] points out the course which ought to be taken for the care and safe custody of insane persons who become chargeable to the parish, viz., by causing them to be conveyed to an asylum or licensed house under the order of the justices.

'But there may be cases in which some short delay must occur before the necessary order of justices can be procured, and the other arrangements made for the conveyance of such lunatics to an asylum. In these instances, it may be desirable for the security as well of the public as of the insane person, that the temporary admission of the latter into the workhouse should be resorted to. The 45th section of the Poor Law Amendment Act, however, forbids the detention of a dangerous lunatic in a workhouse for any longer period than 14 days: and the Commissioners on every ground, both as regards the lunatic and the other inmates of the workhouse, disapprove of the detention for any longer period than absolute necessity may warrant."[2]

It may be asked why, in view of this statement, over 4000 pauper lunatics were still in workhouses eleven years after the Act came into force. The answer lies partly in the insufficient number of county asylums, and partly in the reluctance of individual Boards of Guardians to pay the cost of maintenance in these relatively expensive institutions; but the Com-

---

[1] The Madhouse Act of 1828.
[2] *Official Circulars of Poor Law Commissioners.* Vol. iii, p. 49, July 14th, 1842.

missioners' statement gives the key to the lack of provision for the insane in workhouses. It was clearly not envisaged that they should remain in these institutions for any length of time.

## Medical Attention in Workhouses after 1834.

In 1835, the Poor Law Commissioners laid down the basis on which the system of medical relief was to be organized in each parish. They endorsed the system, already operative in many parishes, in which the post of medical attendant to the workhouse was advertised, and the lowest tender from a medical man accepted. 'Each practitioner should fix the price of his own services under competition.'[1] The acceptance of the lowest tender led frequently to the acceptance of the applicant with the lowest qualifications and the most perfunctory conception of his duties. The Commissioners, obsessed with the danger of hypochondria among the able-bodied, did not regard this as a social danger. In their eyes, the procedure saved money and prevented malingering. Their conception of a healthy community was one in which a free medical service was kept to an absolute minimum, and where 'the evil of sending all parties to the parish doctor for medical relief' was avoided.

The doctors' duties were defined as follows:

'To attend the workhouse . . . as the state of the sick or lunatic patients may render necessary.

'To give all necessary directions as to the diet, classification and treatment of the sick and lunatic paupers, and to provide the requisite medicines.'[2]

We may deduce from this last clause that the Commissioners were not in favour of the system of 'moral management', which would have required a larger staff and better facilities than a workhouse would be likely to possess.

Elsewhere, they gave these directions:

'As soon as the pauper is admitted, he or she shall be placed in the probationary ward, and shall remain there until examined by the medical officer of the workhouse. If the medical officer, upon such examination, pronounces the pauper to be labouring under any disease of body or mind, the pauper shall be placed either in the sick ward, or in the ward for lunatics and idiots not dangerous, as the medical officer shall direct.'[3]

[1] P.L.C. Report, 1834, vol. i, p. 53.
[2] P.L.C. Report, 1834, vol. i, p. 97.
[3] P.L.C. Report, 1835, vol. i, p. 96.

LUNACY, LAW, AND CONSCIENCE

*Accommodation for Pauper Lunatics.*

The 'ward for lunatics and idiots' is mentioned several times in the Orders and Reports published by the Poor Law authorities during this period, and the implication is that most, if not all, workhouses possessed such a ward. In fact, there had never been a statutory provision to this effect, nor had the provision of such accommodation ever been officially suggested. Yet according to the Lunacy Commissioners, accommodation of this kind certainly existed in the large towns by 1844.

'. . . there are numerous workhouses belonging to Parishes and Unions, which are not licensed for the reception of the insane, but which nevertheless contain certain wards exclusively appropriated to lunatics, and receive large numbers of insane persons, dangerous as well as harmless; such as the workhouses at Birmingham, Manchester, Sheffield, Bath, Leicester, Redruth in Cornwall, the Infirmary Bethel at Norwich, and others.'[1]

Here was a clear contradiction of both the letter and the spirit of 1834; yet it was obviously a matter of official policy. The iron control of the Commissioners over the activities of the individual Unions was such that the possibility of a procedure involving extra expense being initiated spontaneously in a number of different areas without official approval or official comment is remote.

The probability is that where such lunatic wards existed, they had been in existence before 1834, and that although they were to be met with in the larger towns, the provision of such accommodation was by no means universal. Why, then, did the Poor Law Commissioners, who must have been aware of these facts, suddenly assume the existence of a lunatic ward in every workhouse? The answer seems to lie in a curious episode in Poor Law policy which occurred in 1838.

*Select Committee on the Poor Law Amendment Act, 1838.*

Among those who gave evidence before this Select Committee was Edward Gulson, the Assistant Poor Law Commissioner. His evidence, like that of his colleagues, was mainly concerned with the effect of the operation of the Act on the able-bodied pauper who was to be forced back into self-maintenance; but in the minutes of this Committee there occurs a remarkable passage[2] in which Gulson attacked the administra-

---

[1] *Report of Metropolitan Commissioners in Lunacy*, 1844, p. 10.
[2] *Report of Select Committee on Poor Law Amendment Act*, 1838, vol. i, pp. 10–11.

tion of the county asylums, and made a plea for the transfer of power over lunatics to the Poor Law Commissioners.

'I conceive a very great evil exists in the law with regard to pauper lunatics. It has always appeared to me that a great improvement might be effected relating to them; at the present time, the expenses of maintaining pauper lunatics in places pointed out by law for lunatic asylums is very great indeed, varying from 8s. to 12s. a week for each person . . . that circumstance operates to a very great degree in keeping individuals in the parishes who ought to be taken care of in a lunatic asylum.'

He recommended—

'in a given group of Unions, a regular lunatic asylum solely for paupers, to which all those Unions should send their paupers, and where they would be kept at one-half or a third or a fourth of the expense at which they are now kept'.

The Chairman of the Select Committee[1] seems to have regarded this proposal as both retrogressive and administratively unworkable:

'Are you aware when you speak of the expense per head in those establishments (county asylums) that those establishments can scarcely be maintained even with that revenue?

'—I am not aware of the fact; but taking it to be so, I am stating distinctly what I conceive to be the best for the paupers, and for the parish purse.

'Then you are aware that the lunatic asylums already established have been built by contributions from the poor rate?

'—I am aware that in a great many instances that is the case, and I am aware that very great jobs have been made of such establishments.

'Are you of the opinion that it would relieve the poor rate to tax them again to build other asylums? . . . are you of the opinion that the houses already established should be suffered to become empty and of no use?

'—As far as paupers I am, unless they were converted to such a purpose as this.

'Are you aware that they have been built specially for the reception of paupers?

'—Yes I am, in some instances.

'Should you think it a wise and prudent policy to abandon those houses and to build others?'

[1] Mr. Fazakerly, formerly a member of the 1827 Committee on Pauper Lunatics.

The Chairman was evidently treating Gulson as a hostile witness, and was driving him into a position from which it was impossible to retreat. Gulson's reply to the last question was:

'If those houses could be converted to such a purpose, and placed under the entire control of the Board of Guardians . . . I think the change would be very much for the general benefit of the people.

'—Then your impression appears to be, that abuses and unnecessary expenditure exist in those houses at present?

'—That is distinctly my impression.

'Are you aware what any of those asylums have cost in the erection?

'—I am aware that a vast sum of money has been thrown away in the erection of some of them, and that very great jobs have been perpetrated in the erection of lunatic asylums.'

The real author of this proposal to bring the county asylums within the scope of the Poor Law was almost certainly Edwin Chadwick. In the hostilities which divided the Poor Law Commissioners from their Secretary at this time, Gulson was always Chadwick's loyal adherent and close friend.[1] Chadwick was engrossed in plans of administrative simplification in which the Poor Law Union would become the primary unit of local authority; he detested administrative complexity, financial waste, and curative medicine. Ashley, now emerging as the leader of the lunacy reformers, was at this time Chadwick's 'arch-enemy'.[2] Moreover, as a Benthamite, Chadwick was bitterly opposed to the humanist approach to social problems, the paternalistic interest in oppressed minorities. The 'greatest happiness of the greatest number' in this instance lay in sparing the pockets of the sane.

Chadwick led, Gulson followed; but by 1838, both were fighting a losing battle against hostile interests. Although Chadwick nominally held office as Secretary to the Commissioners until 1847, the days of his power and prestige in this sphere were over, and this proposal, like so many others which he initiated in those nine years, failed to gain influential support. The Visiting Justices and the Metropolitan Commissioners in Lunacy continued their work unhampered by the claims of Somerset House.

*Summary: Costs and Accommodation.*

The real point at issue between the Poor Law authorities and the

[1] S. Finer, *Life and Times of Sir Edwin Chadwick*, pp. 133, 194, 205, et al.
[2] Finer, op. cit., p 239.

Lunacy authorities was the old one of cure or detention. If the county asylums were looked upon as curative institutions, then their high cost was justified, and they had a legitimate grievance against the Poor Law authorities for refusing to send them pauper lunatics who were susceptible to treatment. If, on the other hand, they were regarded merely as places of detention, the Poor Law authorities could rightly claim that they could do this work much more cheaply.

County asylums were certainly much more expensive to operate than workhouses. A comparison of costs in 1845 shows that the cost of board and clothing alone in county asylums averaged 7s. 3½d. a week for each patient. The highest was Hereford, with a figure of 12s. per week. The figures for workhouses, on the other hand, were still very low, being in many cases little more than they had been a century earlier, in spite of a considerable rise in the cost of living.[1] The average was 2s. 7d. a week, the highest figure of 4s. 1d. being that for Rutland, and the lowest being that for Cornwall—2s. o¼d. The cost of maintenance in the Cornwall Asylum was 5s. 11½d. a week, so that Gulson was strictly accurate when he said that it was possible to maintain lunatics for one-third of the cost under workhouse conditions; but the justification of the county asylums lay not in the fact that they kept costs down, but that they cured their patients. The old argument of the subscribers to the Manchester Lunatic Hospital still held good: that it was better to pay a higher amount for a few months, and restore a patient to self-maintenance, than to pay a lower amount for his entire life-time.

A statement which underlined the unsatisfactory division of functions between workhouses and county asylums was contained in a report published in 1844 by Dr. Boyd, the parish doctor of St. Marylebone.[2] He pointed out that there were seventy-nine patients from that parish in the Middlesex Asylum at Hanwell, all of whom were incurable save four. Among them were twenty-two quiet chronic cases—patients who would be capable of living the normal restricted life of the workhouse without causing alarm or annoyance to the other inmates. At the same time, there were many patients in urgent need of treatment who remained in the Marylebone workhouse because there was no accommodation for them in Hanwell. Some clarification of function and practice, involving close co-operation between the asylum and the workhouse, seemed an obvious necessity.

---

[1] Figures for both workhouses and county asylums taken from 11th *Annual P.L.C. Report*, 1845, pp. 186–9.

[2] Boyd, *Report as to Lunatics Chargeable to the Parish of St. Marylebone*, 1844.

M

By 1842, it seems, the Poor Law Commissioners were anxious to be rid of the whole problem of the pauper lunatic. The attitude expressed in Gulson's statements—if indeed it was ever more than a piece of wishful thinking on the part of the Chadwick faction—was short-lived. In 1842, the Commissioners issued the following directive to Boards of Guardians:

'From the express prohibition of the detention of dangerous persons of unsound mind in a workhouse . . . coupled with the prevalent practice of keeping insane persons in a workhouse before the passing of the Poor Law Amendment Act, it may be inferred that persons of unsound mind, not being dangerous, may be legally kept in a workhouse. It must, however, be remembered that with lunatics, the first object ought to be their cure by means of proper medical treatment. This can only be obtained in a well-regulated asylum; and therefore the detention of any curable lunatic in a workhouse is highly objectionable on the score both of humanity and economy.'[1]

This statement, with its implied division of functions between the Lunacy Commissioners and the Poor Law Commissioners, was satisfactory to both; though the issues involved had still to be fought out between many a Board of Guardians and its local asylum.

#### 4. BETHLEM

After 1828, the authorities at Bethlem seem to have shunned publicity as much as possible. Growing central control constituted a threat to their independence, and incidents which might throw an unfavourable light on the hospital were avoided at all costs. Consequently, very little is known about the conditions in Bethlem from 1828 to 1853, when the Lunacy Commissioners at last assumed control. We know that many patients died in the cholera epidemic of 1832, and that the diet was subsequently improved in order to strengthen the bodily resistance of those who survived.[2] The building which had met with the disapproval of the Select Committee of 1815 was still in use during this period.

#### 5. SINGLE LUNATICS

Despite the provisions of the 1828 Madhouse Act and the constant

---

[1] Printed directions of P.L.C., February 5th, 1842. Quoted in *Report of Metropolitan Commissioners in Lunacy*, 1844, pp. 95–6.
[2] O'Donoghue, *Story of Bethlehem Hospital*, p. 357.

efforts of the parliamentary reformers, no improvement whatever had taken place in the conditions of single lunatics. It was still possible for any person to be confined alone with great secrecy and no public supervision, on the unsupported word of a relative. This constituted the greatest gap in existing lunacy legislation when the reformers again brought the matter before parliament in 1842.

# Chapter Ten

## ASHLEY AND THE ACHIEVEMENT OF REFORM

THE reports which the Metropolitan Commissioners in Lunacy issued between 1829 and 1842 make impressive reading. They show a constant attention to detail, and an increasingly stringent view of their duties. The Commissioners began to inquire as to the character and conduct of the attendants and nurses; they broke with tradition in listening to the patients' grievances and investigating them; they experimented with a system of liberating recovered patients on trial, so that the transition from the sheltered world of the asylum to the world outside could be carefully supervised. The work which the Commissioners did at this time did much to impress the importance of the whole subject on the minds of thinking people. 'The subject of insanity has lately excited much attention,' wrote Ashley in his report of 1839–40; but the whole position of divided authority and divided responsibility was manifestly unsatisfactory. It was clearly necessary to deal with this problem before attempting to further internal reforms.

With the events of 1842–5, the story of lunacy reform enters on a new phase. Ashley was now the acknowledged leader of the reform group.

By 1842, Ashley's reputation as a social reformer was decisively established. He was forty-one years of age; he had been a member of parliament for sixteen years, and a Lunacy Commissioner for fourteen. His unremitting work to improve conditions in the factories and the mines had earned him a place in the minds of the general public. He had become something of a national figure, and to the initial advantage of aristocratic connections had added those of detailed knowledge and practical experience.

Such was Ashley's standing that, but for the personal antipathy which

existed between him and Peel,[1] he might have achieved cabinet office in
the administration of 1841; but Peel offered him only a minor post in the
Royal Household. Ashley was offended.

'Vast numbers are good enough to have confidence in my principles
and character. No one questions the great services I have rendered to the
Conservative cause, and all this was to be henceforth employed in ordering dinners and carrying a white wand! The thing was a plain, cruel,
unnecessary insult.'[2]

Ashley refused the position, and turned to lunacy reform as a channel
for his frustrated talents. It is not suggested that he would have abandoned
the cause of the lunatic if he had taken cabinet office; but inevitably his
time and interest would have been divided, and the main conduct of the
campaign left to lesser men. In the circumstances, he was able to devote
himself to it wholeheartedly.

## I. THE ACT OF 1842

On March 17th, 1842, Lord Granville Somerset rose in the House to
propose that the Commissioners be empowered to carry out an inspection
of all asylums and madhouses in the country, whatever their legal status.
He pointed out the loop-holes in the 1828 Acts—the different systems of
inspection in the metropolis and the provinces, the fact that county
asylums, single lunatics and Bethlem were still not subject to any effective
form of central control. He defined the aims of the 1828 Acts as being
fourfold: the licensing of suitable institutions for the insane, the supervision of their management, the prevention of illegal detention, and the
prevention of detention after recovery; these aims could not be reached
while the Commissioners possessed only a partial jurisdiction.

Somerset stressed that his proposal was only the first stage in the movement to secure a national system of inspection and supervision:

'By doing what he now proposed, there would be laid the foundation
of a better general system, and after the information which the Commissioners would acquire by their communications with the whole
country, the whole subject would be brought to focus by the London
Board. From this a great good would arise, and eventually parliament
would be able to legislate upon this important subject on a broader and
more extensive basis.'

[1] See Hammond, *Lord Shaftesbury*, chapter VI.
[2] Hodder, *Life of Shaftesbury*, vol. I, p. 356—quoting Ashley's *Diary*.

In the debate which followed, the scheme was subjected to a withering attack from Thomas Wakley, the Editor of the *Lancet*. Wakley demanded the introduction of a comprehensive system at once:

'In Scotland, there was one system, in Ireland there was another, and in England there were several, and among them all there was not one which on the whole was entitled to the sanction and approbation of the public, or which was worthy the adoption of the noble Lord.'

He was especially incensed by Somerset's proposal that the two legal Commissioners should undertake the tour—a proposal which he considered 'an insult to the medical profession'.

Ashley rose to answer. He wished that the measure went further, but 'it would baffle the ingenuity of the Member for Finsbury to institute a practicable system of uniformity for all the asylums in the country'. Comprehensive legislation must wait until the House was in possession of all the facts. On the question of whether the tour should be undertaken by the legal or the medical Commissioners, he was outspoken: 'A man of common-sense could give as good an opinion as any medical man he knew.' He may only have meant that the immediate questions to be considered were legal rather than medical in character; but the statement was unfortunate; it so easily lent itself to quotation out of context that it lost him the backing of a large section of the medical profession.

The Bill was ordered on the same day, March 17th, and prepared by Ashley and Lord Granville Somerset. Hansard has no record of further debates in the Commons, so we may infer that the Bill completed all its stages without undue difficulty, and without further major issues being raised.[1] The Bill then went to the Lords, and was returned with several amendments.[2] The Lords still wished to keep official inspection to the minimum, though the climate of public opinion had changed to such an extent that it was impolitic to say so. Consequently, they objected to the proposal that the Commissioners should be empowered to visit all asylums and madhouses twice yearly, giving the strange reason that the medical and legal Commissioners would suffer from 'undue distraction from their other professional pursuits'. Eventually, after much discussion, a compromise was reached; visits were to take place twice a year unless the Lord Chancellor saw fit to direct a less frequent visitation.[3]

[1] The Bill received the backing of the Home Secretary, Sir James Graham. H.C.J., August 2nd, 1842.

[2] H.C.J., July 13th, 1842. The chief spokesman for the Bill in the Lords was the Duke of Buccleuch.

[3] H.C.J., August 1st, 1842.

With this doubtful concession, the Lords had to be content. The Bill became law on August 5th, 1842.

The Act (5 and 6 Vict., c. 87) was to operate for three years in the first instance. Doubtless the supporters of lunacy reform had in mind the substitution of comprehensive legislation within that period, and this was actually achieved by the passing of the 1845 Act at the expiry of the earlier one. There was less finality about a three-year Act; yet at the same time, it gave the Commissioners time in which to carry out their tour and to formulate their findings.

The number of Commissioners was increased. There were to be fifteen to twenty, of whom four were legal Commissioners, and six or seven 'Physicians or Surgeons not practising in Midwifery or Surgery'.[1] The part of the Act relating to the tour of inspection was contained in section 7, which is here reproduced:

'And be it enacted, that in the month of August, or so soon as they shall be able to do so after their appointment in each year, the Metropolitan Commissioners in Lunacy shall meet, and divide England and Wales into districts convenient for visiting, as herein provided, all houses then or within the next twelve months licensed by justices of the peace for the reception of insane persons . . . and that every house so licensed shall be visited by not less than two Metropolitan Commissioners, of whom one at least shall be a physician or surgeon, and one shall be a barrister Commissioner, once at least every six months . . . and such Metropolitan Commissioners, when visiting such house, shall and are hereby required and authorised to inspect every part of the premises included in the then license for the same, and to see every patient then confined therein, and to inquire whether any patient is under restraint, and why; and also to inspect the certificate of admission of every patient who shall have been admitted into such house since the last visit of the Metropolitan Commissioners; and also to consider the observations made in the Visitors' Book . . . and to enter in the Visitors' Book a minute of the then condition of the house so visited, and of the number of patients therein, and the number of patients under restraint, with the reasons thereof as stated, and such irregularity (if any) as may exist in any of the certificates aforesaid. . . .'

Sections 8–11 provided that they were also to report on the efficacy of the non-restraint system in any place where it was practised; on the

[1] Section 2. Presumably because midwifery or surgery might demand their urgent attention at any time, thus distracting them from their duties under the Act.

method of classification adopted; on the effect of occupation and amusements, and especially on the condition of the pauper patients.

The 1832 Act had removed the work of the Commissioners from the
jurisdiction of the Secretary of State for the Home Department, and
placed it within the jurisdiction of the Lord Chancellor. The interests of
the Home Department were now safeguarded by a provision (section 38)
that the Secretary of State, like the Lord Chancellor, might require the
Commissioners to make a special visit to any institution for the insane except Bethlem.

The Commissioners continued to receive £1 an hour for their work in
the metropolitan area; outside it, they were now to be paid at the rate of
five guineas a day. In spite of the arduous nature of the projected tour,
the position of legal or medical Commissioner remained a part-time one,
to be undertaken by a professional man in his spare time.

2. THE TOUR OF INSPECTION

How the asylums and madhouses which had hitherto been exempt from
any real inspection greeted the prospect of the Commissioners' visits, we
may only guess in most cases. The only reliable records available relate to
certain asylums and hospitals; no documents relating to private madhouses
appear to be in existence. In most cases, it does not appear that any very
great effort was made to improve conditions especially for the Commissioners' eyes. The rate of purchase for staple commodities remains
steady. The outstanding exception is the Lancaster Asylum, where a
great change took place as soon as the 1842 Bill was introduced. The cash
book shows a sudden rush of buying; hardware, kitchen utensils, soap,
candles and 'scouring liquors' were bought in large quantities. From May
to September, 1842, £243 was spent on blankets alone, and the former
frequent indents for straw stopped completely. Evidently most of the
patients had previously slept on straw, and were now given proper bedding for the first time.

The sudden change in policy was due not only to panic on the part of
the visiting justices, but also to the effects of the appointment two years
previously of a new and enlightened medical superintendent, Mr. Gaskell.
The use of mechanical restraint had been abolished in June, 1841, on his
orders, and we may conclude that he probably used the threat of inspection as a means to induce the justices to provide the money for a thorough
overhaul of living conditions.

The Commissioners reached Lancaster in October, 1842—only two months after the passing of the Act. It must have been gratifying to Gaskell, in view of his strenuous efforts, to read the Commissioners' report, written in the Visitors' Book; this expressed 'unqualified approbation', commented on the 'skill, zeal and attention' of the staff, and remarked that 'the bedding is good and sufficient, and is arranged with neatness on the bedsteads during the day'.

The significance of the Lancaster episode lies in the fact that it illustrates the double standard which had previously existed in lunacy administration. The Lancaster authorities must have been well aware that the conditions for which they were responsible were well below the standards demanded in the metropolitan area; but it was not until the new Bill was proposed and inspection became imminent that they took steps to remedy this situation. If this could happen in the second largest county asylum in the country, we may readily imagine that it also happened in many provincial private madhouses. The mere threat of inspection was a valuable corrective.

The lay Commissioners, such as Ashley and Somerset, did not take part in the tour; but the actual sifting of the information received and the writing of the final report, published in 1844, was Ashley's work.[1] The tour had two distinct results: it enabled the professional Commissioners to visit institutions formerly outside their control, and to remedy individual cases of abuse; and the mass of raw material received enabled Ashley to draw up a comprehensive picture from the national view-point, and to make recommendations on matters of general policy.

3. THE REPORT OF THE METROPOLITAN COMMISSIONERS, 1844

The report dealt first with county asylums, giving details of conditions in individual asylums, and paying some attention to matters of internal administration, such as heating, diet, and the employment of patients. Other institutions were subsequently dealt with in the same way. There was a section on the nature of insanity, and a classification of its forms; a section on the non-restraint system; and a section on the admission of paupers from workhouses.

From the reader's point of view, this is a muddled report in which details obtrude and the overall picture is not easily grasped. Ashley had little literary ability; but the patient piling of fact on fact provided a sound basis for the recommendations which concluded the report.

[1] With the exception of two sections—those on restraint and medical classification. See pp. 181-3.

LUNACY, LAW, AND CONSCIENCE

*(i) County Asylums.*

The section of the report which dealt with county asylums consisted largely of a mass of domestic detail. There were apparently no outstanding abuses by the time the Commissioners undertook their inspection, but there were many points which they desired to bring to the attention of the Visiting. Committees.

There were twelve county asylums which provided accommodation only for criminal and pauper lunatics, and five 'county asylums united with subscription asylums'—institutions such as those at Stafford and Nottingham, where the cost of construction and maintenance had been raised partly from the county rate, and partly from public subscription. In these latter institutions, paying patients were admitted to offset in part the cost of maintaining paupers.

The Commissioners were disturbed by the sites chosen for many county asylums; in spite of the specific provisions of the 1808 Act, these were often in crowded areas, and without a satisfactory water supply. Bodmin Asylum was frequently short of water, and when visited by the Commissioners, had been totally without water for a whole week. Hanwell had an inadequate supply, and the visiting justices had been forced to sanction the expense of boring a new well. At Nottingham, Dorchester and Lancaster, the asylums were in populous areas, and there was little space where the patients could take exercise. The most serious result of building in towns was that when the asylum became overcrowded, additional accommodation could only be provided at the expense of the gardens and airing-courts.

The cost of county asylums was still very high, and the Commissioners had a cautious word to say about excessive costs:

'Although county magistrates have properly the control of funds to be raised in their own districts, it can scarcely be expected that they should devote so much attention as is really necessary to make them conversant with the various points which involve the convenience, comfort and security necessary to be provided for in large asylums for the insane, and they are therefore liable to be misled as to their proper cost and construction.'[1]

Again, they stated:

'While we have no wish to advocate the erection of unsightly buildings, we think that no unnecessary costs should be incurred for architectural

[1] 1844 *Report*, pp. 29–30.

decoration; especially as these asylums are erected for persons who, when in health, are accustomed to dwell in cottages.'[1]

This emphasis on inexperience and architecture was a polite way of endorsing Gulson's opinion that 'very great jobs have been perpetrated in the erection of county asylums'. At all events, it made a sound basis for Ashley's plan for a central administrative structure to control the design and construction of new asylums:

'It is apparent . . . that although a few of the existing county asylums are well adapted to their purpose, and a very large proportion of them are extremely well-conducted; yet some of them are quite unfit for the reception of the insane, some are placed in ineligible sites, some are deficient in the necessary means of providing out-door employment for their paupers, some are ill-contrived and defective in their internal construction, some are cheerless and confined in their yards and airing-grounds. . . . it appears to be deserving the attention of the legislature, whether the erection of public asylums for the insane poor may not advantageously be regulated by some independent authority . . . pauper lunatics have unfortunately become so numerous throughout the whole kingdom, that the proper construction and cost of asylums for their use has ceased to be a subject which affects a few counties only, and has become a matter of national interest and importance'.[2]

### (ii) Public Lunatic Hospitals.

Some public lunatic hospitals, notably the Warneford Asylum[3] and the Exeter Asylum, had followed Bethlem's example in claiming exemption from visitation. This exemption was granted in 1832.[4] For these asylums, Ashley had a word of reproof:

'We cannot . . . but think that all places receiving and detaining in custody any class of Her Majesty's subjects, should be open to inspection by proper authority.'[5]

The Commissioners commended the administration of the Retreat; St. Luke's they found ill-placed, and deficient in most of the necessary amenities. They were particularly severe about two old pioneer insti-

---

[1] 1844 Report, pp. 11–12.
[2] 1844 Report, pp. 29–30.
[3] Near Oxford, formerly the Radcliffe Asylum.
[4] See 'Refutation of the Assertions made by the Writer of the Article in the *Quarterly Review* for October, 1844'—by the chairman of the Warneford Asylum, 1844.
[5] 1844 Report, p. 33.

tutions—the Bethel Hospital at Norwich and the Manchester Lunatic Hospital, which were 'very ill-adapted for receptacles for the insane'.[1]

### (iii) *Licensed Madhouses.*

There were thirty-seven licensed madhouses in the metropolitan area; these had, of course, been within the jurisdiction of the Metropolitan Commissioners for the past fourteen years, and so were familiar to them; but there were ninety-nine houses in the provinces which the Commissioners visited for the first time on their tour of inspection. Their chief impression was not of widespread cruelty and neglect, but of a common evasion of the law. In many houses, the law relating to the registration of certified persons was evaded by declaring that the patient was merely suffering from 'nerves', and did not therefore require certification. Some houses took 'low-spirited or desponding' patients as 'boarders'. It should be said here that these patients were probably equivalent to the 'Voluntary' patients suffering from psychoneuroses who now form a large part of the admissions to mental hospitals. The fault may have been in the law, which made no provision for the treatment of those who were not certifiable. The licensing laws were also evaded; it frequently happened that a proprietor would keep patients in several different houses, although he had a licence only for one. This increased the difficulties of inspection.

Proprietors of private madhouses often took their responsibilities lightly. At Cranbourne, in Dorset, two Commissioners visited a house on three separate occasions, and the proprietor was away each time, the house being left to the care of a solitary female servant. At Belle Grove House, Newcastle, there was a repetition of an incident which the Commissioners had encountered during their first year of office: the house was being administered by a man who knew nothing whatever about the treatment of insanity, merely because he happened to be the chief creditor of the former owner.

The effect of some years' systematic and thorough inspection in the metropolitan area had been wholly good; the Commissioners were especially pleased to report that Warburton's houses were greatly improved:

'We have visited few, if any, receptacles for the insane in which the patients are more kindly or more judiciously treated . . . the abuses which existed in this and some other asylums previously to the year 1828

---

[1] 1844 *Report*, p. 33. The Norwich Bethel Hospital was apparently a development of the old workhouse 'bedlam'.

led to the introduction of the system of visitation by commissioners in the metropolitan district. The houses at Bethnal Green, which were among the worst, now rank with the best receptacles for the insane'.[1]

There were three houses on which the Commissioners felt themselves bound to pass 'almost unqualified censure'. These were the asylums at Haverfordwest, where patients existed in an almost unbelievable state of filth and neglect, a house at West Auckland in similar conditions, and St. Peter's, Bristol. There was no doubt that, like most of the other old pioneer institutions, St. Peter's was now totally out of date. The airing ground was 'utterly unfit', the site 'totally unfit for an asylum'; there was no system of classification of patients, no plan for exercising them, and no arrangements for employing them. The Commissioners who visited this institution concluded roundly, 'the entire body of lunatics ought to be removed to more spacious premises, and to a more airy and healthy situation.'[2]

Previous suspicions that the local magistrates were not in all cases taking their duties under the Lunacy Acts seriously were now confirmed. In four cases, the Commissioners found that the magistrates did not visit at all; in one, they invariably sent for the visitors' book beforehand, so that the proprietor was forewarned of their intentions.

Where the Commissioners found grounds for complaint in the conduct of an asylum, they communicated with the Chairman of the Quarter Sessions, calling his attention to the abuses which they had in mind; in almost every case, a subsequent visit showed that no action had been taken. On the very day on which the Commissioners visited the house at West Auckland, the local magistrates also visited. The Commissioners found the house 'utterly unfit'; the magistrates, only an hour or two before, had recorded 'everything in good order'.

Some magistrates did attempt to carry out their duties conscientiously, but in almost all cases they were content to inspect the bodily condition and cleanliness of the patients, and made no inquiries concerning diet, medical treatment, employment of patients, or whether any of them were fit to be released.

Again Ashley returned to his main theme: the only remedy for these diverse and unsatisfactory conditions was the creation of a powerful national inspectorate on a permanent basis. He quoted Samuel Tuke:

'We shall not secure efficient visitation until we have an appointment

[1] 1844 Report, p. 44.
[2] 1844 Report, p. 53.

of a number of competent persons to visit, under the authority of Government, all the places of whatever description, chartered or unchartered, in which the insane are confined.'[1]

### (iv) Workhouses.

Since they were under the control of the Poor Law Commissioners, workhouses lay outside the Lunacy Commissioners' terms of reference; at the same time, a consideration of the relations between the two branches of administration made it imperative that they should form a picture of the state of pauper lunatics as a whole. They contented themselves with visiting 'such as lay in our road'—the workhouses at Redruth, Bath, Leicester, Portsea and Birmingham. All these were large workhouses possessing a special lunatic ward; there is no information about those which did not.

There were 21 insane persons—this term still including the mentally defective—at Redruth, 21 at Bath, 20 at Leicester, 26 at Portsea and 71 at Birmingham. Many of them were dangerous. At Leicester alone, the lunatic ward included 'a noisy maniac, very cunning', a man 'subject to maniacal attacks . . . raving mad . . . constantly fastened to his bed at night', another 'violent and passionate and tried to cut others with knives', 'a destructive and dangerous idiot', and 'an abusive and dangerous lunatic'.

In spite of the injunctions of the Poor Law Commissioners, section 45 of the Poor Law Amendment Act was still apparently not being observed in many places. The Metropolitan Commissioners found, as might have been expected from previous evidence, that some patients whose condition would have been curable had they been passed to the county asylum within the statutory fourteen days were still being detained in workhouses. In Cornwall, they noted,

'. . . it had been the custom . . . not to send a patient to the asylum until he had become, either from dirty habits or dangerous propensities, unmanageable in a workhouse or in lodgings'.[2]

At Nottingham:

'The result of our latest enquiries . . . has been that, since the new Poor Law came into operation, an increased reluctance has been exhibited

---

[1] 1844 Report, p. 71—quoting from S. Tuke's introduction to Jacobi's Treatise on Hospitals for the Insane.
[2] 1844 Report, p. 223.

on the part of the parish authorities to send their poor to an asylum, and the patients frequently come in a very debilitated and exhausted state. Great advantage is said to be taken of the use of the word "dangerous" in the 45th section of the Poor Law Amendment Act, and many curable cases are detained in Union workhouses in the rural districts.'[1]

In Surrey, the Poor Law authorities were responsible for the patients being 'sent into the asylum in some cases to die'.

Ashley concluded his general consideration of this problem by attacking the implications of section 45:

'The clause which is supposed to sanction the confinement in work-houses of lunatics, without adverting to the probability of their being curable or not, is, in our opinion, impolitic and open to serious objection'.[2] He was probably understating the case when he said that the local Boards of Guardians were 'under some misconception as to the condition of lunatics in workhouses'.

*(v) Mechanical Restraint.*

The section of the Report which deals with experiments in non-restraint was not Ashley's work. Ashley was known to be a firm supporter of the non-restraint system, and as early as 1842 had publicly praised the work done in this connection at Hanwell. He 'could not speak too highly either of the system itself, or of the manner in which it was carried out by the talented superintendent, Dr. Conolly'.[3]

The Report did not reflect that attitude. It summarized the main arguments for and against restraint with a show of fairness, but it is quite clear that the writer was actually in favour of coercion, though only as a last resort.

The main arguments for absolute non-coercion were that it soothed the patient, and was thus more humane than mechanical restraint, which tended to degrade and humiliate him; that the use of restraint gave the keepers an opportunity of abusing and neglecting their charges; that the only requisite was an increase of staff, which ought not to be refused merely on the grounds of expense; and that experience showed that the general tone of the asylum improved when restraint was abolished.

The arguments in favour of moderate coercion involved diametrically opposed claims: that slight restraint frequently induced tranquillity in an

[1] 1844 *Report*, p. 226.
[2] 1844 *Report*, p. 99.
[3] Hansard, July 16th, 1842.

otherwise restless patient; that the only real alternative to restraint in the case of an excited or dangerous patient was solitary confinement, which could be even more degrading; that it was impossible for the staff, however great their devotion to duty, to exercise an unwearying surveillance; and finally, that experience showed that the best approach to the insane was that in which kindness was mingled with a show of authority.

The Commissioners' experience at Lincoln and Hanwell evidently led them to support the latter view; they found that the non-restraint system did not always produce the tranquillity and high moral tone claimed by its advocates. At Lincoln, they found 'unusual excitement prevailing in the disorderly ward on the female side'. At Hanwell:

'. . . a violent female lunatic who had been endeavouring to bite other persons as well as herself was seized by four or five nurses, and after a violent and protracted struggle forced with great difficulty into . . . one of the cells. During this scene, there was much confusion in the ward, and the great efforts of the patient to liberate herself must have greatly exhausted her'.

They saw a female patient push an elderly patient to the ground; a woman who lacerated her arm from wrist to elbow as a result of thrusting it through an unbarred window; and a male patient who had recently killed another. The Commissioners may have felt that there was some justification for the attitude of the anonymous but reverend gentleman who, while a patient at Hanwell in 1841, addressed the following lines to his member of parliament:

We have in this asylum, sir,
Some doctors of renown,
With a plan of non-restraint
Which they seem to think their own. . . .
All well-meaning men, sir,
But troubled with a complaint
Called the monomania
Of total non-restraint. . . .'[1]

The question of the authorship of this section of the report was raised in the House of Commons by Wakley, soon after its publication. He believed that 'there almost lurked about it something of a sneer at the Hanwell Lunatic Asylum' and stated flatly that it was obviously not the

[1] *Epistle to Mr. Ewart, M.P., by a Rev. Gentleman lately a patient in the Middlesex Asylum,* 1841—Hume Tracts.

work of Ashley.[1] Although Ashley was present in the House at the time, he made no reply. An answer was given by his fellow-Commissioner, Vernon Smith.[2]

It may be relevant here to record Wakley's reaction to the statements of the Report concerning coercion:

'But, said the report, those who employ as well as those who do not employ mechanical restraint, adopt an equally mild and conciliatory method of managing their patients. The deuce they did; it was the oddest in the world. So that a man who whipped his child every morning before breakfast adopted just as mild a system of treatment as the father who endeavoured to admonish his child into the path of duty and happiness!'

Wakley's attitude to the subject was also Ashley's; but on this occasion, Ashley's ideas were at variance with the experience of the professional Commissioners.

*(vi) Forms of Insanity.*

Eleven pages of the Report were occupied with definitions of insanity and classification of its forms. The medical terminology used has now fallen into disuse, and the whole of this section would be of interest only to a medical historian; but the recognition in an official document of the fact that insanity comprises a complex of causes and effects—not merely one disease with a single cause—was indicative of the advance which had taken place in the community's understanding of the whole subject.

*(vii) Suggestions for the Amendment of the Law.*

The Commissioners' recommendations, or perhaps it would be more correct to say Ashley's recommendations, had two primary aims: to secure the unification of the forms of statutory control exercised over asylums and madhouses, and to extend the Lunacy Laws to all institutions of whatever character in which the insane were detained. Recommendations having these aims in mind may be briefly summarized as follows:

1. Each county should be required to build a county asylum for its own pauper lunatics. (The previous Acts were of course permissive.)
2. All asylums and hospitals for the insane should be subject to inspection by the statutory authority; they should also be required to

[1] Hansard, July 23rd, 1844.
[2] Robert Vernon Smith, 1800–73, was a nephew of Sidney Smith: Secretary of State for War and the Colonies, 1839–41. Baron Lyveden, 1859. He worked with Ashley on the Lunacy Commission for many years.

N

keep records and case-books of a prescribed type, which should be the same for all institutions.

3. All authorities responsible for the care of the insane should be required to furnish certificates of the admission, discharge or death of a patient within two days of the event. These should be forwarded in all cases to the statutory authority.

4. A new, more detailed, and standardized form of medical certification should be devised.

5. The person who certified a patient's insanity should not be allowed also to sign the certificate of consignment. (This was to obviate the situation which arose when a patient was certified by a medical practitioner who was also a relative, and thus in a position to sign both documents. The 1828 Madhouse Act had provided safeguards against collusion between the certifying doctor and the madhouse proprietor; this recommendation was designed to prevent collusion between the certifying doctor and the relatives.)

Recommendations which concerned the relation between workhouses and county asylums may be classified under three heads:

6. County asylum authorities should be empowered and encouraged to make separate provision for incurable lunatics who were paupers, in order to make room for a greater number of curable cases in the asylum.

7. Pauper patients should not be sent to workhouses unless their condition was definitely incurable; in that case, they should be sent only to certain specified workhouses which could make special provision for them.

8. The lunacy authority should be responsible for visiting and reporting on the condition of all pauper patients, whether in workhouses or county asylums.

These measures would have the effect of giving the Lunacy Commissioners a power of supervision, and therefore to some extent of removing pauper lunatics from the grip of the Poor Law.

9. A board or authority should be set up, to be responsible for the approval of sites, plans and estimates for all new asylums to be built at the public expense. This proposal broke new ground, since it proposed an entirely new kind of function for the central authority. It was designed as the final answer to critics of the financial policy of visiting justices.

## 4. EFFECT OF THE 1844 REPORT

'July 2nd, finished at last, Report of the Commission in Lunacy. Good thing over. Sat for many days in review. God prosper it! It contains much for the alleviation of physical and moral suffering.'[1]

Thus wrote Ashley at the conclusion of his task. The writing of the Report, however, was only the first stage in the process which was to culminate in legislative action. From the first, it was apparent that there would be action within a relatively short space of time; Peel, who had consistently supported the reformers, was now Prime Minister of an administration which, though Tory in name, was Liberal in social policy. Social reform was in the air, and the reformers were no longer handicapped by the necessity of struggling against the weight of public indifference.

The Lunacy Report, in spite of its turgid and unimaginative form, attracted a good deal of attention. The *Westminster Review* in particular published a detailed analysis in which the new note of social responsibility was sounded.[2] The writer stated that the Report was highly creditable to the Commissioners, but 'at the same time humiliating to us as a nation. Our feeling of humiliation, however, ought to give way to thankfulness that such facts are brought to light'.

On the vexed question of the high cost of county asylums, the writer pointed out that their construction was necessarily an expensive matter; if the dormitory principle were approved as being cheaper than separate sleeping accommodation for each patient, it would still be necessary to construct a certain number of separate cells for violent and dangerous patients; and it was essential, in view of the fact that some patients might have tendencies towards incendiarism, to have the building fireproofed. When allowance was made for these considerations, the writer thought the construction cost average of £200 per person for a county asylum, as against £40 per head for a workhouse, not unreasonable. He also pointed out that a comparison of maintenance costs was both meaningless and misleading. It was usual in workhouse accounts to express the weekly cost per head in terms of food, clothing and fuel only; in county asylums, on the other hand, computation of weekly maintenance costs included not only these items, but also staff wages and the cost of household replacements.

[1] Quoted by Hodder, *Life of Shaftesbury*, vol. II, p. 61.
[2] *Westminster Review*, March, 1845.

The *Westminster Review's* correspondent also championed the visiting justices of the various county asylums against the oft-repeated charge of extravagance. Commenting on the Commissioners' view that 'no unnecessary cost should be incurred for architectural display', he replied:

'No unnecessary expense should be incurred in architectural display, but . . . buildings destined for the reception of the afflicted in mind should not be devoid of taste and ornament . . . regard should be had to the patients, and to them only.'

The writer felt strongly that the welfare of the patients was not, as it should be, the focal point of the Lunacy Laws. Confinement in the interests of the sane was still the ruling motive.

'Do we not discover the protection to the public rather than the cure of the sufferer is the predominating principle inculcated in our Acts of Parliament? The guardians of the poor are instructed to send patients to the county asylum when they become dangerous . . . our county asylums have thus become, and the evil is daily increasing, places of security rather than curative establishments.'

All this covered relatively familiar ground; but the writer then proceeded to an analogy which, though common to-day, must have been novel to his readers. He inquired of them what would be the reaction of the general public if patients suffering from acute physical ailments, such as inflammation of the lungs, were commonly sent to workhouses, and allowed to remain there until the disease was incurable before being sent to hospital; and he stressed that the insane person was a sick person, urgently in need of specialized treatment. The questions which the Poor Law authorities commonly asked themselves in cases of insanity—is he dangerous? and, how much will it cost?—were irrelevant and anti-social. The true interest of the community lay in the achievement of a speedy cure.

The similarity between mental and physical illness was repeatedly stressed by references to 'patients', 'hospitals', and 'nurses', avoiding the derogatory and emotionally-coloured terms then still in common use. With reference to such official phrases as 'order for admission', 'commitment papers' and 'keepers', the writer commented:

'Does not this savour of transport to prison rather than of removal to hospital? We recommend the total disuse of these terms.'

This humane and enlightened study of the subject surpassed even Ashley's aims and standards. The attitude expressed evidently found a response in the minds of the educated public, for the article was reprinted and subsequently sold as a pamphlet.

## 5. ASHLEY IN PARLIAMENT, 1844–5

Meanwhile, Ashley was attempting to translate sentiment into action. On July 23rd, 1844, he brought forward in the House of Commons a motion praying that the Lunacy Report might be taken into consideration. In a lengthy speech, he recapitulated the findings of the Report, and ended:

'These unhappy persons are outcasts from all the social and domestic affections of private life . . . and have no refuge but in the laws. You can prevent, by the agency which you shall appoint, as you have in so many instances prevented, the recurrence of frightful cruelties; you can soothe the days of the incurable, and restore many sufferers to health and usefulness . . . I trust, therefore, that I shall stand excused, though I have consumed so much of your valuable time, when you call to mind that the motion is made on behalf of the most helpless, if not the most afflicted, portion of the human race.'

It was unfortunate that this undeniably moving speech should have been made at an inopportune moment. Ashley appears to have known little about parliamentary tactics, and not to have realized that he had committed a blunder in bringing the matter forward at the end of a session. He had evidently not consulted the administration before acting, for the Home Secretary rose in answer to urge him not to press the motion at that stage, and to promise Government support at a later date. Ashley agreed, and the whole matter was allowed to lapse until the following session.

This abortive move had a surprising result. *The Times*, which had hitherto confined its interest in lunacy reform to brief summaries of events and speeches, published in its editorial of July 25th an outspoken commentary. Ashley's inconclusive actions were described as 'humbugging and being humbugged'.

'We have no wish to be severe on Lord Ashley: we have the greatest respect for his humanity, his zeal, his industry, his abilities, his piety. But he is not a political leader . . . we think that Lord Ashley only exhibited his own weakness by allowing himself to bring forward the question of the treatment of pauper lunatics at this period of the session, with the certainty of being obliged to give up the matter to Government. The question was his own; the Home Secretary acknowledged himself unable to discuss it with him on the ground of want of acquaintance with detail. Why did not Lord Ashley keep it in his own hands?'

Ashley's own explanation, that he had brought the matter forward at the end of the session in order that 'these weighty matters should be maturely considered during the recess'[1] was politically naïve. He had temporarily lost the initiative, though *The Times* was unduly pessimistic in supposing him incapable of regaining it.

Contrary to reasonable expectation, public interest in lunacy questions increased in the next few months, and showed no sign of decreasing until positive action had been taken. A study of *The Times* from August, 1844, to June, 1845, when the Lunacy Bill was finally ordered, shows that the subject of insanity was repeatedly introduced in items of news and in the correspondence columns. In the last quarter of 1844, a number of letters expressing opinions on the efficacy or otherwise of the existing legal framework were published. 'The farce of Lord Ashley's medical and non-medical Commissioners may proceed,' wrote a sceptic who signed himself 'One Who Could Say More'.

'All acquainted with the subject know that it is only an expensive humbug; and if it were withdrawn altogether, there would be more real protection for the wretched inmates of these asylums, because the public would not then have the opinion that they were legally inspected, and would be more vigilant over these dens.'[2]

'It needs no enquiry into the merits of particular cases,' wrote 'S',

'to perceive that these laws are manifestly erroneous and absurd . . . the public should have guarantees for the treatment of insane patients far better than any which now exist, or could be devised under the present system.'[3]

These letters and others, some endorsing Ashley's efforts, and some demanding an unspecified but improved form of protection for the insane, published in September. In October, a lunatic named Big Hester escaped from confinement at Edderton, and was alleged to have devoured a girl's arm.[4] In November, the facts concerning a new case of

[1] Hansard, July 23rd, 1844.
[2] Ibid.
[3] *The Times*, September 26th, 1844.
[4] *The Times*, October 7th, 1844.

illegal detention were published.[1] Throughout the winter, *The Times* Law Reports gave details of a series of inquisition cases, in which the sanity of a wealthy individual was held in question by his relatives in order to protect the estate. An Act of 1842 had greatly simplified the procedure for a writ *de lunatico inquirendo*, and consequently the number of cases increased considerably at this time.[2] The two most notable cases in the winter of 1844–5 were those of Dyce Sombre, an Asiatic whose wife was apparently anxious to be rid of him,[3] and Thomas Telfer Campbell, who alleged that he had been wrongfully detained in a private madhouse in order to weaken his mental resistance to suggestions of insanity.[4] The Dyce Sombre case provided several precedents in the law relating to Chancery Lunatics.[5]

In February, 1845, allegations were made concerning the treatment of a pauper patient in the Bodmin Asylum, and this led to a lively and protracted correspondence on the subject of pauper lunatics in general.[6] There were further inquisition cases in April, May and June, and on the day on which the Lunatics Bill finally passed the Commons, there was an account of a lunatic who ran amok in Pimlico, 'declaiming in the most horrible and blasphemous language.'[7]

The Editor of *The Times* apparently made no effort to shape this mass of material, or to produce a definite reaction in the public mind. The facts, however diverse, were reported simply because anything connected with lunacy was a matter of public interest. Undoubtedly the attitude of *The Times* helped to maintain that interest, in addition to satisfying it. Thus, when the administration, in furtherance of Graham's undertaking, supported Ashley in bringing forward his Bill in June, the proceedings had almost an air of anti-climax. All that could be said had been said already; most thinking people supported the Bill, and some doubted whether its provisions would go far enough.

On June 6th, 1845, the motion for the ordering of the Bill was at last brought forward. 'Sir,' said Ashley in his opening speech,

'it is remarkable and very humiliating, the long and tedious process by which we have arrived at the sound practice of the treatment of the

---

[1] *The Times*, November 8th, 1844.
[2] See Appendix II.
[3] *The Times*, August 7th, 1844 *et seq.*
[4] *The Times*, September 23rd, 1844 *et seq.*
[5] See *English and Empire (Law) Digest*, vol. 33, pp. 189-230.
[6] *The Times*, February 11th, 1845, *et seq.*
[7] *The Times*, July 24th, 1845.

insane, which now appears to be the suggestion of common sense and ordinary humanity.'

He dwelt at some length on the work of Pinel in France:

'This was indeed a man to be honoured by every nation under heaven . . . the system passed from France to this country[1] . . . we are mainly indebted for it to the Society of Friends, and that remarkable family of Tukes who founded the Retreat at York soon after the victories of Pinel in France.'

. . . and he spoke vehemently on the subject of the plight of the single lunatic:

'I have said it before, and I say it again, that should it please God to afflict me with such a visitation, I would greatly prefer the treatment of paupers . . . to the treatment of the rich'.

Graham seconded the motion on behalf of the Government, giving it his full support and approval.

'I have the satisfaction of stating that the measures which my noble friend wishes to introduce are introduced with the Lord Chancellor's entire approbation . . . we determined to give the Bill, as a Government, our most cordial support.'

The Lunatics Bill was ordered to be prepared by Ashley, Graham, and Vernon Smith. Since Graham's ignorance of the deeper issues involved was well-known, and Ashley's personality virtually dominated those of the other Commissioners, we may reasonably suppose that the Bill, like the Report which preceded it, was his work.

Unexpectedly, in view of the circumstances, the Bill encountered some opposition. Petitions were received from the Retreat and from York Asylum opposing it on the grounds that charitable hospitals were not a suitable sphere for statutory control;[2] it was also opposed in the House by Thomas Duncombe,[3] who took up the attitude of the *Times* correspondent who signed himself 'One Who Could Say More'—that the entire system of inspection was useless, and that it merely served to lull

---

[1] An article in the *Edinburgh Review* for April, 1803, took the opposite view. It appears in fact that the work of Pinel and that of the Tukes existed independently of each other for some years. See D. H. Tuke, *Hist. of the Insane*, pp. 133-4, and H. C. Hunt, *A Retired Habitation*, p. 11.

[2] H.C.J., July 10th and 11th, 1845.

[3] H.C.J. and Hansard, July 3rd, 1845.

the general public into a false sense of security. It was at this point that he introduced, among others, the petition of Lewis Phillips, but his purpose in doing so was not clear. That these abuses could occasionally arise, the House already knew; this was precisely what the new Bill was designed to obviate.

The Lunatics Bill passed the Commons on July 23rd, and went to the Lords; the Lords returned it on August 1st with several amendments, the chief of which was a clause exempting Bethlem from all its provisions. These amendments were agreed to, and the Bill became law on August 4th as 8 and 9 Vict., c. 100.

A subsidiary Bill, dealing with the erection and management of county asylums, was introduced at the same time; this suffered only minor amendments by the Lords, and received the Royal Assent on August 8th (8 and 9 Vict., c. 126).

### 6. THE LUNATICS ACT OF 1845

The new Lunacy Commissioners—formerly the Metropolitan Commissioners in Lunacy—were named by the Act. They included five laymen—Lord Ashley, Lord Seymour (formerly Lord Granville Somerset), Vernon Smith, Robert Gordon and Francis Barlow; three medical Commissioners—Thomas Turner, H. H. Southey, and J. R. Hume; and three legal Commissioners—James Mylne, John Hancock Hall, and Bryan Proctor, better known as 'Barry Cornwall', the writer. These constituted a permanent full-time inspectorate. The medical and legal Commissioners were to receive a salary of £1500 a year, and were debarred from holding any other office. The lay Commissioners were unpaid. All held their positions during good behaviour, and were bound by an oath of secrecy unless called upon to divulge information by legal authority. In the case of death, dismissal or resignation, the Lord Chancellor was to make further appointments, which must maintain the existing proportion of lay, legal and medical Commissioners.

The chairman was to be a lay member, elected by the other Commissioners. A small secretariat was provided for by the appointment of a secretary—the stipulated salary of £800 a year suggests that this was a post carrying responsibility—and two clerks.

The work of the Commissioners was an extension of that of the old Metro- politan Commissioners—that is to say, it consisted of three main functions—inspecting, licensing, and reporting.

The duty of inspection was now extended permanently to cover all hospitals and licensed houses in the country. A legal and a medical Commissioner were to visit each hospital once a year, each licensed house in the metropolis four times a year, and each licensed house in the provinces—where the justices would also continue to visit—twice a year. They had power to visit by night, and to inspect all buildings and outhouses; they were to inquire about each patient under restraint, and to inspect all the prescribed records; they could discharge patients (apart from criminal or Chancery cases) on their own authority after two visits at an interval of seven days.

Thus far, the powers granted to the Commissioners were mainly a ratification of those granted on a three-year basis in 1842; but three other clauses extended the right of inspection in such a way that it covered all the insane in whatever type of institution they might be confined. The Commissioners were specifically empowered to visit gaols and workhouses—making a separate report to the Poor Law Commissioners in the latter case—and were also given a general power to visit any other institution not named in the foregoing clauses. In addition, the Home Secretary and the Lord Chancellor retained the right to order a special visitation in any circumstances in which they saw fit. Bethlem was not exempted from this last clause.

The Commissioners retained their licensing function in the metropolitan area; licensing in the provinces remained in the hands of the local magistrates, but a copy of every provincial licence was to be sent to the Commissioners for their information.

The reporting function of the Commissioners formed a permanent link between their work and that of the Lord Chancellor's office. They were to report in all three times in the year: once every six months to furnish routine particulars of the number of visits undertaken and the establishments visited, and annually in June to supply details of the state of institutions visited in the foregoing year.

The new Commission was, then, a development of the old—the chief differences being the extension of the inspectorate to cover the entire country and all types of institutions, and the appointment of full-time salaried Commissioners.

*Certification.*

A more detailed form of certification was devised, which, while not abolishing the distinction between pauper and private patients, increased the legal safeguards against wrongful detention in each case. The form of petition for private patients given in Schedule B of the Act was as follows:

'I, the undersigned, hereby request you to receive A.B., a lunatic (or insane person or idiot or person of unsound mind) as a patient in your house (or hospital). Sub-joined is a statement concerning the said A.B.'

The person making the petition was required to append his signature, details of his occupation, address, and the degree of relationship with, or other circumstances connected with, the patient; this was followed by a list of requirements designed to furnish a rudimentary medical and social history of the patient:

> Name of patient.
> Sex and Age.
> Condition of life and previous occupation (if any).
> Previous place of abode.
> Religious persuasion (if ascertainable).
> Duration of attack.
> Whether first attack.
> Age (if known) on first attack.
> Whether subject to epilepsy.
> Whether suicidal or dangerous to others.
> Previous place of confinement.

A comparison between this detailed form of petition and those in previous use shows that this was a considerable advance on former practice.

The two medical certificates were to be signed in a form prescribed in Schedule C:

'I . . . hereby certify that I have this day, separately from any other medical practitioner, visited and personally examined A.B., the person named in the accompanying statement, and that the said A.B. is a lunatic (or an insane person or an idiot or a person of unsound mind) and a proper person to be confined, and that I have formed this opinion from the following fact or facts, viz.:

(signed).

The form of petition for a pauper patient, which had, as before, to be signed by a justice of the peace or officiating clergyman of the parish, and also by the Relieving Officer or overseer (Schedule D), was similar in form, and required the same detailed statement.

*Records.*

All institutions for the treatment of the insane were now required to possess an Admission Book, in which the name of the patient had to be entered within two days of his reception, and the diagnosis of his complaint within seven; a book in which to enter the cause of a patient's removal from the institution, whether by death, discharge, transfer or escape; a Medical Visitation Book 'to include details of restraint, seclusion, medical treatment, injuries and acts of violence'; a Medical Case-Book, a Visitors' Book, which was to contain the reports of those who had made an official or unofficial inspection; and a Patients' Book, in which the visitors or Commissioners might make observations on the condition of individual patients.

In addition, the proprietor or superintendent was made legally responsible for forwarding notice of each individual reception, death, discharge, escape or transfer to the Commissioners within seven days of the occurrence, and if the institution was outside the metropolitan area, to the justices in addition. Thus there were five different sets of documents to be dealt with, and five sets of records to be kept. This was all in addition to the documents required for the original consigning procedure, which had to be seen by the superintendent, though not actually completed by him.

It might be asked whether such an insistence on record-keeping was either necessary or effective. Unnecessary complication of paper-work tends to defeat its own ends, for when the law becomes so complex that it may be transgressed unwittingly, deliberate evasion is easily explained away. Ashley, however, in the light of his experience in the metropolitan area, believed implicitly in the value of documentation as a safeguard against irregular practice.

*Single Lunatics.*

The provisions of Gordon's Act concerning the registration of those confined alone had remained a dead letter because there had been no real means of inspection. Now a distinction was drawn between single patients received for profit, and those detained by relatives and friends. The latter remained unprotected, but the detention of the former now required the same order and medical certificates as were necessary for a private patient in an institution. The patient was to be visited by an independent medical practitioner once every two weeks, and a Medical Visitation Book was to be kept. Notices of reception and removal were to be sent to the Commissioners within seven days, and the patient could be visited at any time by the direction of the Lord Chancellor. It would seem that section 112 of the Act, which, as already mentioned, gave the Commissioners power to visit any patient not included in the categories of establishment specifically dealt with, could also be interpreted to give them power to visit single lunatics on their own authority if they thought fit.

So ended the first stage of reform.

'One of the minor, but not the least valuable, fruits of the session' was the comment of the *Annual Register* on the Act. The writer added that 'the feeling of the House was strongly in favour'.

Legislation for a minority—particularly an anti-social minority—is not usually of great import to the majority; and it is in some ways surprising that so great a degree of public interest was aroused and maintained on behalf of the insane. There was, it is true, some opposition to the Act; but this came almost entirely from people who believed that its terms did not go far enough. The dead weight of apathy and reaction which defeated earlier attempts at reform was now finally overcome.

Ashley and his colleagues had roused the conscience of mid-Victorian society, and had set a new standard of public morality by which the care of the helpless and degraded classes of the community was to be seen as a social responsibility.

The victory was unquestionably Ashley's, and is commonly associated with his name; but the reform which had taken place in the care and treatment of the insane was not merely one man's work. The 1845 Act marked the culmination of a slow process of social evolution which transformed the 'Lunatick or mad Person' of 1744 into the 'person of unsound mind' of 1845.

# EPILOGUE

THE basic structure of Lunacy Law was complete by 1845; the national inspectorate had been achieved, and institutions of all types came under its supervision. The reformers had achieved their objects; and yet in one sense, it might be said that the work of reform had only just begun. The period from 1845 to the present day has seen changes no less momentous than those of the preceding century.

A detailed discussion of this latter period is outside the scope of this book, and it will be sufficient to indicate briefly the main threads of development.

The 'landmarks' of the last hundred years have been:

    (i)  The Lunacy Act of 1890.
   (ii)  The mental deficiency legislation of 1913–27.
  (iii)  The Mental Treatment Act of 1930.
  (iv)  The National Health Service Act of 1946.

These enactments have reflected not only the growing sympathy and insight of the general public, but also the very great advances which have taken place in the fields of psychiatry and abnormal psychology. New and improved methods of classification, treatment and cure are now possible, and the psychiatrist now possesses new resources in drugs, neuro-surgery, and psycho-analytic techniques, which were not available to the 'asylum doctor' of the nineteenth century.

## (i) 1845–90.

After 1845, the county asylum became the basis of the new system. The subscription hospitals tended to revert to their original purpose—that of providing treatment at moderate fees for members of the middle classes. In most cases, they ceased to receive pauper patients.

The question of the relationship between the Lunacy Commissioners and the Poor Law Authorities remained a vexed one until 1874. In that

EPILOGUE

year, a grant-in-aid was introduced, four shillings per week being paid from the Consolidated Fund for every pauper maintained in an asylum. This acted as an incentive in inducing the Guardians to send their insane paupers to the asylum for treatment, and reversed the principle of 1808 and 1845—that pauper lunatics were to be maintained solely by means of the county rate and local subscriptions. This marks the first assumption of financial responsibility by the State in this field.

The Lunacy Commissioners, in their report of 1875, were pessimistic about the results of the 'new financial arrangements'; and certainly the separation of the poor from that of the mentally ill has never fully been achieved. Even to-day, there are many senile cases in 'Part III Accommodation' under the National Assistance Act.

Despite the stringent provisions of the 1845 Act, some licensed houses continued to evade the regulations, and in the period 1845–90, the Commissioners were repeatedly criticized in Parliament and in the Press for their apparent inability to exercise adequate control. Charles Reade's novel, *Hard Cash*, published in 1863, drew the attention of the public to the subject, and Reade in his preface stated that he had personal knowledge of a number of cases of abuse which the Commissioners seemed powerless to prevent.

Ashley (who became the 7th Earl of Shaftesbury in 1851) remained Chairman of the Commissioners until his death in 1885. He lived on into a period in which the general public, once apathetic to the claims of the insane, became almost morbidly aware of the social implications of their treatment. As D. H. Tuke said, 'Waves of suspicion and excitement . . . occasionally pass over the public mind in regard to the custody of the insane.'[1] Shaftesbury, faced with a mixture of genuine concern and irresponsible sensationalism which he was unable to understand, was forced on several occasions to defend the work of the Commissioners against attacks in the House of Lords.[2]

Amending Acts of comparatively minor importance were passed in 1853 (16 and 17 Vict., c. 70, c. 96 and c. 97), and 1862 (25 and 26 Vict., c. 111). The latter was a result of a Select Committee constituted to consider the operation of the Lunacy Laws in 1859.

In 1877, another Select Committee, known as Dillwyn's Committee, was formed; like its predecessor, it vindicated the Commissioners from all charges of laxity and negligence, but recommended certain changes in the

[1] D. H. Tuke, *Hist. of Insane*, p. 190.
[2] See Hammond's *Lord Shaftesbury*, pp. 191-200 for a sympathetic treatment of this period of his life.

197

state of the law. No immediate legislation resulted from the recommendations of this committee.

The last 'wave of suspicion and excitement' in the nineteenth century was roused in 1884 by the case of Weldon v. Winslow, in which Mrs. Georgiana Weldon sued Dr. Forbes Winslow, the proprietor of a private asylum, for wrongful confinement. Much litigation ensued, and it would appear from the Press reports[1] that Mrs. Weldon was at least a woman of extreme eccentricity; but aided by the Lunacy Laws Amendment Association, she conducted her own cases, and won. The judge in Weldon v. Winslow (Baron Huddleston) stated that he was 'astonished that a person could be confined in an asylum on the statement of anybody, providing that certain formalities were gone through . . . it was positively shocking that such a state of things should exist.'

On May 5th, 1884, Lord Milltown rose in the House of Lords to move that 'in the opinion of this House, the existing state of the Lunacy Laws is unsatisfactory, and constitutes a serious danger to the liberty of the subject'.

Shaftesbury, then eighty-four years of age, rallied his failing strength to defend the operation of the existing laws. 'Overwhelmed by anxiety and labour in the matter of this lunacy business,' he wrote in his diary. Eighteen years of effort had gone into the making of the Act, and for forty years, he had laboured to preserve it. It seemed as though 'the toils, the anxieties, the prayers of more than fifty years' would be swept away. He rose in parliament to answer Lord Milltown, stating that he 'thought it necessary and almost a point of duty, to explain the state of things and calm the public mind'. At one point in the controversy, he attempted to resign from the Lunacy Commission, but was induced not to sever his contact with this, his first and most abiding interest.

Shaftesbury died in 1885. Two years later, a Lunacy Acts Amendment Bill, containing the highly controversial clause requiring an order from a justice of the peace before certification could take place, was introduced. A Bill containing this clause and other minor amendments became law in 1889 as 52 and 53 Vict., c. 41. The Lunacy (Consolidation) Bill which consolidated the 1845 Act with all subsequent legislation was speedily passed in the following year as 53 Vict., c. 5. This Act has not yet been repealed *in toto*, and most of its provisions still apply to certified mental patients.

---

[1] Full reports are given in *The Times* for March, 1884.

EPILOGUE

(*ii*) *Mental deficiency legislation, 1913-27.*

The distinction between the 'idiot' and the 'lunatic' had long been known in principle; but it was not until after 1845 that attempts were made to provide separate institutions and separate forms of treatment for the mentally defective. The first known institution of this kind was at Bath, where a school was started for four cases by the Misses White in 1846. Earlswood—which grew from a small 'idiot asylum' in Highgate— opened in Redhill in 1855, and by 1861, had 561 inmates. Other asylums soon followed—notably Starcross, near Exeter, and the Northern Counties Asylum for Idiots and Imbeciles at Lancaster. This last institution was founded as a result of a donation of £2000 from a member of the Society of Friends, who may have been Daniel Hack Tuke.[1]

In 1877, a sub-committee of the Charity Organization Society under Sir Charles Trevelyan recommended that the State should supplement charitable effort in this direction. The result was the permissive Idiots Act of 1886, which empowered local authorities to build institutions specifically for mental defectives, and guaranteed a capitation grant similar to that given for pauper lunatics.

A Royal Commission sat in 1904-8 to consider the existing methods of dealing with mental defectives, and came to the conclusion that there was no general provision for them. Defectives were scattered up and down the country in county asylums, in prisons, in inebriate reformatories, in workhouses, and in the community at large. The Commission considered seriously the social implications of mental deficiency, particularly with reference to drunkenness and illegitimacy, and came to the conclusion that the provision of suitable institutions, especially for female defectives of child-bearing age, was an urgent necessity.

The Act of 1913 (3 and 4 Geo V, c. 28) outlined the circumstances which rendered defectives 'subject to be dealt with', and prescribed a form of procedure for their committal to institutions. Local authorities were to provide institutions, and to appoint suitable officers. The central authority was the Board of Control, a body set up under this Act to take over the functions of the existing Lunacy Commissioners in addition to the duties of inspecting and reporting on the new mental deficiency institutions.

The 1913 Act recognized four grades of mental defectives—idiots, imbeciles, the feeble-minded, and 'moral defectives', and defined mental defectiveness as 'a condition of arrested or incomplete development exist-

[1] See Tuke, *Hist. of Insane*, p. 306.

ing from birth or from an early age'. The 1927 Act (17 and 18 Geo. V, c. 33) substituted 'before the age of eighteen years'—a more exact definition which permitted the inclusion of cases of disease or brain injury during childhood or adolescence.

The duties of the central authority had been defined in 1913 as 'supervision, protection and control'. Now the significant words 'training and occupation' were added. Many advances in the care and treatment of defectives had taken place in the interim, and the problem was now seen as primarily one of education.

An amending Act of 1925 (15 and 16 Geo. V, c. 53) had made it possible for defectives to be restored to the community under a statutory form of guardianship. Since that time, the general trend has been to replace institutional care by community care when possible. Despite this fact, mental deficiency institutions to-day suffer badly from overcrowding, and there is still a great shortage of suitable accommodation for low-grade defectives.

Mention should also be made of the report of the Wood Committee of 1929—an interdepartmental committee which considered the educational aspects of dealing with mental defectives of all grades.

*(iii) The Mental Treatment Act, 1930 (20 and 21 Geo. V, c. 23).*

By 1930, the county asylum—as it was still called—was the normal channel of treatment for the mentally ill. Its use was not confined to pauper patients, and it was felt, following the recommendations of the Macmillan Commission of 1926, that a wider basis for treatment was advisable. The Mental Treatment Act of 1930 introduced two new categories of patients who might be received without certification— 'Voluntary' patients, who would enter the hospital of their own volition, and might leave at any time after giving seventy-two hours' notice; and 'Temporary' patients, who might be expected to regain the power of volition within six months. Treatment as a temporary patient might be extended by two periods of three months each, but could in no case last longer than a year from the original date of entry.

This Act also reorganized the personnel and qualifications of the Board of Control, and gave a statutory blessing to the provision of out-patient clinics. Psychiatric clinics, usually attached to general hospitals, had developed during the war of 1914–18, and were now a valuable bridge between life in the community and life in the asylum. Patients might be introduced to psychiatric care through the clinic; and they might also receive after-care there following a period of hospitalization.

# EPILOGUE

Perhaps the most striking part of the Act was its recognition, long over-due, of the terminological changes which had taken place. The terms 'pauper', 'asylum' and 'lunatic' were discontinued, being replaced by 'rate-aided person', 'mental hospital' and 'person of unsound mind'. 'If this Act means anything at all,' said the Minister of Health,[1] 'it means that we have ceased to think of mental disease as something that is so in-decent that it has to be kept in a separate category of its own . . . you asked for these powers: you have got them: I hope you will use them.'

The 1930 Act gave an immense impetus to what was now becoming known as the mental health movement. The Report of the Feversham Committee on the Voluntary Mental Health Services, published in 1939, showed that four main voluntary associations were carrying out work in this field. There was the Mental After-Care Association, founded by Shaftesbury in 1879; the Central Association for Mental Welfare, which dealt with mental defectives; the National Council for Mental Hygiene, which was engaged in public enlightenment and preventive measures; and the Child Guidance Council, founded in 1927.

The main recommendation of the Feversham Report was that these organizations should amalgamate; and in 1942, the three last-named united to form the Provisional National Council for Mental Health. In 1946, the National Association for Mental Health was formed. Operating from headquarters in Queen Anne Street, London, the Association now fulfils many functions in supplementing the work of the statutory bodies, and in organizing training-courses. Mental Health, like other fields of social service, is now becoming increasingly specialized, and a variety of pro-fessional trainings are available for those interested in this work.

*(iv) The National Health Service Act of 1946 (9 and 10 Geo. VI, c. 81).*

The Royal Commission of 1926 had resolved 'that the treatment of mental disorder should approximate as nearly to the treatment of physical ailments as is consistent with the special safeguards which are indispensable when the liberty of the subject is infringed'. The National Health Service Act made this a reality. While retaining the categories of Certified, Volun-tary and Temporary patients, it placed the treatment of the mentally ill and mentally defective on a par with that of the physically ill and disabled. Both mental and general hospitals now come under the authority of the new Regional Hospital Boards; both are ultimately the responsibility of the Minister of Health; and only a few 'registered hospitals'—the old

---

[1] Mr. Arthur Greenwood. Address to a Conference held in 1930 between the Board of Control and representatives of mental hospitals and local authorities.

subscription hospitals—remain outside the Health Service.[1] Among these are the Retreat and Cheadle Royal (the former Manchester Lunatic Hospital).

Bethlem, which did not come within the scope of the national inspectorate until 1853, is now a Teaching Hospital. Removed to ideal premises in Kent, it operates for the benefit of Health Service patients in connection with the Maudsley Hospital, and has built up an international reputation.

A debate in the House of Commons on February 19th, 1953—the first full-dress debate on the subject of mental illness for twenty-three years—raised a number of problems for the future. There is still an acute shortage of nurses, of beds, of money. Many of our buildings are mid-nineteenth-century edifices, built to last—and to call them 'centres for psychiatric in-patient treatment' does not disguise the fact that they were originally conceived as county asylums. It will be many years before a true parity of esteem between mental and general hospitals can be achieved.

At the time of going to press, a Royal Commission, headed by Lord Percy of Newcastle, is considering the question of the consolidation and amendment of the laws relating to mental disorder and mental deficiency. The terms of reference of this Commission, which was set up in February, 1954, are as follows:

'To inquire as regards England and Wales into the existing law and administrative machinery governing the certification, detention and care (other than hospital care or treatment under the National Health Service Acts, 1946–52), absence on trial or licence, discharge and supervision of persons who are, or are alleged to be, suffering from mental illness or mental defect, other than Broadmoor patients; to consider as regards England and Wales the extent to which it is now or should be made statutorily possible for such persons to be treated as voluntary patients, without certification; and to make recommendations.'

We cannot yet write 'Finis' to the story of reform, for there is still much to be done; but as we reach the point where history shades into present policy and future aspirations, we may derive confidence, if not complacency, from the achievements of the past two hundred years.

---

[1] There is also a steadily-decreasing number of licensed houses. Only 24 are now still in existence.

# *Appendix One*

## CRIMINAL LUNATICS

C RIMINAL lunacy before 1807 has been treated briefly as part of the general history of the insane,[1] because it was not at that time understood as a condition for which separate provision should be made. A consideration of this subject raises two main questions—'What is criminal insanity?' and 'How are the criminally insane to be confined?' No totally satisfactory answer has yet been found to either question, so that a consideration of nineteenth-century views is not without present-day significance.

Lunatics who committed minor crimes presented no real difficulty. Before 1807, they went to the county gaol or Bridewell in almost all cases; after the development of the county asylum movement, they went to those institutions in increasing numbers. The term 'criminal lunatic', however, is usually limited in application to those who have committed major crimes, and whose continued existence constitutes a more or less permanent danger to society. The view taken of this class, and the treatment provided for it, forms a distinct stream of development.

### I. DEFINITION OF CRIMINAL INSANITY

Reference has already been made to Mr. Justice Tracey's enunciation of the 'Wild Beast Test'.[2] This belief that only total and unabated violence or fatuity could exempt a man from the consequence of his actions was a rigorist view in which there was no comprehension of forms of insanity which could leave the intellect partially or seasonally unimpaired.

[1] See pp. 22-5 and 69.
[2] See p. 24.

# LUNACY, LAW, AND CONSCIENCE

*R. v. Margaret Nicholson* (1786).

The rigorist view was not always maintained in practice. A case in point was that of Margaret Nicholson, who made an attempt on the life of George III in 1786. She was found on arrest to be perfectly lucid, but suffered from the delusion that she was the rightful heir to the throne, and that England would be deluged in blood for a thousand years if her claims were not publicly acknowledged. It may have been the King's knowledge of his own precarious sanity which led him to intervene on her behalf. 'The poor creature is mad; do not hurt her; she has not hurt me.' She was sent to Bethlem, where the Duke of Dorset later visited her, and reported that she was 'very quiet'.[1]

*R. v. Hadfield* (1800).

It was not until James Hadfield or Hatfield made a similar attempt on the life of the King that some clarification of the legal position occurred, and the possibility of an insane person having periods of lucidity was admitted in law.

Hadfield was undoubtedly insane. He had been a private in a dragoon regiment, and had received several sabre wounds in the head while in action.[2] He had an excellent military record, but evidence was given at the trial that he had been discharged from the Army on grounds of insanity, being subject to delusions and fits of maniacal frenzy.[3]

He concealed himself in the Drury Lane Theatre, and fired two shots at the Royal Box as the King entered before the performance. Both shots went wide, and no harm was done. On being arrested, he said that he was tired of life, and hoped that an apparent attempt on the life of the King would result in his execution; he had not intended to harm the King, and had deliberately fired wide. Counsel for the Defence gave at the trial the following explanation:

'He (Hadfield) imagined that he had constant intercourse with the Almighty, Author of all things; that this world was coming to a conclusion, and that, like our blessed Saviour, he was to sacrifice himself for its salvation; and so obstinately did this morbid image continue, that you will be convinced that he went to the theatre to perform, as he imagined, the blessed sacrifice, and because he would not be guilty of suicide, though

[1] F. H. Jesse, *Memoirs of the Life and Reign of George III*, vol. III, p. 145.
[2] *Sketches in Bedlam*, p. 14.
[3] W. Norwood East, *Forensic Psychiatry*, pp. 47–8, from which the following account is taken.

called upon by the imperious will of heaven, he wished that, by the appearance of crime, his life might be taken away from him by others.'

Hadfield's military record showed that his mental condition was a direct result of service to his country. The defence was that no crime had been intended. On the other hand, he did not come within the definition of the 'Wild Beast Test'—'a man that is totally deprived of his understanding and memory'. The Duke of York, who saw the prisoner immediately after his arrest, testified that he appeared perfectly calm, and that his conversation was quite lucid. His Counsel said of the 'Wild Beast' definition: 'No such madman ever existed in the world.'

Thus for the first time the question was raised of what came to be termed 'partial insanity'. Was it possible for a man who appeared sane after committing a crime to have been insane at the moment of the criminal act? Or was it possible for a man who was perfectly reasonable in some respects to harbour a delusion which would justify a responsible authority in describing him as insane? More than the fate of Hadfield hung on the answers to these questions.

The presiding judge thought that 'partial insanity' existed. He directed the jury to base its verdict on its view of Hadfield's state of mind at the precise moment when he raised his arm to fire at the Royal Box. 'To be sure, if a man is in a deranged state of mind at the time, he is not criminally answerable for his acts; but the material part of the case is whether, at the very time the act was committed, the man's mind was sane.'

Hadfield was found 'Not Guilty', and ordered to be confined in Bethlem. There he killed another patient, and subsequently made his escape. Recaptured, he spent a period in Newgate, and was then returned to Bethlem, where in 1823 he was said to be 'engaged in making handsome straw baskets which he is permitted to sell to visitors'.[1]

### R. v. Bellingham (1812).

The leniency showed to Hadfield did not form a precedent. On May 10th, 1812, Bellingham shot Spencer Perceval in the lobby of 'the House of Commons, and although some evidence of a deranged state of mind was brought to the trial, he was subsequently executed.[2]

Bellingham was well known in political and diplomatic circles as a malcontent. He had lived in Russia for some years, and at one time approached the British Ambassador, Lord Granville Leveson-Gower, for

---

[1] *Sketches in Bedlam*, pp. 14–18.
[2] A full account of the Bellingham trial was published in *The Times*, May 12th–16th, 1812, from which this account is taken.

protection against the Russian authorities. When the Ambassador discovered that Bellingham was alleged to owe the sum of two thousand roubles to a Russian subject, and that he had been held in custody for a legal cause, he declined to intervene.

The rights and wrongs of the matter are obscure. It appears that Lord Granville assisted Bellingham in every way consistent with the limits of diplomatic influence. He sent him money, and was successful in having him repatriated after a few months of imprisonment; but, back in England, Bellingham became obsessed with the idea that the British Government owed him compensation for the treatment he had suffered at the hands of the Russians. When the Government made it clear that it did not share this view, he shot the Prime Minister as a protest.

With the curious logic of the insane, he regarded this as a necessary and blameless action. After the shot, he said, 'I am the man who shot Mr. Perceval,' and surrendered himself without offering resistance.[1]

The conduct of the trial was subsequently subject to much adverse comment in legal circles. A request from Counsel for the Defence for a postponement so that he might bring witnesses in Bellingham's favour was refused, and Lord Chief Justice Mansfield,[2] in summing up, gave a clear direction to the jury: 'The question is whether you—the jury—are satisfied that he—the prisoner—had a sufficient degree of capacity to distinguish between good and evil, and to know that he was committing a crime when he committed this act; in that case, you will find him guilty.'[3]

The whole trial bears the marks of extreme haste, for the shooting took place on May 11th, the trial occupied only two days, May 14th and 15th; the prisoner was found guilty, and was hanged on May 18th—only a week after committing the crime. The judgment as to his state of mind was almost certainly influenced by four factors: his previous career had been detrimental to British prestige abroad; his victim was the Prime Minister; his shot found its mark; and the general public demanded a life for a life.

## R. v. Bowler (1812).

Bowler was a farmer who shot at a neighbour named Burrows.[4] The victim was not seriously wounded, and recovered sufficiently to give

---

[1] Crosby's *Parliamentary Record*, p. 85.
[2] Sir James Mansfield (1733–1821) was a contemporary and associate of Lord Eldon.
[3] Norwood East. *Forensic Psychiatry*, p. 50.
[4] See *The Times* reports June 8th, 11th and 24th, 1812.

evidence at the trial. It was proved that Bowler had suffered from epilepsy, and was subject to fits of mental confusion in which he was not fully responsible for his actions; but premeditated intention was proved. Bowler admitted saying before witnesses, 'Damn that Burrows, I will burrow him before long. I will be the death of him if I am hanged for it the next minute, so sure as my name is Bowler.' It might be questioned whether this was the cold-blooded statement of an intending murderer, or merely the irritable outburst of a short-tempered individual; but again, the summing-up was in favour of the prosecution. Bowler was found guilty and executed.

## R. v. Oxford (1840).

'Bowler was executed, I believe, and very barbarous it was.' This was the verdict of one of the judges in the Oxford case twenty-eight years later.[1] Edward Oxford, a pot-boy, earned a brief notoriety by shooting at Queen Victoria on Constitution Hill. The story is well-known from Victoria's point of view, but perhaps less so from Oxford's.[2]

The accused was a half-caste, and appears to have been, in later terminology, a sociopath. He could read and write, and was considered 'a good scholar', but was totally lacking in responsibility or in a sense of the significance of his actions. At the time of the incident, in June, 1840, he was eighteen or nineteen years of age. There was some doubt, not resolved in court, as to whether the two pistols were ever loaded with bullets, or whether they had merely contained powder. The shots went wide, and the person most affected was apparently Prince Albert, who, according to Oxford, 'got up as if he would jump out of the carriage, and then sat down as if he thought better of it.' A series of extraordinary documents purporting to relate to a society which plotted the assassination of the Queen was found in the boy's pockets, but these were accepted by the prosecution as being entirely fictitious.

The trial caused great public interest, *The Times* reporting that 'additional seats were placed in the body of the court, which were speedily filled by a highly respectable and anxious auditory'.

Among the witnesses were three medical practitioners, including Dr. John Conolly, the medical superintendent of the Middlesex Asylum. All three concurred in stating that Oxford was mentally abnormal, but their evidence was cut short by the judges, who stated that the experts should not be allowed to state positively whether the prisoner was of unsound

---

[1] Baron Alderson, *The Times*, March 6th, 1840.
[2] See *The Times*, July 10th and 11th, 1840.

mind or not, this being for the jury to decide. A typical passage occurred during the examination of Dr. Birt Davis:

'Mr. Bodkin (Junior Counsel for the Defence): Looking at the manner in which the crime was committed, and the whole circumstances of the transaction, what is your opinion of the state of the prisoner's mind?

'The Attorney-General objected. . . .

'Mr. Bodkin: From the evidence you have heard, what is your opinion of the sanity or otherwise of the prisoner at the Bar?

'Lord Denman: That question is still worse than the former ones. You cannot put this witness in the place of the jury and make him give a verdict for this point, which is so clearly for them.

'. . . Lord Denman said, he was clearly of the opinion the question could not be put. It was like asking a witness to pronounce a verdict for the jury.'

Perhaps the greatest factor in Oxford's favour was his complete indifference to his action and to its consequences. When asked by Conolly whether he was 'not conscious of having committed a great crime in shooting at Her Majesty', he replied that he 'might as well shoot at her as at anyone else'.

The jury appears to have been perplexed by the legal technicalities of the case. After deliberating for three-quarters of an hour, its members came back with a muddled verdict to the effect that Oxford was guilty of discharging two pistols at the Queen, but that they did not know whether the pistols were loaded or not, and that they considered him to have been insane at the time. 'After much discussion' they were sent out again, and came back an hour later with the verdict that they 'found the prisoner guilty, he being at the time insane'.

'Mr. Baron Alderson: Then you find the prisoner guilty, but for his insanity?

'The foreman: We do, my lord.

'Lord Denman: The court asked you this question: Do you acquit the prisoner on the ground of insanity?

'The foreman: Yes, my lord, that is our intention.

'Lord Denman: Then the verdict will stand thus: not guilty on the ground of insanity.'

Oxford was sent to Bethlem, where he remained until the criminal patients of the institution were transferred to Broadmoor in 1864. O'Donoghue records: 'The arrangements of the South-Western Railway were so admirable that the transfer was unattended by any sensational incidents. Among the last to wave farewell to the dome was Edward Oxford, who discharged two pistols at Queen Victoria in 1840'.[1]

## R. v. McNaughton, 1843.[2]

Within three years, legal minds were again exercised on the problem of criminal insanity in the case which has become famous as forming a precedent for legal judgments on insanity. Daniel McNaughton shot Edward Drummond, the secretary of Sir Robert Peel, then Prime Minister, in broad daylight, and in view of a number of passers-by. The incident took place in Parliament Street, Drummond having just left the apartments he occupied in 10 Downing Street, in the company of the Earl of Haddington.

McNaughton was immediately seized and taken into custody. He was taken to Tothill Fields, where, it was reported, he 'ate well and laughed'. Drummond lingered on for five days but finally died on January 25th, when McNaughton was formally charged with his murder; he was subsequently tried at the Central Criminal Court.

It was established at the trial that the prisoner was decidedly abnormal. He was twenty-seven years of age, a turner by trade, and came from Glasgow. An illegitimate child, he had quarrelled with his father some years before, and had developed markedly asocial tendencies. Witnesses declared that he 'avoided society', was 'parsimonious', 'a radical in his politics and inclined to infidelity in his religion'. Two years before the murder of Drummond, he had informed his landlady in Glasgow that he was being followed by devils in human form, and his member of Parliament that he was hunted by 'Tory persecutors'. He then vanished for two years. His former acquaintances saw him again only a few days before he shot Drummond, and could obtain from him no explanation of his absence save that he had been in France.

When McNaughton was examined at Bow Street, he made the following statement: 'The Tories in my native city have compelled me to do this: they follow and persecute me wherever I go, and have entirely destroyed my peace of mind. They followed me to France, into Scotland, and all over England; in fact they follow me wherever I go; I can get no rest for them night or day . . . I believe they have driven me into a consumption. . . . They have everything in their power to harass and

---

[1] O'Donoghue, *Story of Bethlehem Hospital*, p. 345.
[2] See *The Times*, January 21st–March 6th, 1843, from which the following account is taken unless otherwise indicated.

persecute me, in fact they wish to murder me. It can be proved by evidence—that's all I wish to say at present.'

The newspapers seized upon two aspects of the case: was McNaughton sane or insane? And, whom did he intend to kill? Doubt arose in the latter case because Drummond bore a physical resemblance to Peel, and had in fact been mistaken for him some months previously. It later transpired that McNaughton was actually under the impression that he had shot the Prime Minister.

*The Times* believed that McNaughton was sane, and that his delusions of persecutions were assumed. 'It appeared to be the general opinion of many persons who were present during the examination of the prisoner (at Bow Street) . . . that in making the statement he did, it was his wish to lead the public to infer that he was labouring under insanity, though his previous conduct and behaviour, coupled with his general appearance, entirely negatived such a supposition.'[1]

If McNaughton was sane, what was his motive? Obviously a political one. *The Manchester Courier* suggested that he might be an agent of the Anti-Corn Law League—'a combination dangerous in its tendency, and suspicious in its acts'.[2] At all events, a verdict of 'Wilful Murder' was returned against McNaughton at the inquest, and he was indicted for murder.

At the trial, the prosecution brought forward proof of intent: McNaughton had purchased the pistols six months earlier, and had been seen loitering in the vicinity of Downing Street for some period before the crime took place. The Curator of the Mechanics' Institute at Glasgow testified that McNaughton was normally intelligent—that he had attended courses of lectures and borrowed books, and knew members of the Socialist Society.

The defence was able to bring forward incontrovertible proofs of insanity. Among the lay witnesses were McNaughton's Glasgow landlady and the minister of the parish of Gorbals, both of whom considered him insane; the Member of Parliament to whom he had complained—who had actually written back, 'I fear you are labouring under an aberration of mind'; and the Commissioner of Police for Glasgow, who stated that he had known the prisoner for ten or twelve years, during which time McNaughton had complained on a number of occasions that 'the police, the Jesuits, the Catholic priests, and the Tories were all leagued against him'.

[1] *The Times*, January 24th, 1843.
[2] Quoted *The Times*, January 31st, 1843.

# APPENDIX I

Medical witnesses included Dr. Edward Thomas Monro of Bethlem; Sir Alexander Morison of Bethlem and the Surrey Asylum; the physician of the Royal Lunatic Asylum at Glasgow, and Dr. John Bright, who was a Metropolitan Commissioner in Lunacy. All concurred without hesitation that McNaughton was insane, and that he thought he was acting in self-defence. The Lord Chief Justice summed up in the prisoner's favour, McNaughton was found formally not guilty, and removed in custody.

There now seems little doubt that the verdict was a just one; but comparison with previous trials shows that it was not altogether the verdict which might have been expected. As in Bellingham's case, there was a tremendous public outcry in the Press against the accused in view of the eminent position of his victim: and it might have been expected, in view of what happened at Oxford's trial, that medical evidence would carry comparatively little weight. Yet the statement of Counsel for Defence that 'the question of insanity . . . was a question the most difficult, upon which men not scientifically acquainted with the subject could not be called upon to decide, and upon which the greatest deference should be paid to those who had made the subject their particular study' went uncontested.

The newspapers threw all their influence against McNaughton. 'Of the twenty million persons who compose the population of the British Empire,' wrote the editor of the *Sunday Times* in the issue of March 12th, 1843, 'we will ask who, beside the judge and jury who tried McNaughton and the witnesses who swore to what they considered the proofs of his insanity, considered him insane? How many persons are of the belief . . . that he was not perfectly aware that he was, when he shot Mr. Drummond, committing a foul and detestable murder? . . . no miscreant ever more richly deserved to expiate his crime on the gallows at Newgate. . . . Can Sir Robert Peel feel his life worth a week's purchase after this acquittal?'

The *Weekly Dispatch* of the same date published some verses which showed that the old fear of the insane as irresponsible agents still existed in the public mind:

> Ye people of England: exult and be glad,
> For ye're now at the will of the merciless mad.
> Why say ye that but three authorities reign—
> Crown, Commons and Lords? You omit the insane!
> They're a privileged class, whom no statute controls,
> And their murderous charter exists in their souls,

Do they wish to spill blood—they have only to play
A few pranks—get asylum'd a month and a day,
Then heigh! to escape from the mad-doctor's keys
And to pistol and stab whomsoever they please.

Among the more responsible periodicals, there was a diversity of opinion. The *Jurist* of March 11th published a *reductio ad absurdum* asking whether every criminal might not be said to be abnormal—in which case, every prison should be converted into an asylum. 'A few weeks' labour at the treadmill is no remedy for that disease of the brain which causes the monomania of picking pockets . . . such treatment ought not, therefore, to be adopted.' The *Lancet*, in a more balanced article published on March 18th, mentioned 'the difficulty of holding, with a just hand, the balance between the compassion which is due to a miserably afflicted human being, and the value of an infinite number of lives which may be sacrificed to his hallucination.'

On July 19th, 1843, following a debate in the House of Lords, all the High Court judges attended, and a number of questions were propounded to them concerning the legal aspects of criminal insanity. Their replies, which constitute the 'McNaughton Rules' included these points:

1. A criminal is punishable if he knows that what he did was contrary to the law, notwithstanding the insane delusion.

2. If the accused person is deluded, his culpability must be judged as if the delusion was in fact true: thus, if he supposes that a man intends to kill him, and kills that man, believing his action to be one of self-defence, he is exempt from punishment: but if he believes only that the man has damaged his reputation, and kills him, the accused is punishable by law as if he were sane.

3. The decision as to the prisoner's sanity or otherwise must be made by the jury, since it 'involves the determination of the truth of the facts deposed to, which it is for the jury to decide: and the questions are not mere questions upon a matter of science, in which case such evidence is admissible'.

4. The onus of proving insanity rests with the defence—that is to say, the accused person is presumed sane until it is proved that he is not.

5. The prisoner must be proved to have been insane 'at the time when the crime was committed'. It is at least theoretically possible for a person previously certified insane to bear full responsibility for a crime committed in a lucid interval.

The McNaughton Rules are still in force; at the time when they were originally formulated, legal opinion was very much in advance of the views of the general public, who wanted McNaughton executed as a deterrent to other would-be murderers. From the present point of view it is interesting to note that had something like the McNaughton Rules been applied in the earlier trials, the verdicts would probably have stood un-altered. The nature of Margaret Nicholson's delusion was such that she did not regard her action in firing at the King contrary to the law, for in her eyes, as the rightful occupant of the throne, she was above the law. If Hadfield's contention that he had not meant to harm the King, but merely by a devious method to commit suicide, was accepted, then he could not be accused of attempted murder. The interesting factor of this case is that the jury believed Hadfield's statement, although they found him insane. If he had intended to kill the King, the nature of his delusion would not have been sufficient grounds on which to secure his acquittal.

Bellingham indubitably had a delusion that the Government had treated him wrongly, but even if this had been true, it would not have been sufficient grounds for committing homicide against a man he did not know. Bowler had suffered from epilepsy and mental confusion in the past, but it was not proved at the trial that the balance of his mind was disturbed at the time the crime was committed. Given the legal premise that attempted murder should be punishable by death, the decision was a just, though not a merciful one. Oxford had no specific delusion which justified—in his own eyes—an attempt to kill the Queen, but he was proved to have been totally lacking in moral responsibility at the time of the act; hence his acquittal.

Public opinion is often against the insane murderer, and particularly so when his victim is an eminent person, or one who easily calls forth sympathy. The position in law is determined by totally different considerations, and despite the superficial inconsistency of the decisions recorded here, closer examination shows that the criteria of judgment were fundamentally constant throughout this period.

### ACCOMMODATING THE CRIMINALLY INSANE

The question of finding suitable accommodation for those who had been found criminally insane was not settled satisfactorily until Broadmoor was constructed. As that falls outside the period under review, it remains to indicate what expedients were used to deal with the situation in the years before 1844, and the reasons adduced by the Metropolitan

Commissioners in that year for recommending an institution of the Broadmoor type.

As we have seen, criminal insanity as such was not recognized before 1800, and insane persons committing crimes were held in law to be fully responsible for their actions. After the Hadfield case, with its recognition of 'partial insanity', the position was materially altered, and an Act to deal with the situation was formulated hastily within a few weeks of the trial.

*Criminal Lunatics Act of 1800.*[1]

The Bill listed four sets of circumstances in which a person might be detained as a criminal lunatic, introducing for the first time the concept of detention 'during His Majesty's pleasure'.

(i) In the case of a person tried for treason, murder or felony, where evidence was given to the effect that the prisoner had been insane 'at the time of the commission of such offence', the jury was to 'find specially whether such person was insane'. As we have seen, this provision was ultimately included in the McNaughton Rules.

(ii) Where a person was arrested for any other crime, a jury 'lawfully impanelled for that purpose' might judge the prisoner insane upon arraignment, without trying him for the specific offence.

(iii) Any person 'discovered or apprehended under circumstances that denote a derangement of mind and a purpose of committing some crime for which, if committed, such person would be indicted' could be sent to a place of confinement on a justice's warrant as 'a dangerous person suspected to be insane'.

(iv) Any person attempting to gain entry to one of the royal palaces could be committed into custody by the Privy Council or a Secretary of State pending an inquiry into his state of mind.

These last two clauses drew a protest in the House of Lords from Earl Stanhope, on the grounds that they constituted an attack on the liberty of the subject.[2] The question of whether a person was about to commit a crime was an extremely difficult one to decide in some circumstances, and the latter clauses held possibilities of victimization. Stanhope moved a series of amendments providing that persons committed under the Act

---

[1] Act for the Safe Custody of Insane Persons Charged with Offences (39 and 40, Geo. III, c. 94), July 28th, 1800. Hadfield's attempt on the life of the King had taken place on May 15th, of the same year.

[2] Woodfall's *Parliamentary Reports*, July 23rd, 1800.

APPENDIX I

should not be denied medical or legal assistance, the use of writing materials, or reasonable access to their friends; but both Houses of Parliament appear to have had recent events rather than future contingencies in mind, and the Bill received no other opposition of note. This is not surprising when one recalls that the same administration had shortly before carried out the suspension of Habeas Corpus among other repressive acts. The word 'liberty' was politically suspect during the war with Jacobin France, and Earl Stanhope was a Foxite who supported the revolutionary doctrines.[1]

The Act raised more problems than it purported to solve, the most obvious one being that of accommodation. Criminal lunatics found guilty of a capital offence might be sent to the common gaol, but the gaol was not a suitable place of confinement for those found insane upon arraignment, or those taken into protective custody. County gaols were usually very small, and already overcrowded.

*Criminal Lunatics in Prisons, 1807.*

The first appendix to the 1807 Report showed that only fourteen counties made returns of lunatics known to be detained in gaols at the end of 1806, and thirteen counties of those detained in houses of correction. Dr. Halliday found none in Suffolk, and only seven in Norfolk. The county of Middlesex—which seems to have made fairly accurate returns, since it housed criminal and pauper lunatics from the metropolitan area, where facts and figures were more easily checked than in the remoter parts of the kingdom—registered five lunatics in gaol and twenty-seven in houses of correction. Consequently we may infer that criminal lunatics were far fewer in numbers than pauper lunatics, though the problems involved in their detention aroused a correspondingly greater degree of public interest.

*Criminal Lunatics, 1808-27.*

After the introduction of the county asylum principle, the position became complex. In those counties where an asylum was constructed, criminal lunatics normally went to the asylum. In others, their place of detention was decided by considerations of expediency. Some were sent to Bethlem, if the cost of transport was not too great; others went to the local gaol or the Bridewell.

The general course of prison reform appears at this time to have had little effect on the condition of criminal lunatics in penal institutions. The

[1] Holland, *Memoirs of the Whig Party*, vol. I, pp. 33-4.

work of Romilly, Whitbread and Fowell Buxton passed them by, and even Elizabeth Fry, that 'spiritual dictatress among Quakers'[1] appears to have confined her ministrations at Newgate to those prisoners who were capable of improvement. When in 1812 James Neild, the treasurer of the Debtors' Relief Society, carried out his tour of the prisons in imitation of Howard, he made no study of the subject of the insane in prisons, and his report[2] rarely mentions their existence.

It was at this time that Bentham's scheme for the 'Panopticon' aroused public interest. This plan for an institution where each inhabitant would occupy a separate cell, and all would be under the constant supervision from the 'inspector's lodge' at the centre was, Bentham claimed, 'applicable . . . to all institutions whatsoever in which . . . a number of persons are meant to be kept under inspection. No matter how different or even opposite the purpose: whether it be that of punishing the incorrigible, guarding the insane, reforming the vicious, confining the suspected, employing the idle, maintaining the helpless, curing the sick, instructing the willing in any branch of industry, or training the rising race in the path of education.'[3] He suggested that prisons built on this system would obviate the difficulties inherent in the imprisonment of the criminally insane—the necessity for special staff and special accommodation—by giving them 'an apartment exempt from disturbance and adapted to their wants'.[4]

From the administrative point of view, the only objection to this scheme was its prohibitive cost; from the point of view of common humanity, it was wholly objectionable. Bentham defended the principle of solitary confinement by the statement that 'a fund of society would thus be laid up for them (the prisoners) against the happy period which is to restore them to the world'.[5] This offered no hope for the sufferer from a chronic form of insanity. The whole conception was essentially a punitive one—a typical product of the neat and impersonal mind which found it possible to refer to children as 'unripe hands'.

Bentham suggested in one of his letters that Lord Sydney (formerly the younger Thomas Townshend)[6] might 'find some little assistance lent to the humane and salutary regulations for which we are chiefly indebted

[1] Clay, *Memoirs of Rev. John Clay, B.D.*, p. 81.
[2] Neild, *Account of the Various Prisons of England and Wales*, 1802.
[3] *Works of Jeremy Bentham*, vol. IV, p. 40. The 'Panopticon' was first published in 1787.
[4] Op. cit., vol. IV, p. 61.
[5] Op. cit., vol. IV, p. 75.
[6] See page 37. Sydney was Home Secretary in the younger Pitt's first ministry, and died in 1800.

to his care'.[1] This somewhat misleading reference to the Madhouse Act of 1774 illustrates only Bentham's complete lack of knowledge of the subject of accommodating the insane; since that act referred only to private madhouses and was in any case largely unworkable. It is difficult to see what relevance the 'Panopticon' scheme could have possessed to it.

Sir George Paul and Reginald Pole Carew were among Bentham's supporters in his scheme.[2] He made an attempt to interest George Rose, and failing, concluded that 'the man was passionate, rough and coarse'.[3] In 1811, the plan, which had hung fire for several years, was finally crushed by a parliamentary committee, and Bentham was paid £23,000 for contracts unfulfilled.[4]

The 'National Penitentiary' was constructed on the Millbank site chosen for the Panopticon; it was intended as a reformatory prison where inmates would undergo imprisonment as an alternative to transportation. There is no indication that those who were found insane at the time of their trial were accommodated there, but some of the prisoners certainly became insane during their confinement 'under the combined influences of solitude, malaria and Calvinism'.[5]

Following the introduction of a new dietary in 1822 it was found that, within six months, 448 of the 880 prisoners were suffering from scurvy, and of these some 110 were totally incapacitated.[6] A Select Committee was constituted to inquire into conditions there,[7] and in 1824, all the male prisoners were transferred elsewhere and all the females given a free pardon.[8] There is no record of what happened to those who were insane.

### The Position in 1827.

The annual report of the Society for the Improvement of Prison Discipline published in 1827, stated that there were still twenty-nine counties in which gaols and houses of correction contained criminal lunatics. This Society, which, in spite of its forbidding title, did much to carry on the work of prison reform started by John Howard, had reported only four years earlier that 'there yet exist prisons in nearly the same state as Howard left them'.

---

[1] *Works of Jeremy Bentham*, vol. 4, p. 60.
[2] Op. cit., vol. XI, p. 101. See also Clay, *Memoirs of Rev. John Clay, B.D.*, pp. 74–5.
[3] Op. cit., vol. XI, p. 103.
[4] Op. cit., vol. XI, p. 106.
[5] Clay, *Memoirs of Rev. John Clay, B.D.*, p. 77.
[6] *Report of the Society for the Improvement of Prison Discipline*, 1823, Appendix.
[7] Select Committee to inquire into the present state of the Penitentiary at Millbank, 1823.
[8] *Report of the Society for the Improvement of Prison Discipline*, 1827, p. 91.

# LUNACY, LAW, AND CONSCIENCE

The plight of insane prisoners was dealt with at some length in the Society's report of 1827 in the following terms:

'There is not upon earth a more affecting spectacle than an imprisoned lunatic. In viewing the ordinary inmates of a gaol, our sense of pity is in some degree counteracted by a feeling of justice; but in the criminal lunatic we behold an object of unmixed compassion—an irresponsible agent suffering under punishment, a sufferer from disease the most terrible, without the means which can alone contribute to his cure. Under circumstances the most favourable to recovery—when mitigated by all that skill can dictate and kindness can suggest—how awful are the maladies of mind! Other evils admit of relief from the promises of religion, the approbation of conscience, and the consolations of friendship; but the lunatic is estranged from every comfort by which man is sustained in the hour of affliction; and if, as in the treatment of the criminal and pauper insane, the miseries of disease be aggravated by indigence and neglect, then is the measure of human calamity indeed full.

'In prison, the lunatic receives no medical aid adapted to his condition. He is usually confined with, and for the most part treated as, other prisoners; and he is too frequently the object of violence and sport to the brutal and depraved. These circumstances inevitably strengthen the excitement of his feelings, and the alienation of his mind; and it is very rare that imprisonment fails to prolong his disorder and perpetuate his sufferings during life. Obvious as is the cruelty of such treatment, it becomes still more apparent by the fact, that an early attention to mental disease affords the most certain, and in most cases the only, means of cure . . . as there are yet but a small number of county asylums, this unhappy class of persons is too generally doomed to lasting suffering, and their connections to deplore the loss of a husband, a father, or a friend. . . . There are in fact no institutions, in the increase and good management of which the interests of humanity are more deeply concerned, than in county lunatic asylums; nor will Britain be exempt from reproach, while any district throughout the Kingdom shall be deficient in provision for these most helpless and most suffering classes of our fellow-creatures.'

The Society had found many insane prisoners confined under the most pitiable conditions. At Barking County Bridewell, according to the appendix to the 1827 report, its investigator found cells six yards long and three yards wide. 'In one of the cells was an insane prisoner; he had been three weeks in custody—committed as "dangerous to be at large"; he has occasionally been subject to paroxysms, and on one recent occasion, he made a dangerous attack on another prisoner with an iron fender, which obliged the keeper to seclude him from the other prisoners. Insane prisoners are very frequently to be met with in this Bridewell. There is no county lunatic asylum, and it is in most cases very difficult to discover to what parish they belong'. At York, there were three 'dark solitary cells', and a refractory lunatic had recently been shut up in one of them for an uninterrupted period of ten days—'at the end of which he was quite orderly, and afterwards continued very submissive'.

It seems clear that in many counties, detention 'during His Majesty's pleasure' meant only confinement of indefinite duration under conditions similar to those designed as a deterrent for criminals who were fully responsible for their actions.

*Criminal Lunatics Acts of 1838 and 1840.*

The Criminal Lunatics Act of 1838 (1 and 2 Vict., c. 14) amended the 1800 Act by drawing a distinction between lunatics who had actually committed a crime, and those who were 'apprehended under circumstances that denote a derangement of mind and the purpose of committing a crime'. It made it possible for the latter to be sent to an asylum on a warrant from two justices, accompanied by a medical certificate, or alternatively to be released into the custody of a friend or relation who was prepared to enter into recognizances for his future peaceable behaviour. A patient sent to an asylum under this Act might be liberated by the asylum authorities in the usual way upon recovery.

The 1840 Act (3 and 4 Vict., c. 54) stated that any prisoner who was found to be insane either before or after trial might similarly be sent to a county asylum; but in the case of a prisoner who had been sane when sentenced, he was to be returned to prison upon recovery to serve the unexpired portion of the sentence.

These two Acts increased the scope of the county asylums and reduced the number of prisoners who came under the category of those detained 'during Her Majesty's pleasure' in prisons.

*The 1844 Report.*

The position in 1844 was as follows: 139 criminal lunatics were confined in county and private asylums, 85 in Bethlem, and 33 in gaols. After investigation the Commissioners came to the conclusion that although the county asylums were not designed for major offenders, their inmates included not only those charged with crimes such as larceny and minor assault, but also those convicted of serious offences. At Lancaster, for example, the asylum contained no less than seven patients who had committed murders, and several of the county asylums contained at least one patient who had been accused of arson.[1] From the point of view of the asylum authorities, this was probably the most dangerous type of patient; in a crowded institution where all doors were kept locked and the evacuation of the building at short notice was practically impossible, the threat of fire was an even greater danger than the threat of murder.

The Commissioners found that in practice it was hardly ever possible to provide a separate ward for criminal patients, and that as a result they were frequently in the company of other patients who were unaware of their tendencies, and might thus be unwittingly exposed to personal risks. Moreover, if the other patients were to be allowed any liberty of movement at all, there was always the possibility that a criminal patient might escape. The unsatisfactory nature of the system of sending homicidal patients to asylums was underlined by an occurrence at Gateshead Fell. A criminal patient escaped from this asylum, murdered his wife and daughter—and was then readmitted to the asylum because there was nowhere else to send him. The Commissioners were particularly concerned with the problems which arose in an asylum such as Hanwell, which practised total non-restraint and concluded, 'it is highly desirable that arrangements should be made for the separated care and custody of criminal lunatics.'[2]

Since it had been proved by experience that insane persons charged with serious offences could not be satisfactorily detained either in gaols, where their insanity made them a danger to the other prisoners, or in asylums, where their criminal tendencies made them a danger to the other patients, the only solution was the construction of a special establishment which would combine the medical facilities of an asylum with the precautions against escape or violence to be found in a prison. It was to fill this need that Broadmoor was eventually founded.

[1] 1844 *Report*, p. 275—a table showing 'cases of atrocious offences'.
[2] 1844 *Report*, pp. 197-9.

# *Appendix Two*

## CHANCERY LUNATICS

CHANCERY Lunatics form a small but distinct category of the insane —those possessed of considerable means, whose estates have been placed under statutory supervision. They did not come within the scope of the ordinary Lunacy Acts until 1845.

The procedure for dealing with Chancery cases had its origin in the *Praerogativa Regis* of Edward II, which made the following provisions:

'The King shall have custody of the lands of natural fools, taking the profits of them without waste or destruction, and shall find them their necessaries, of whose fee soever the lands be holden. And after the death of such idiots, he shall render them unto the right heirs; so that by such idiots no alienation shall be made, nor shall their heirs be disinherited.

'The King shall provide, when any happen to fail of his wit, as there are many having lucid intervals, that their lands and tenements shall be safely kept without waste and destruction, and that they and their households shall live and be maintained completely from the issues of the same; and the residue beyond their reasonable sustention shall be kept to their use, to be delivered unto them when they recover their right mind; so that such lands and tenements shall in no wise within the time aforesaid be aliened. . . .'[1]

This procedure provided protection for the property of an insane or mentally deficient person, but not for the person himself. By the middle of the eighteenth century, it had crystallized into an administrative pattern: the heirs and relatives would petition the Lord Chancellor to inquire into the condition of an alleged lunatic or idiot, usually in order to prevent him from wasting a fortune. If the Lord Chancellor was satisfied

[1] Quoted D. H. Tuke, *History of the Insane*, pp. 287–8.

that there was a prima facie case, he then issued a writ *de lunatico* or *de idiota inquirendo* to the sheriff of the county, requiring him to try the case by jury. If the allegation was found proved, the property then passed into the protection of the Crown, and was administered from the Lord Chancellor's office.[1]

The procedure was a lengthy one, and involved heavy legal costs. For this reason, it was rarely employed, since the costs might well take the whole of a small estate. Moreover, until public opinion was aroused in the early nineteenth century, it was a comparatively easy matter to have an inconvenient relative confined in a madhouse—unless he was of such social standing that questions were likely to be asked by disinterested persons.

In 1833, an Act (3 and 4 Will. IV, c. 36) was passed 'to diminish the inconvenience and expense of commissions in the nature of writs *de lunatico inquirendo*, and to provide for the better care and treatment of idiots, lunatics, and persons of unsound mind found by such inquisitions'. Gordon's Acts, five years earlier, had provided some kind of supervision for all the insane with the exception of this class, and this Act attempted to remedy the defect. Under its terms, the Lord Chancellor was empowered to cause commissions in the nature of writs *de lunatico* to be addressed to any one or more persons he should direct. He was also to appoint three official visitors—two medical men and a barrister or solicitor—who were to visit lunatics and idiots so found, as he directed. These were to serve in a part-time capacity, the medical visitors receiving £500 a year, and the legal visitor £300. Persons so found were to be visited at least once a year, and the visitors were to make a report in writing to the Lord Chancellor.

No previous Acts were recited, so it may be assumed that this was the first attempt to put on a statutory basis a procedure which had grown up piece-meal.

It appears from the evidence of the next Act that the Lord Chancellor's duties in the matter of causing commissions to be issued, and also of supervising estates, were delegated to the Masters in Chancery. In 1842 came an Act (5 and 6 Vict., c. 84) which transferred these duties to two new officials—two barristers of not less than ten years' standing who were to be known as the 'Commissioners in Lunacy'. The title naturally led to some confusion with the Metropolitan Commissioners in Lunacy, whose functions were quite different. The 'Commissioners in Lunacy' were full-time officials, who received a salary of £2000 each. They became *ex officio* visitors of lunatics and idiots so found, in addition to the

---

[1] See D. H. Tuke, *History of the Insane*, pp. 289–91.

visitors appointed under the Act of 1833. A secretariat was established for them.

It seems clear that the second Act was made necessary by the first: since the procedure had been simplified and the cost reduced, the number of commissions sought had greatly increased, so that a full-time and permanent body was now necessary to deal with them. A study of the legal columns of *The Times* between 1833 and 1842 shows that this increase had in fact taken place, and that the procedure of applying for a writ *de lunatico* or *de idiota* was no longer confined to cases involving persons of very great wealth. Another factor may have been the new stringency in the matter of certification under the 1828 Madhouse Act. Cases were now brought to light which would formerly have been solved by quietly putting away a person whose sanity was in doubt.

The Lunatics Act of 1845 preserved the distinction between Chancery Lunatics and others, and no common form of administration was devised. Under this Act the previous 'Commissioners in Lunacy' became the Masters in Lunacy, the former title being given to Ashley and the others who took over the extended work of the Metropolitan Commissioners in inspecting and supervising the condition of the insane as a whole. Where Chancery Lunatics were admitted to institutions which came within the scope of the Lunatics Act, their conditions and treatment were regulated by the provisions of that Act; but the new Commissioners in Lunacy had no power to discharge Chancery Lunatics, who continued to be visited according to the terms of 5 and 6 Vict., c. 84.

The following is a list of outstanding cases which during this period contributed to a definition of the position of the Chancery Lunatic in Law:

Oxenden *v.* Compton (Lord) (1793). Dealings with lunatic's property. Lunatic's benefit to be first consideration.

*Ex parte* Fletcher (1801). Masters in Chancery not to be member of Committee of Estate.

*Re* Wykeland (1823). Alleged lunatic out of the country may be brought back.

*Re* Howell (1824). Next of kin order to attend inquiry.

*Re* Early (1837). Procedure where lunatic has no next of kin.

*Re* Bariatinski (Princess) (1843). Commission of Lunacy may issue against an alien.

*Re* Dyce Sombre (1844). Person found sane by competent foreign tribunal.[1]

---

[1] See *English and Empire Digest*, vol. 33. Also, in most cases, reports in the legal columns of *The Times* for the relevant year.

# Appendix Three

## THE INCIDENCE OF INSANITY

ONE of the questions which preoccupied nineteenth-century writers on the subject of insanity was, 'Is the number of the insane increasing?' They commonly answered this question in the affirmative, pointing to the great increase in asylum accommodation in their own day. Thus Esquirol drew attention to the fact that public provision for the insane in Paris hospitals doubled between 1801 and 1821; and Halliday, writing in 1828, thought that the number of the insane in England had tripled in the previous twenty years.

Browne believed that the increase was due to the development of 'mechanical civilization' and thought that there was a particularly high ratio in America, attributable to 'the luxurious social habits to which the good fortune of our transatlantic brethren has exposed them'. Elsewhere, he states that 'the occupations, amusements, follies, and above all the vices of the present race are infinitely more favourable for the development of the disease than any previous period'. Pinel, on the other hand, blamed the French Revolution.[1]

George Burrows had a sharp and sensible word to say on this subject. He pointed out that this belief in a correlation between civilization and insanity was primarily a result of the 'nature-cult' of the late eighteenth century, and the romanticism of the early nineteenth. The 'noble savage' was actually no more than a fiction; and the reason that no insane people were detected among primitive tribes was largely due to the fact that primitive tribes destroyed them without compunction.[2]

The beliefs of Browne and Pinel have been echoed in various forms

---

[1] See Browne, *What Asylums Were, Are, and Ought to Be*, pp. 51–5—a summary of views on this subject.

[2] Burrows, *Commentaries on the Causes, etc. of Insanity*, 1828.

right down to the present day. Thus it is regarded as axiomatic in many quarters that modern Western civilization has produced a high rate of neurosis, and that tensions now exist which were unknown in a simpler and more leisured age. Again, we find the World Health Organization's Expert Committee on Mental Health stating that:

'Certain workers who have attempted a study of this matter in economically under-developed countries have the strong impression that psychiatric disorders are much less prevalent in some of these areas. The view has been put forward, for instance, that incidence of psychiatric disorders in tribal Africans is one-tenth of that usually found in Western Europe and North America.'[1]

This seems like a return to the belief in the 'noble savage', and it is interesting to read that 'other workers . . . hold the view that . . . psychiatric disorders have a rather constant frequency in all societies.'[2]

In fact, it is doubtful whether we possess at present any adequate data on which to form a judgment. The number of the insane in England has certainly increased during the past two hundred years; but several considerations require to be taken into account before it is possible to make an informed judgment on this subject.

1. An increase in total numbers is not necessarily an increase in proportion. The population of England has increased to an unprecedented extent since 1744. As the net reproduction rate rose, and the expectation of life increased, so the number of the insane naturally rose also.

2. A need is frequently not seen to exist until provision is made for meeting it. Thus it was not until the Paris hospitals made provision for the insane that the insane came forward to fill the places. The experience of the early English county asylums, which were overcrowded almost as soon as they were opened, was of a similar nature. It will be remembered that Bedfordshire reported that there were no lunatics within its boundaries in 1806, yet found no difficulty in filling an asylum in 1814.

3. We have never had a stable definition of what 'insanity' or 'mental illness' is, on which to base an assessment. All authorities agree that the difference between the psychologically normal and the abnormal is a matter of infinite gradation, and the line between the two has gradually been pushed back in succeeding generations. In the eighteenth century, only the 'furiously and dangerously mad' were considered to be abnormal; to-day, they form a very small part of the population of a mental

---

[1] W.H.O. *Technical Report Series*, 1953, no. 73, p. 3.
[2] Ibid.

hospital. The recognition of the psychoneuroses and of psychosomatic illnesses has pushed back the dividing-line still further in our own generation, until to-day some 42% of all Health Service beds are designated as 'mental beds'. This does not necessarily mean that the incidence of mental illness has increased: merely that we have learned to recognize certain conditions for what they are.

It will not be possible to determine whether the prevalence of mental disorder varies from generation to generation until we have a sufficiently stable definition to be able to compare figures over a period of forty to fifty years. Comparison between the Western countries and simpler societies similarly depends on the workers concerned having a clear-cut idea of what they are looking for.

Few statistics of any kind have been given in this book, because they are generally unreliable. Subscription hospitals and county asylums issued many sets of figures giving the number of patients cured, the duration of treatment, the mortality rate, and other relevant information. These had an immediate propaganda value, but are not now worthy of serious consideration, since 'Cured' and 'Relieved' are at best only relative terms, and have no general meaning.

# BIBLIOGRAPHY

*Public General Statutes.*

| | |
|---|---|
| 43 Eliz., c. 2. | Poor Law Act, 1601. |
| 17 Geo. II, c. 5. | Vagrancy Act, 1744. |
| 14 Geo. III, c. 9. | Act for Regulating Private Madhouses, 1774. |
| 39 and 40 Geo. III, c. 94. | Criminal Lunatics Act, 1800. |
| 48 Geo. III, c. 96. | County Asylums Act, 1808. ('Wynn's Act') amended by: |
| | 51 Geo. III, c. 79 (1811). |
| | 55 Geo. III, c. 46 (1815). |
| | 59 Geo. III, c. 127 (1819). |
| 9 Geo. IV, c. 40. | County Asylums Act, 1828. |
| 9 Geo. IV, c. 41. | Madhouse Act, 1828. |
| 2 and 3 Will. IV, c. 107. | Lunatics Act, 1832. |
| 4 and 5 Will. IV, c. 76. | Poor Law Amendment Act, 1834. |
| 1 and 2 Vict., c. 14. | Criminal Lunatics Act, 1838. |
| 3 and 4 Vict., c. 54. | Criminal Lunatics Act, 1840. |
| 5 and 6 Vict., c. 84. | Lunatics Property Act, 1842. |
| 5 and 6 Vict., c. 87. | Lunatic Asylums Act, 1842. |
| 8 and 9 Vict., c. 100. | Lunatics Act, 1845. |
| 8 and 9 Vict., c. 126. | Lunatic Asylums and Pauper Lunatics Act, 1845. |
| 16 and 17 Vict., c. 70. | Lunacy Regulation Act, 1853. |
| 16 and 17 Vict., c. 96. | Lunatics Care and Treatment Amendment Act, 1853. |
| 16 and 17 Vict., c. 97. | Lunatic Asylums Amendment Act, 1853. |
| 25 and 26 Vict., c. 111. | Lunatics Law Amendment Act, 1862. |
| 52 and 53 Vict., c. 41. | Lunatics Law Amendment Act, 1889. |
| 53 Vict, c. 5. | Lunacy (Consolidation) Act, 1890. |
| 3 and 4 Geo. V, c. 28. | Mental Deficiency Act, 1913. |
| 17 and 18 Geo V, c. 33. | Mental Deficiency Act, 1927. |
| 20 and 21 Geo. V, c. 23. | Mental Treatment Act, 1930. |
| 9 and 10 Geo. VI, c. 81. | National Health Service Act, 1946. |

*Official Papers.*

Journals of the House of Commons, 1547–1867.
Journals of the House of Lords, 1509–1830.
*The Parliamentary History of England from the earliest period to the year 1803*, 34 vols.
    4to. London, 1806–19.

# LUNACY, LAW, AND CONSCIENCE

*Woodfall's Parliamentary Debates,* by W. Woodfall, etc., 1794–1803, 33 vols.
London.

*Hansard's Parliamentary Debates,* vols. 1–41 (1804–20). New Series, vols. 1–25
(1820–30), Series 3, vols. 1–356 (1831–91). London.

Reports of Select Committees of the House of Commons:
On Madhouses, 1763 (also published in H.C.J.)
On the State of Criminal and Pauper Lunatics in England and Wales, 4to, 1807.
On Madhouses, 1815. (3 reports published May–July and subsequently bound
as one volume, the page-numbers running consecutively), 8vo.
On Madhouses, 1816. (3 reports published April–June and subsequently bound
as one volume, each report numbered separately), 8vo.
On Pauper Lunatics in the County of Middlesex, and on Lunatic Asylums, 4to,
1827.
On the Poor Law Amendment Act of 1834, 4to, 1838, 50 vols., bound in 3 vols.

Statutory Reports of the Metropolitan Commissioners in Lunacy, 1830. (Unpublished, handwritten. In Public Records Office, London.)

Report of His Majesty's Commissioners for Inquiring into the Administration and
Practical Operation of the Poor Law, 4to, 1834.

1st Annual Report of the Poor Law Commissioners, 1835.

11th Annual Report of the Poor Law Commissioners, 1845.

Official Circulars of the Poor Law Commissioners, 1835–54, 2 vols.

Report of the Metropolitan Commissioners in Lunacy to the Lord Chancellor,
1844, 1 vol., 8vo.

*Standard Works of Reference.*

*The Annual Register,* 1758–1862, 104 vols.

*The Royal Kalendar,* 1799–1846, 8vo. London. Vols. for 1814, 1815 and 1816
published as the *London Kalendar.*

*Dictionary of National Biography,* 8vo. London, 1885–1900.

*Burke's Peerage and Baronetage.* London, 22nd edition, 1860.

*Cockayne's Peerage. The Complete Peerage,* by G. E. C. 2nd edition, 1910–45, ed.
Vicary Gibbs and others.

*English (Law) Reports,* 174 vols. Edinburgh, 1900–32.

*English and Empire Digest* . . . being a complete digest of every English case reported from early times to the present day. . . ., 48 vols, 8vo. London, 1919–30.

*Halsbury's Laws of England* . . . being a complete statement of the whole law of
England, 2nd edition, under the general editorship of Viscount Hailsham,
37 vols. Butterworth, London, 1931–42.

*Newspapers and Periodicals.*

*Edinburgh Review* (quarterly).

*General Evening Post* (daily). (Certain issues only in the Burney Collection at the
British Museum.)

*Gentleman's Magazine* (quarterly).

*Lancet* (weekly).

*Manchester Mercury* (daily).

*Nottingham Evening Post* (selected cuttings only).

# BIBLIOGRAPHY

*Quarterly Review* (quarterly).
*The Times* (daily).
*Westminster Review* (quarterly).
*York Courant* (weekly).
*York Herald* (weekly).

*Unpublished Papers (in manuscript).*
Records of meetings of the trustees or visiting committees, visitors' books, case-books, household accounts, etc., of the following institutions:
The Retreat (at the Retreat).
Cornwall Asylum (at St. Lawrence's Hospital, Bodmin).
Manchester Royal Infirmary and Royal Lunatic Hospital (at Manchester Royal Infirmary).
Nottingham Asylum (at Saxondale Hospital, Radcliffe-on-Trent).
Lancaster Asylum (at County Records Office, Preston).
Stafford Asylum (at St. George's Hospital, Stafford).
Medical Biographies: The Lectures of Sir George Thane, Professor of Anatomy in the University of London, 1877-1919. Notes taken by Dr. H. A. Harris, in the Library of University College Hospital, London. Undated.


*Books.*

AINGER, CANON A. *Charles Lamb.* English Men of Letters Series (Macmillan, London, 1902).
AINSWORTH, W. HARRISON. *Jack Sheppard: a romance* (London, 1879), illustrated by Cruickshank.
ALBERT, E. *History of English Literature* (Harrap, London, 3rd edition, 1926).
APOTHECARIES. *A Statement by the Society of Apothecaries* (London, 1844).
ASPINALL, A. *Politics and the Press, 1780-1850* (Home and Van Thal, Ltd., London, 1949.)
AUBREY, JOHN. *Natural History of Wiltshire.* (Written 1656-91, ed. Britton, and published by the Wiltshire Topographical Society, 1847).

BAINES, E. *History, Directory and Gazeteer of the County of York* (pub. *Leeds Mercury* Office, 1823).
BATTELLE, M. *Rapport au Conseil Général des Hospices de Paris sur les établissements aliénés d'Angleterre, et sur ceux de Bicêtre et de la Salpêtrière* (Paris, 1845).
BATTIE, DR. *Battie on Madness* (London, 1758).
BENTHAM, J. *Letters on the Management of the Poor* (Dublin, 1796), (including the 'Panopticon').
*Works of Jeremy Bentham,* ed. Bowring, 11 vols. (London, 1843).
BETHLEM. *Charters of the Royal Hospitals of Bridewell and Bethlem* (London, 1807).
BETHLEM. *Sketches in Bedlam,* by a Constant Observer (London, 1823).
BICKERTON, T. H. *A Medical History of Liverpool from the earliest days to the year 1920* (Murray, London, 1936).
BOWLEY, A. L. *Wages in the United Kingdom in the Nineteenth Century* (Cambridge University Press, 1900).

# LUNACY, LAW, AND CONSCIENCE

BOYD, R. *Report as to Lunatics Chargeable to the Parish of St. Marylebone* (London, 1844).

BRAIN, W. R. and STRAUSS, E. B. *Recent Advances in Neurology and Neuro-Psychiatry* (J. and A. Churchill, Ltd., London, 5th edition, 1945).

BRISTOL. *Bristol Corporation of the Poor.* Selected Records, 1696–1834, ed. E. E. Butcher. (Bristol Record Society Publications, 1932).

BROCKBANK, E. M. *A Short History of Cheadle Royal from its Foundation in 1766* (Sherratt and Hughes, Manchester, 1934).

BROWNE, T. *What Asylums Were, Are, and Ought to Be* (Black, Edinburgh, 1837).

BUTLER, SAMUEL (Bishop of Lichfield). *The Analogy of Religion* (1736).

BURTON, ROBERT. ('Democritus Junior'). *The Anatomy of Melancholy.* Written 1676, 1821 edition, 2 vols. (London).

BUCKHAM. *Insanity considered in its Medico-Legal Relations* (Philadelphia, 1883).

BURROWS, G. M. *Commentaries on the Causes of Insanity* (Underwood, London, 1828).

CAPPE, CATHERINE. *Thoughts on the Desirableness of and Utility of Ladies Visiting the Female Wards of Hospitals and Lunatic Asylums* (London, 1816).

CHAPLIN, A. *Medicine in England during the Reign of George III.* (Fitzpatrick Lectures delivered at the Royal College of Physicians), 8vo (London, 1919).

CHARLESWORTH, E. P. *Considerations on the Moral Management of Insane Persons* (London, 1828).

CHEYNE, G. *The English Malady, or, A Treatise of Nervous Diseases of all Kinds* (London, 1733).

CLARK, D. STAFFORD-. *Psychiatry To-day* (Penguin Books, Ltd., 1952).

CLARK, SIR J. *Memoir of Dr. Conolly* (Murray, London, 1869).

CLAY, W. L. *Memoir of the Rev. John Clay, B.D.* by his son (Macmillan, London and Cambridge, 1861).

CONOLLY, J. *An Inquiry Concerning the Indications of Insanity* (London, 1830).
*On the Treatment of Insanity; the treatment of the insane without mechanical restraints* (London, 1856).

CROSBY. *Crosby's Parliamentary Record of Elections in Great Britain and Ireland, with Select Biographical Notices and Speeches of Distinguished Statesmen*, 1 vol., 12mo. (Leeds, 1847).

CROWTHER, BRYAN. (Surgeon to Bethlem and Bridewell.) *Practical Remarks on Insanity* (London, 1811).

CROWTHER, CALEB. (Senior Physician to the West Riding Asylum.) *Observations on the Management of the Insane* (London, 1838).

DAVIS, O. C. and WILSHIRE, F. A. *Mentality and the Criminal Law* (Simpkin Marshall, London, 1935.)

EAST, SIR W. NORWOOD. *An Introduction to Forensic Psychiatry in the Criminal Courts* (J. and A. Churchill, London, 1927).

EDEN, SIR FREDERICK. *The State of the Poor, or, a History of the Labouring Classes in England, etc.*, 3 vols. (London, 1797).

ELLIS, SIR WILLIAM C. *A Letter to Thomas Thompson, Esq., M.P. containing considerations on the Necessity of Proper Places being provided by the Legislature for the Reception of all Insane Persons* (Hull, 1815).

# BIBLIOGRAPHY

*A Treatise on the Nature, Causes, Symptoms and Treatment of Insanity* (London, 1838).
EPISTLE TO MR. EWART, M.P. See HANWELL.

FERRIAR, J. *Medical Histories and Reflections*, 3 vols. (Warrington, 1792).
FINER, S. E. *Life and Times of Sir Edwin Chadwick* (Methuen, London, 1952).
FLUGEL, J. C. *A Hundred Years of Psychology, 1833-1933* (Duckworth, London, 1933).
FOSS, E. *The Judges of England from the Time of the Conquest*, 9 vols. (London, 1848-70).

GARDINER HILL. See HILL, R. GARDINER.
GERARD, JAMES, and others. *An Address to the Magistrates of the County of Lancaster on the Situation Proposed for the intended County Lunatic Asylum* (Liverpool, 1810).
GOLDSMITH, M. *Franz Anton Mesmer: The History of an Idea* (Arthur Baker, Ltd., London, 1934).
GRAY, B. KIRKMAN. *A History of English Philanthropy from the Dissolution of the Monasteries to the Taking of the First Census* (London, 1905).
GRENVILLE. *The Grenville Papers*, ed. W. J. Smith, 2 vols. (Murray, London, 1852).
GREVILLE. *The Diaries of Robert Fulke Greville*, ed. F. McKno Bladen (Bodley Head, 1930).

HALÉVY, E. *A History of the English People in the Nineteenth Century*, vol. I, England in 1815; 2nd English edition (Benn, London, 1949).
HALLIDAY, SIR ANDREW. *A General View of the Present State of Lunatics and Lunatic Asylums in Great Britain and Ireland, and in some other Kingdoms* (London, 1828).
HAMMOND, J. L. and B. *Lord Shaftesbury*, 4th edn. (Penguin Books, 1936).
HANWELL. *An Epistle addressed to Mr. Ewart, M.P. on his withdrawing his Notice of Motion for an Enquiry into the Total Abolition of all Restraint on the Pauper Lunatics at Hanwell*. By a Rev. Gentleman not under Restraint (Hanwell, 1841). (Hume Tracts, University College Library, London).
HART, B. *Psychology of Insanity*. Cambridge Manuals of Science and Literature, vol. 45 (Cambridge University Press, 1912).
HARTLEY, D. *Observations on Man*, 6th edn. (London, 1734).
HASLAM, J. *Observation on Madness and Melancholy* (London, 1809).
*Considerations on the Moral Management of Insane Persons* (London, 1817).
HERBART, F. *Lehrbuch zur Psychologie*. 1816. (Translation in International Education Series, pub. New York, 1891.)
HIGGINS, GODFREY. *A Letter to the Right Honourable Earl FitzWilliam respecting the Investigation which has lately taken place into the Abuses at the York Lunatic Asylum, together with various Letters, Reports, etc.* (Doncaster, 1814).
HILL, R. GARDINER. *The Non-Restraint System of Treatment in Lunacy* (Simpkin Marshall, London, 1857).
HODDER, E. *Life and Work of the Seventh Earl of Shaftesbury*, 3 vols. (London, 1886).
HOLLAND, LORD. *Memoirs of the Whig Party*, 2 vols. (Longmans, London, 1854).
*Further Memoirs of the Whig Party*, ed. Lord Stavordale (Murray, London, 1905).
HOWARD, JOHN. *State of the Prisons in England and Wales, with Preliminary Observations and an Account of some Foreign Prisons*. 2 parts in 1 vol. (Warrington, 1777-80).

R

HUME, D. *An Inquiry Concerning the Principles of Morals;* contained in vol. 2 of *Essays and Treatises on Several Subjects,* by David Hume, Esq. (Edinburgh, 1804).
HUNT, H. C. *A Retired Habitation. A History of the Retreat, York.* (H. K. Lewis, London, 1932.)

JESSE, J. HENEAGE. *Memoirs of the Life and Reign of George III,* 3 vols. (London, 1867).
*Memoirs of Celebrated Etonians,* 2 vols. (London, 1875).
JONES, L. CLARK. *Clubs of the Georgian Rakes* (Columbia University Press, 1942).

KIRKMAN GRAY. See GRAY, B. KIRKMAN.
KNIGHT, PAUL SLADE. *Observations on the Causes, Symptoms and Treatment of Derangement of the Mind. (Knight on Insanity),* (London, 1827).

MACKENZIE, I. *Social Activities of the English Friends in the First Half of the Nineteenth Century:* a dissertation (New York, 1935).
MAHON, LORD (Philip Henry Stanhope, 5th Earl). *History of England, comprising the Reign of Queen Anne until the Peace of Utrecht . . . 1701-13* (London, 1870).
MANCHESTER LUNATIC HOSPITAL. *An Account of the Rise and Present Establishment of the Lunatic Hospital in Manchester* (J. Harrop, Manchester, 1771).
—A fuller edition, 1778.
MANCHESTER ROYAL INFIRMARY *Rules for the Government of the Infirmary, Lunatic Hospital and Public Baths in Manchester* (1791).
MENNINGER, W. C. *Psychiatry* (Cornell University Press, 1948).
MIDDLEBROOK, S. *Newcastle-on-Tyne, its growth and achievements.*
MITFORD, J. *Crimes and Horrors of Kelly House,* undated, c. 1828-30. (Hume Tracts, University College Library, London.)
*Crimes and Horrors of Warburton's Private Madhouses,* undated, c. 1828-30. (Hume Tracts, University College Library, London.)
MONRO, J. *Dr. Monro's Reply to Dr. Battie* (London, 1758).
MONRO, T. *Observations of Dr. Thomas Monro upon the Evidence taken before the Committee of the Hon. House of Commons for Regulating Madhouses* (printed at Bridewell, 1816).
MURRAY, MARGARET A. *The Witch-Cult in Western Europe* (Clarendon Press, Oxford, 1921).

NEILD, JAMES. *An Account of the Various Prisons of England and Wales together with An Account of the Rise, Progress and Present State of the Society for the Discharge and Relief of Persons Imprisoned for Small Debts . . .* (London, 1802).
NICHOLLS, J. *Recollections and Reflections . . . as connected with Public Affairs during the Reign of George III,* 2nd edn., 2 vols. (London, 1822).

O'DONOGHUE. *The Story of Bethlehem Hospital from its Foundation in 1247* (London, 1913).

PATERNOSTER, R. *The Madhouse System* (pub. by the Author, London, 1841).
PAUL, SIR GEORGE ONESIPHORUS. *Suggestions of Sir George Onesiphorus Paul, Bart., to*

# BIBLIOGRAPHY

*Earl Spencer, 1806*, published as Appendix IV of the *Report of the Select Committee of 1807 on Criminal and Pauper Lunatics*, q.v.

*Doubts concerning the Expediency of Immediately Proceeding to Provide a Lunatic Asylum for the County of Gloucester* (printed at the Office of the *Gloucester Journal,* 1813).

PERCY, REUBEN and SHOLTO (pseud.). *The Percy Anecdotes,* 3 vols. (London, 1870).

PINEL, PHILIPPE. *A Treatise on Insanity,* trans. of Pinel's *L'Alienation Mentale,* by D. D. Davis, M.D. (Sheffield, 1806).

PISTORIUS, H. A. *Notes and Additions to Dr. Hartley's Observations on Man,* trans. from the German, 3rd English edition (Warrington, 1801).

RAFFALD, E. *Raffald's Manchester Directory.*

RETREAT. *State of an Institution called the Retreat for Persons Afflicted with Disorders of the Mind.* Anon. (Whitby, 1803).

RIGBY, E. *Further Facts Relating to the Care of the Poor in the City of Norwich, 1812.*

ROSE, RT. HON. GEORGE. *Diaries and Correspondence of the Rt. Hon. George Rose,* ed. Vernon Harcourt, 2 vols. (Bentley, London, 1860).

*Observations on the Poor Laws and on the Management of the Poor,* 2nd edition (Hatchard, London, 1805).

SEMELAIGNE, RENE. *Philippe Pinel et son œuvre.* (M.D. Thesis for the Medical Faculty of Paris), (Paris, 1888).

SHAFTESBURY. *The Life, Letters and Philosophical Regimen of the Third Earl of Shaftesbury,* ed. Rand (New York, 1900).

SKETCHES IN BEDLAM. See BETHLEM.

SOCIETY FOR THE IMPROVEMENT OF PRISON DISCIPLINE. *5th and 7th Reports of the Society,* pub. London 1823 and 1827 respectively.

SPRIGGE, S. S. *Life and Times of Thomas Wakley* (Longmans Green, London, 1897).

STAFFORD-CLARK. See CLARK, D. STAFFORD-.

SUMMERS, M. *The History of Witchcraft and Demonology* (Kegan Paul, London, 1926).

SURREY ASYLUM. *Rules of Surrey Asylum.* Printed together with *Reports of Visiting Justices of Surrey Asylum, 1844–6* (London, 1847).

THURNAM, J. (Medical Superintendent of the Retreat.) *Observations on the Statistics of Insanity* (Simpkin Marshall, London, 1845).

TUKE, D. H. *Chapters in the History of the Insane in the British Isles* (Kegan Paul, London, 1882).

TUKE, SAMUEL. *Description of the Retreat* (York, 1813).

WARNEFORD ASYLUM. *Refutation of the Assertions made by the writer of an Article in the* Quarterly Review *for October, 1844 . . . as far as they relate to the Conduct and Practice of the Warneford Asylum* (Oxford, 1844).

WEBB, SIDNEY and BEATRICE. *English Poor Law Policy* (Longmans Green, London, 1910).

*English Poor Law History,* 3 vols., being vols. 7–9 for the series *English Local Government from the Revolution to the Municipal Corporations Act,* 9 vols. (London, 1909–29).

WESLEY, JOHN. *Primitive Physick, or, An Easy and Natural Way of Curing Most Diseases.* 1st edition (London, 1780).

WILLEY, B. *The Eighteenth-Century Background* (Chatto & Windus, London, 1940).

WILSON, J. *Biographical Index to the Present House of Commons* (London, 1808).

WORKHOUSES. *An Account of Several Workhouses in Great Britain in the year 1732, shewing their original number and the particular management of them at the above period. With many useful remarks on the state of the poor.* Anon. 3rd edn. pub. 1786.

ZILBOORG, G. and HENREY, G. *History of Medical Psychology* (Norton, New York, 1941).

# INDEX

# INDEX

'Carlton House Set', 41-3
Central Association for Mental Welfare, 201
Certification of patients of unsound mind, 39, 76-8, 107, 143, 184, 192-3, 198, 200
Chadwick, Edwin, 67, 166
Chancery Lunatics, 189, Appendix II *passim*
Charlesworth, Dr. E. P., 140, 150-3
Cheadle Royal—see Manchester Lunatic Hospital
Chesterfield, Lord, 8
Child Guidance Council, 201
Churchill, Charles, 33, 46
Clapham Sect, 67, 129 n.
Clergy, attitude to insanity, 6-7
Clive, Edward, 28
Collins, William, 47
Conolly, Dr. John, of Hanwell, 154-6, 181, 207
Cornwall County Asylum, Bodmin, 116-7-8-9, 123-4, 157, 189
County Asylums, 69, **73-8**, 111, **116-126**, 145, **149-60**, 164-8, **176-7**, 183-4, 185-6, 199, 200-2. See also Cornwall, Lancaster, Middlesex, Northampton, Stafford, Surrey
Cowper, William, 46-7
'Crib-room cases of Bethnal Green', 137-8
Criminal Lunatics, 9, 24-5, 69-70, 76, Appendix I *passim*. See also Prisons
Crowther, Dr. Bryan, of Bethlem, 92-93, 129
Crowther, Dr. Caleb, of West Riding Asylum, 156-8

Dashwood, Sir Francis, 33
Delarive, Dr., 58-9, 61
'Devil's Claw', 2

Diet:
  Bethlem, 16, 114
  County Asylums, 122, 152
  Manchester Lunatic Hospital, 55
  Prisons, 23, 217
  Retreat, 63-4
  St. Luke's, 97
  Workhouses, 19, 114
Dundas, Charles, 72
Dunston, Dr. John, of the White House, 104, 137-8
Dunston, Thomas, Master of St. Luke's, 97-8, 104, 105

Eden, Sir Frederick, 3
*Edinburgh Review*, 65, 128
Eldon, Lord (Sir John Scott), 110-11, 141
Ellis, (Sir) William, of W. Riding Asylum, 129-30, 157
Evangelical humanism, influence of, 66-7

Fazakerly, Nicholas, 27
Ferriar, Dr. John, 53, 129
Feversham Report, 201
Fitzwilliam, Earl , 79, 91
Friends, Society of, 57-9, 61, 64-5

Gardiner Hill, Dr. R.—see Hill, Dr. R. Gardiner
*Gentlemen's Magazine*, article on private madhouses, 32, 51
  First published, 128
  Obit. of George III, 45-6
  Obit. of J. Haslam, 112
George III, King, **40-6**, 204
Goldsmith, Oliver, 47
Gordon, Robert, **133** *et seq.*, 141-4, 191

236

# INDEX

# INDEX